SURVIVORS BECOME THE STRONG

Truths & Lessons of Asian and Global Economic Crises

SURVIVORS BECOME THE STRONG

Truths & Lessons of Asian and Global Economic Crises

Copyright © 2015 by Man-Soo Kang

First edition published on November 25, 2015

Author: Man-Soo Kang
Publisher: Samsung Economic Research Institute
Publisher & CEO: Ki-Young Chung
Publication Registration: 302-1991-000066
Date of Registration: October 12, 1991
Address: 30th Fl. Samsung Life Insurance Seocho Tower, 4,
         Seocho-daero 74-gil, Seocho-gu, Seoul
         Tel: 82-2-3780-8153 (Planning), 82-2-3780-8084 (Marketing)
         Fax: 82-2-3780-8152
ISBN: 978-89-7633-958-4 03320

You can find more information on SERI publications at www.seri.org.
Homepage (http://www.seri.org) 〉 Books 〉 SERI Books

Printed in the Republic of Korea

Truths & Lessons of Asian and Global Economic Crises

SURVIVORS BECOME THE STRONG

Man-Soo Kang
Former Finance Minister & Senior Economic
Advisor to the President of Korea

SAMSUNG ECONOMIC RESEARCH INSTITUTE

ACKNOWLEDGEMENT

The ebb and flow of global liquidity and the associated fluctuations in financial conditions has been a constant backdrop to the global economy following the advent of financial globalization. Many countries and regions have been touched by the ebb and flow of global liquidity but few countries have been affected as much as Korea. It was one of those countries most severely affected by the Asian financial crisis of 1997–1998 and it was again at the sharp end of the global financial crisis unleashed in 2008 after the bankruptcy of Lehman Brothers.

It was Man–Soo Kang's fate to be standing at the helm of the ship that was the Korean economy on both occasions, steering the ship through treacherous waters—as the Vice Minister of Finance during the Asian crisis and then as the Finance Minister during the global financial crisis of 2008, having spent the intervening ten years in the political wilderness. In this extraordinary book, Man–Soo Kang has produced a gripping account of the two financial crises that has shaped the modern

Korean psyche viewed from the ship's bridge.

The book details the build-up of vulnerabilities and gives a unique glimpse into the frantic days following the outbreak of crisis and the political and diplomatic deals that officials struck to quell the crisis. Throughout the book we are given the sketch of an official with the steely determination to do the right thing, even if it means courting short-term unpopularity.

On a personal note, I had the privilege of serving alongside Man-Soo Kang on the President's staff in Korea in 2010, and many of the personal traits that I admired and learned from during those times are on display in the pages of the book.

Basel, Switzerland

Hyun Song Shin

Economic Adviser and Head of Research

Bank for International Settlements

and

former Professor of Economics at Princeton University

FOREWORD

「In a system of government, if a statesman is determined to describe a straight line, and in all things to go against the inclinations of the people, such rigor must make his administration odious; and, on the other hand, if he suffers himself to be carried along with their most erroneous motions, the government will soon be in a tottering and ruinous state.」
(From Plutarch's Lives)

The Asian financial crisis of 1997 severely traumatized Asians and the 2008 global economic crisis inflicted similar damage to everyone in the global village.

Some inconvenient truths and many lessons came out of these crises along with dejection experienced in Asia and suffering in the global arena situated between center and periphery countries, Korea tasted the Asian suffering and the global pains as well, and in the process she learned painful truths as well as useful lessons.

I had to confront the Asian Financial Crisis while serving as Korea's Vice Minister of Finance in 1997 and the Global Economic Crisis in 2008, when I was Finance Minister. While my governmental portfolios didn't tolerate any missteps on these matters of national response, I had to engage in a lonely fight on an uncharted path and amid relentless criticism.

The public cried out while politicians raised their voices of criticism. Plutarch's wisdom during the Roman era 20 centuries ago seemed poignantly relevant even today —resisting populism will threaten the government but embracing it can mortally wound the nation.

The Asian Financial Crisis centered on fluidity brought on by excessive desire for growth, whereas the Global Economic Crisis was a manifestation of imbalance caused by excessive appetite for gains. Deep-rooted in such fluidity and imbalance were the inconvenient truths of greedy speculative capital and an unstable global financial system. The Asian Financial Crisis was a regional earthquake that originated in Tokyo. The Global Economic Crisis was a worldwide earthquake that erupted in New York and shook the entire global village.

Yet, Koreans did not seem to be seriously upset by the global upheaval, unlike their bitter memories of the Asian crisis. Perhaps it was because the global crisis was an expected war fought outside the nation's borders but the 1997 turmoil was an unexpected struggle that Koreans had to confront on their own territory.

After fighting the Asian crisis of 1997, I stepped away from government service as Korea underwent a political shift and regime change. I spent the next decade as an outsider without any official portfolio but in 2008, I returned to the government, this time as Minister of Finance, by participating in the birth of a new administration of my liking. As Minister, I was able to summon the lessons learned from the 1997 crisis and devise and carry out "preemptive, decisive, and sufficient" measures from both external and internal threats in the wake of the 2008 crisis. In particular, I had to take countermeasures against the over-valued exchange rates, excessive capital flows, high tax rates, and slackening investment into R&D. Korea survived the crisis and became stronger. Subsequently, I closed some 40 years of my public service for Korea, a country that now stands tall as the world's seventh-largest exporter.

Koreans surmounted dejection and suffering from the two crises by marshaling a strong will and undaunted determination. Having had the rare experience of dealing with the crises, first as Vice Minister of Finance and later as Minister, I am offering this book as a look at economics in practice. It is not an outsider's view, relying on analyses of aggregate data. Nor is the book a personal memoir. Instead, this book is an insider's factual account of the challenges and battles fought during the crises.

While chronicling the dire situations that Korea faced and I had to resolve, I tried to take a global perspective anchored in the middle ground between center and periphery countries, underscoring the import of leadership of the former and offering encouragement to the latter. And in recording my experiences, I discovered inconvenient truths, where all these deemed critically relevant to common prosperity of all in today's global community.

As a bureaucrat on the frontline of policymaking I was a natural target for second-guessing and criticism. As the crises unfolded, I often had to resort to imperative obligations rather than to textbook theories, especially when unprecedented conditions meant no prior experience could be consulted. In this approach, I admit I may have committed some theoretical errors and inconsistencies or contradiction in reasoning. It's my sincere wish that these errors and inconsistencies serve as lessons to future public officials as well as examples of reference for scholars. For my energetic desire to present a factual recording that's believed to serve the bigger cause, I also might have hurt some persons in the field, especially in the center states, though unintentionally. To them, if any, I offer my genuine apologies.

I also acknowledge that there might be some deviations from certain facts and statistics that I am unaware of since I relied primarily on my own personal experience, various reports prepared by my colleagues in the government, and Korea's official governmental documents. New York's *The Wall Street Journal* and London's *The Economist* were very helpful for general information. Also very helpful to my writing, with insights, were the Korean journalist Jeong-tae Park's *Asian Economic Crisis* and Professor Nouriel Roubini's *Crisis Economics*.

My appreciation goes to my colleagues in the Korean government who toiled beside me day and night during the crises. Thanks are due to the many colleagues in charge of foreign exchange, taxation, budgeting, and policy coordinating at the Ministry of Finance during the 2008 turmoil, in particular:

Vice Minister Jung-gyung Choi, Assistant Minister Je-yun Shin, Director General for Economic Policies Jong-yong Yim, and Director General for International Finance Jong-gu Choi. Lastly, I send my heartfelt thanks to Professor Jae-won Lee, Ms. Hana Byun, Ms. Jeong-min Seo and Mr. Ted Chan for their efforts in translation and editing.

『Enter through the narrow gate. For wide is the gate and broad is the road that leads to destruction, and many enter through it. But small is the gate and narrow the road that leads to life, and only a few find it.』(Matthew 7:13-14)

November, 2015,
Man-Soo Kang

CONTENTS

CHAPTER 4 _ **2008 GLOBAL ECONOMIC CRISIS**

CHAPTER 5 _ KOREA'S RESPONSES IN 2008

CHAPTER 6 _ POLITICAL ECONOMICS TO ADVANCE

PROLOGUE

『There have been two miracles in the history of mankind—
Korea achieving industrialization and democratization in a
single generation and the Jewish people rebuilding a nation
after losing their homeland and wandering for 2,500 years.』

As a country with nothing to lose, Korea achieved the miracle,
sweeping away the ruins of war, and escaped from poverty
and jettisoned authoritarianism solely armed with a tenacious
spirit. But its grit was not enough to evade the Asian and global
financial crises. They inflicted enormous frustration and deep
wounds, and we suffered heavy losses.

My public career began in 1970 and spanned 43 years, except
for 10 years outside of government service. I lived through the
most revolutionary years in Korea's history, when the miracle
of industrialization and democratization in one generation was
achieved. Between 1960 and 2008, the per capita income of Korea
multiplied from US$80 to US$20,000, and its economy became 30

times larger while the world economy was expanding six-fold. By 2010, Korea was the world's seventh-largest exporter. This is quite miraculous, considering that during the same period the US, Japanese, and Chinese economies expanded by five, eight, and 20-fold, respectively. Born in the year that marked the end of World War II and having lived in a country that ascended from a state of absolute poverty to a developing country, and to a state on the doorstep of an advanced economy, my generation has witnessed events that took more than a century in other countries. I have to say that my generation has had the most trying years of our history.

I joined the Ministry of Finance in the 1970s when the second Five-year Economic Development Plan to escape from poverty was being implemented. I worked in fiscal and financial areas, introducing the value-added tax system and the real-name financial transactions, dealing with development funding and liquidating insolvent companies, and spearheading financial market opening and the reform in the financial supervisory system. In 1997, I had to fight to overcome the currency crisis which hit Asia. I left government service in 1998 when the opposition party began its 10-year hold on power for the first time in Korea's history and joined efforts to reclaim the administration from the leftists. Starting from 2008, I fought to overcome the global economic crisis as Minister of Finance and Senior Economic Advisor to the President. I engaged in financial management as Chairman of the Korea Development Bank Financial Group from 2011 and retired from public life in 2013.

"No food, one problem." When hunger loomed over the

nation, the only issue was how to be better off. During the 1970s, policies were selected based on rationality to modernize the state. When the value-added tax system and the real-name financial transactions were introduced, and financial supervision was reformed, rational conclusions could be drawn despite controversies and wrangling. We considered diligence and saving virtuous, and achieved a high economic growth rate of around 10%. Shadows of political conflict lingered in the process of pursuing economic efficiency, but I believe this period was the era of *"growth" economics* during which rationality preceded sensibility.

Beginning in 1962, Korea implemented five Five-year Economic Development Plans. The plans encountered several crises due to investment levels that exceeded savings and capital-goods imports that surpassed exports. With its financial market not opened yet, the turmoil was overcome through exogenous variables such as special demands rising from the Vietnam War and the Middle East construction boom. The 1997 Asian currency crisis spread to Korea because of the rapid outflows of short-term foreign funds, which had poured into the nation after its financial market opened in the1990s. A decade later, the country was swept up by the global economic crisis caused by the subprime-mortgage crisis of the United States.

Crises occur repeatedly. A boom-bust cycle probably existed in one form or another in ancient times, and certainly has repeated itself since capitalism began to develop in the 18th century. Bubbles were created indiscriminately in the New World, involving railroads, mines, and slave trade.

I fought the 1997 Asian financial crisis as Vice Minister of Finance (then the Ministry of Finance and Economy) and faced the 2008 global economic crisis as Minister of Finance (then the Ministry of Strategy and Finance). It was a lonely battle amid criticism, in an environment of all talk and no action. The opinions of economic experts turned out to be incorrect. The only option was to rely on experience and intuition in adopting countermeasures. Meanwhile, those who had created the conditions for the crises kept a low profile as the public threw stones and politicians complained loudly about those who were visible on the frontline fighting the crises. Because of the time lag in economic policies, those who sowed the seeds of recovery faced political punishment, while those who picked the fruits were complimented.

Continued peace and abundance brings about indolence and decadence among people, eventually leading to a crisis. When faced with a disaster, people display their inner attributes: they point fingers at one another, perform an exorcism, and embark on witch-hunts. Catastrophes such as Black Plague, Great Depression, and wars terrify people, and wise men appear, claiming they warned of such disasters and raising voices for punishment. After punishment is meted out and a new order is established, people forget the catastrophes and once again careen toward another crisis. This repeated cycle is well described in *Crisis Economics*.

The Asian financial crisis directly resulted from a maturity mismatch of liquidity. But the core cause of the global economic crisis was structural problems in household, fiscal and international balance sheets. A liquidity problem is a short-term acute disease that can be cured with injections into the money supply, but a structural issue is a long-term chronic disease that can be resolved only through structural improvement. The 1997 Asian financial crisis traumatized Korea's psyche because it involved warfare against an occupation force that had silently invaded our land. We had no knowledge of the hidden truth behind short-term capital. However, we did not endure such pain in the 2008 crisis because it was a matter of repelling an invasion and we applied our experience. Based on lessons learned in 1997, I pushed ahead with preemptive, decisive, and sufficient measures in exchange rates, financial sector, and public finance in the face of the 2008 crisis. It was a global game of survival in which the strong do not always survive, but the survivors become the strong. In the end, Korea was the first country to overcome the crisis, and took a leap forward to become the seventh largest exporter in the world.

I feel the 1997 crisis was caused by over-eagerness of businessmen, inexperience of bureaucrats, and helplessness of politicians, while the global economic crisis was caused by greediness of bankers, complacency of bureaucrats, and populism of politicians. The bubble of instability, created by hubris and lack of economic acumen, led to the Asian financial crisis. Then the bubble of uncertainty formed by greed and overconfidence in speculative income resulted in the global economic crisis. If the Asian financial crisis was a regional earthquake that shook Asia with Tokyo as the epicenter, the global economic crisis was a global earthquake that rocked the whole world with New York as the epicenter. *Crisis Economics* tells us that carry trade, which allowed low-interest short-term borrowing from the US, Japan, and Europe to finance expensive long-term loans of Asia, was the conduit for greed.

In many cases, effective election promises are bad policies and policies that don't win votes don't make good pledges. I designed the 2007 presidential election campaign platform to reclaim the administration seized by the leftist party in 1998. Election promises need to earn public sentiment and votes. Public sentiment is influenced not by what is right and wrong but by what is good and bad, and it has a tendency to shift in accordance with personal interests rather than for the benefit of a nation's future. Political populism to win votes is the reality of election marketing and an inevitable political cost of democracy. Populism places popularity and the possibility of gaining votes ahead of efficiency and legitimacy, and it appeals to emotion rather than reason. The 2002 campaign platform to move Korea's capital to Sejong city was an archetype of political populism, and the cost will be staggering. *Election economics* tells us that a populist campaign platform serves as the hotbed of fiscal deficit and bubble creation.

Policies essential for the future but not vote-getters also had to be shelved. For Korea, such policies included issues regarding high schools standardization, wasteful welfare spending, and labor market flexibility. Advanced economies are no exception to populist election promises that even lead to spending tax money of future generations. The average national debts of the member states of the Organization for Economic Co-operation and

Development (OECD) exceeded their gross domestic product (GDP). Voters prefer populism disguised as good intentions which, unfortunately, the electoral engineering encourages us to use. But lo and behold, the road to hell is paved with good intentions!

"Much food, many problems." Some say it is more difficult to endure jealousy than to stand hunger. This tendency is magnified if one is more educated or richer. While serving as Minister of Finance, it was more difficult for me to resolve conflicts than to fight the global economic crisis. Normalizing excessively overvalued exchange rates and lowering corporate tax rates that were higher than those of competing countries were dismissed as accommodating *chaebols* (conglomerates). Lowering exorbitant income tax rates or reducing the comprehensive real estate tax that was equal to a form of political violence was denounced as tax cuts for the rich. Not only politicians but also economists joined in, and emotion trumped reason. I have lived a life that had no reason to protect *chaebols* or the rich. I have never seen a case in history where a minister responsible for public finance employed tax cut policies simply to reduce tax revenues. Tax cuts, in the long term, are to increase tax revenues. What I observed was *"co-destructive" economics* filled with jealousy and hatred.

One scholar even went so far as to say that a blogger named "Minerva," who recklessly criticized government policies on the internet in 2008, "should be hailed as a national mentor." Public prosecutors revealed that Minerva was not someone who had majored in economics and that he simply patched together relevant internet posts. I insisted on abolishing the comprehensive real estate tax, a form of political violence under the name of taxation, and received not only criticism but also condemnation. Benevolent criticism leads people down the right path, but condemnation out of spite drives their souls towards destruction. I eschewed political rhetoric and clearly stated what was right and what was wrong to the public and to the politicians. This led to even more criticism.

A government official is required to walk the path that serves the interests of the nation, impervious to public criticism. The public truly does not want a government official who is helpless or idle. When I was appointed Minister of Finance in 2008, I set three goals: normalize exchange rates, turn the current account deficit into surplus, and abolish the comprehensive real estate tax. I accomplished the first two goals, but ended up with only reducing the comprehensive real estate tax. During my lonely battle, businessmen remained silent and politicians amplified conflicts disguised as righteousness. Soaring crude oil prices fueled the fire and the public rebuked policymakers as the rising exchange rates led to an increase in prices and the amount of remittances to their children studying overseas. The opposition party's political attacks to dampen the spirits of the new administration by taking advantage of the situation was crafty, and some of the ruling party members who joined a rising tide of criticism were despicable. They all clung to their interests and votes with no regard for the future of the nation. I fought this solitary battle against the crisis with the thought that it would be my last service for my country.

Primary responses in the domestic arena regarding the fight against the crisis were harsh criticism and political punishment. After I left office, the current account balance turned to a surplus and Korea became the first country to turn around to a positive growth among OECD member states. Now, the critics of the past are silent and the public, without recognizing the time lag in economic policies, praise those in office at the time when the outcome was achieved. You cannot pick the fruits without sowing the seeds. Compliments on Korea's achievement began coming from abroad. A Bloomberg article said, "Hats off to officials in Seoul," and the International Monetary Fund (IMF) praised Korea's countermeasures against the crisis as a "textbook example."

I have recorded the fight against the two financial crises that was mounted solely on grit, along with criticism. I am writing this faithful record of what I witnessed from a global perspective to promote the get-up-and-go spirit and development of the global village, hoping that Korea's experience as an intermediate nation will encourage those in periphery nations to exert strenuous efforts and cooperation and those in affluent center economies to display tolerance and leadership.

I consider myself a rightist, a "fieldist" who resolves market failures based on principles of free markets, and a pacifist who believes in the common prosperity of center and periphery countries. My life in public service has been about blaming ourselves than others, and it was a process of learning from advanced countries to lift Korea out of poverty. There has been inconvenient truth regarding moral hazards of the international financial order and the IMF's bailouts, and although we were deeply hurt by speculative capital, it was speculative money that I hated, not the IMF or the supplier countries. Nonetheless, speculative funds and the originating countries were sometimes difficult to distinguish!

One thing I would like to say is that it was more difficult to deal with the economics of center nations than the crisis itself. The economics of countries that can print reserve currencies and are equipped with the best technology or resources cannot be the same as the economics of countries that lack technology and resources and are forced to suffer a crisis due to a shortage of US dollars. The thoughts of those who had studied the economics of affluent Pax Americana full of technologies, resources, and dollars resembled a fossilized dinosaur to Korea. Center nations could print reserve currency and arrange currency swaps during a crisis, but periphery countries were shoved into a crisis if they could not hold out any longer with foreign exchange reserves.

During a year-end party of the press corps in 2008, amid a continuous series of numerous countermeasures to overcome the global economic crisis, one journalist recalled, "I have worked as a journalist for 18 years, and I have written more articles during this one year than I did for the past 17 years." Three years after I retired from the Minister of Finance post, I received the following plaque of appreciation from the press corps.

『The Korean economy is a history of challenge that has blossomed amid hardship and crises. You have always stood at the forefront in facing challenges. During the 2008 global financial crisis, you led the Korean economy as Minister of Finance to rise from the crisis. You were unskilled at persuasion, but didn't give up or circumvent. Time passes by, but policies with soul last. Your devotion will be long remembered. We, the press corps who criticized sometimes and defended other times, present you today with this small plaque of appreciation.」

November 15, 2012

Members of Press Corps at the Ministry of Finance

during the time of global financial crisis

CHAPTER 1

CRISES REDUX

Boom and Bust Cycle

My public career was with money. I faced the Asian crisis as a vice minister, and the global crisis as Minister of Finance. Liquidating numerous insolvent enterprises and financial institutions, I thought about the meaning of money. Water and fire were driving forces behind human development, but when they were improperly managed, a dyke collapsed and a fire erupted. Money also, if not managed well, leads to troubles. As water flows downwards, money also flows to a place where risk is low. However, when greed leads to risk, the water level can become too high. Eventually the dyke collapses. Egoism that follows reason has propelled the development of mankind, but when greed turned into over-speculation, disaster appeared.

Crises have always existed. The history of capitalism has seen an endless cycle of bubbles fed by too much greed and then collapse. In the past, when people were confronted with a disaster, they took out their frustration with witch-hunts. After the 18th century, when human knowledge was advanced further, beggar-my-neighbor policies emerged as a new form of witch-hunt, sometimes providing causes for war. Various analyses trace the roots of World War II to the Great Depression in the US and the subsequent economic downturn in Germany.

Economic crises in the past occurred primarily in the English-speaking world, especially in Europe and the US where capitalism was developed. Asia, before the rise of capitalism in the region, didn't even have a market in which crises could occur. The Asian economy, at the level of self-sufficiency, flowed on an instinct for survival. There were only a few pockets of capital and targets for speculation. After the world was connected into a global village, a crisis occurred first in Asia. Subsequently, crises spread to center countries. What does the 1997 Asian financial crisis, the first of its kind in periphery countries, mean? What does the 2008 global economic crisis in center economies mean? What meaning do the dollars scattered by the US and the yen printed by Japan have? Can the cycle of crises end?

| Recurring crises

Bubbles probably existed even in antiquity in one form or another, but since the rise of capitalism in the 18th century, the boom-and-bust cycle has repeated itself, causing huge waves. Since the 18th century, financial crises usually began in the financially developed English-speaking world, and spread to other countries.

The UK was the epicenter of crises several times. The 1720 South Sea Crisis when stock prices crashed after investments went into a mirage of South American trade. The Panic of 1825, regarded as the birth of the modern economic crisis, was a case of over speculation and fraud in Latin America; many people invested in a mirage, the Republic of Poyais. And the Panic of 1837 caused by the bankruptcy of short-term money market.

In the 19th century, the center of crisis crossed the Atlantic to the US: The Panic of 1857 caused by speculation in slaves; the Panic of 1873 caused by rampant speculative investment in railroads; the Bankers' Panic of 1907 caused by trust companies' investment in stocks; and the Great Depression of 1929 triggered by a rumor-based stock market crash all started in the US.

Some analyses trace the repetitive financial crises since the 18th century to excessive credit expansion of financial institutions and greedy speculation of people. Speculative investments driven by greed were made in all areas, including textile, railroads, mines, stocks, real estates, and slaves. These episodes of financial contagion were like novels with hollow endings.

For more than 50 years between the end of World War II and the 1997 Asian financial crisis, the global economy enjoyed its fastest growth ever, under the Bretton Woods System. This period saw sovereign bankruptcies in South America in the 1980s and the so-called "Lost Decade" of Japan in the 1990s, but China's embrace of a market economy after 1980 offset the negative impact of those events and the world economy continued to make rapid progress. Also, the inception of the World Trade Organization (WTO) and digital revolution founded on the development of the Internet in the 1990s connected the whole world into a single global community, expanding the trade volume of goods and services and facilitating faster movement of capital.

The 1997 Asian financial crisis was the first upheaval in the new era of a single global community and easy movement of capital. It also was the first financial contagion largely confined to non–English–speaking periphery countries. The global economic crisis of 2008 was unprecedented as it was the largest crisis ever, engulfing both center and periphery nations.

The reason why financial crises broke out primarily in the English–speaking world in the past can be assumed that with English becoming the main language in international trade, London and New York naturally became financial centers and with their abundant opportunities for profits, magnets for speculative investors. The Asian financial crisis in 1997 occurred only after Asia was incorporated into the financial circle of London and New York with the opening of the region's financial markets. Moreover, the 2008 global crisis easily spread across the world as financial transactions of center countries were connected to the rest of the world.

| 1997 Asian crisis: Temptation and mismatch

On July 2, 1997, the day after the return of Hong Kong to China after more than 150 years, the Asian financial crisis, the first of its kind since the globalization of the world economy, began with the collapse of the Thai baht. The day also marked the beginning of a new ordeal for the world economy which had achieved remarkable growth without a severe downturn since the establishment of the Bretton Woods System on July 1, 1944.

The two events intersected at a turning point in history. Hong Kong, which had transformed itself from a small fishing town into the Asian financial hub, exemplified the two faces of a colony and the 1800s East India Company—civilization and exploitation. The crisis in Thailand, which was growing rapidly through foreign capital, showed the two faces of the opening up and globalization—development and setback.

Thailand requested a bailout from the IMF on July 28, with Indonesia and Korea requesting rescue packages on October 8 and November 21, respectively. Malaysia tackled the crisis head-on with policies that contained the flow of foreign capital and the Philippines ended up requesting bailout loans in 1998. Hong Kong and Singapore were able to weather the crisis thanks to their advantage of being the Asian financial centers. Taiwan had ample foreign exchange reserves, and China was relatively unscathed because its economy was less open.

The IMF injected a total of US$118.5 billion—US$17.2 billion for Thailand, US$43 billion for Indonesia, and US$58.3 billion for Korea—in collaboration with the International Bank for Reconstruction and Development (IBRD), the Asia Development Bank (ADB), and major advanced economies, such as the US and Japan. The IMF bailout packages came with the economic programs that demanded financial restructuring, fiscal and financial austerity, and price and economic stabilization.

Their objectives were to accelerate economic opening and further develop market economies. The programs, which were prerequisites for the bailouts, led to closure of financial institutions, bankruptcy of enterprises, layoffs, and economic slowdown. But the wounds left Thailand, Indonesia, and Korea with a tolerance for enduring the 2008 global economic crisis.

I believe that it is appropriate to label the 1997 Asian crisis a financial crisis in view of its direct causes: excessive inflow of short-term funds from Japan, the US, and Europe to drive economic growth; maturity mismatch resulting from long-term lending by borrowing short-term funds; and current account deficit caused by the importation of capital goods. Although it can vary among countries, from a structural perspective, a drop in price competitiveness following China's transition to a market economy in the 1980s and low productivity despite economic growth through labor and capital injection could be seen as common causal factors.

According to the OECD's estimates, a total of US$207.3 billion bank loans which were made up of US$86.7 billion from Japan, US$98.6 billion from the European Union (EU), and US$22 billion from the US, were provided in 1997 to five crisis-affected countries — Korea, Thailand, Indonesia, Malaysia, and the Philippines. In particular, a sudden outflow of yen-carry funds by Japan, the largest lender that provided 42% of the loans to the region, and subsequent collapse in their currencies' value were immediate causes. The excessive flow of speculative capital was a bigger problem than economic fundamentals. US$87 billion in yen-carry funds to the five countries served as the main fuel for the crisis.

| 2008 global crisis: Imbalance and burst bubble

The bankruptcy of Lehman Brothers on September 15, 2008 burst a huge bubble of financial derivatives and plunged the global community into an economic crisis. The Great Moderation that began in the 1980s under Federal Reserve Chairman Alan Greenspan's low interest rate policy and expansion of credit, ruptured in 2008, two years after he retired. Behind the Great Moderation were the US's fiscal and trade deficits, imbalances masked by an unlimited supply of cheap goods from China's transition into a market economy. Greenspan's Great Moderation propelled the birth of bubbles and imbalance. "No such thing as a free lunch in economy" was proved once again.

With the establishment of the Bretton Woods system in 1944, when World War II was nearing its end, the US dollar became the most powerful key currency, and the opening of financial markets starting from the late 1900s made capital from all around the world flow into New York. Financial transactions in New York became linked to the rest of the world, and the crisis in New York thus easily spread to the world.

Commercial banks and investment banks in New York achieved a stellar growth in the late 20th century. Mergers and acquisitions that occurred mainly in the stock market of New York led to the emergence of financial behemoths such as Citigroup, JPMorgan Chase, Goldman Sachs, Lehman Brothers, and AIG. These financial behemoths led the way for financial market opening in emerging economies and created a wave of globalization, expanding their business networks to all parts of the world, and created colossal profits through reckless expansion of credit and wild speculation. Meanwhile, bankers and stock traders earned exorbitant performance-based bonuses and stock options. The untouchable financial behemoths created too-big-to-fail conditions for themselves in the US economy, and as they reached out to the global financial market, they created too-interconnected-to-fail status.

Although the 2008 global crisis began as a financial crisis, I believe that it should be viewed as an economic crisis, given that two fundamental reasons behind the crisis were economic imbalance and the limitation of international financial order. In 2009, the global economy suffered negative growth, and the situations were even worse in advanced economies. It became difficult for center countries alone to manage and resolve the global economic crisis since the world is now so interconnected. In the face of the subprime mortgage crisis, the US injected around US$9 trillion, 90% of its GDP, for financial bailouts and economic stimulus measures, while the EU, Japan, and China also infused a massive amount of capital. As international cooperation became inevitable to overcome the global economic crisis, the Group of Twenty (G-20) was born along with the Bretton Woods system.

The root cause of subprime mortgage crisis was an enormous bubble of financial derivatives, which presumably was fueled by speculative money shifting to New York from East Asia.

In 2005, the Austrian school of economics pointed out that speculative capital, which drove East Asia and then the whole world into a crisis, was rooted in low interest rates and excessive money supply. I believe that the 2008 global crisis may not be the last banquet of speculators unless the imbalance between excessive-spending countries and excessive-saving states is resolved. If the crisis could be tackled by easing money, wouldn't a high-performance money printing machine be more efficient than Fed Chairman Ben Bernanke or his Bank of Japan counterpart, Kuroda Haruhiko?

| Crises in Korea: Trial and error

Korea reached the doorsteps of an advanced nation in a single generation relying solely on a get-up-and-go spirit, rising from the ashes of 1950-53 Korean War. Between 1960 and 2008, its per capita income increased from US$80 to US$20,000 and the size of its economy expanded 30-fold while the world economy grew by 6 times. This transformed Korea into the world's seventh largest exporter in 2010.

Korea faced a number of crises in executing five Five-year Economic Development Plans from 1962. The culprits were foreign capital inducement to supplement investments that exceeded domestic savings, and current account deficits arising from imports of capital goods that were scarce in the domestic market. During the 1997 Asian currency crisis, Korea had to cope with a sudden outflow of short-term foreign funds that had poured into the market after the nation's financial market opening in the 1990s, and overcame the crisis albeit with many wounds through the IMF bailout of US$58.3 billion. When the subprime mortgage crisis broke out in the US in 2008, Korea could withstand it without much hardship thanks to what it learned from the Asian financial crisis.

The first crisis in Korea occurred when the trade deficit reached US$1.12 billion as a result of importing raw materials and capitals in the process of implementing the first Five-year Economic Development Plan that began in 1962, and it was resolved through US$800 million of reparation funds from Japan paid upon the restoration of Korea-Japan diplomatic relations in 1965. The second crisis broke out as the country recorded trade deficit of US$6.26 billion during the second Five-year Economic Development Plan (1967-1971). Korea overcame its shortfall in foreign exchange reserves by dispatching troops to Vietnam War in 1966 and thus becoming Asia's provider of supplies and services to the US. Foreign exchange reserves again became an issue in the third crisis; the trade deficit rose sharply to US$4.58 billion from 1974 and its foreign reserves dropped to below US$1 billion in 1975 due to the first oil shock in 1973. The country surmounted the crisis thanks to a jumbo loan of US$200 million underwritten mainly by Citibank and Chase Manhattan Bank of the US. The fourth crisis was a currency crunch. The trade deficit, which had been accumulated through excessive investment in the heavy chemical industry during the fourth Five-year Economic Development Plan (1977-1981), ballooned to US$14.95 billion in 1979 as a result of the second oil shock. This shortfall in foreign exchange was resolved by the US$4 billion Korea–Japan economic cooperation fund signed in 1982. The fifth crisis was caused by wrongful appreciation of the Korean won as the current account deficit swelled to US$38 billion between 1994 and 1997 and was overcome with a US$58.3 billion IMF bailout loan.

Although there have been five crises in Korea, we resolved them by relying on exogenous variables such as reparation funds from Japan, demands for military supplies on the occasion of the Vietnam War, and construction boom in the Middle East. There was no lucky exogenous variable during the 1997 currency crisis, and Korea had to pay a severe price to overcome the crisis by accepting the IMF bailout.

02

Bubbles
Eventually Burst

From the moment that mankind was expelled from the Garden of Eden, we were destined to work and sweat to survive. Martin Wolf of *Financial Times* referred to one of Aesop's Fables to explain the nature of the global economic crisis; he compared Germany, China, and Japan to hardworking ants, and the US, the UK, and Spain to the listless grasshoppers. He wrote that the ant countries should spend more and the grasshopper countries should spend less to resolve the problem, and that the ants should not lend to grasshoppers.

Prolonged abundance and peace makes people fall into indolence and decadence; indolence and decadence is followed by speculation and greed; and excessive speculation and greed always lead to troubles. History tells us that this is the ways of the world. Although people are aware of such history, they remain undeterred until they encounter headwinds. Only then do they repent.

After World War II, affluence spread amid more than a half

century of global peace although there were still regional wars. Optimism buoyed on the back of Japan's 30-year Great Growth that began in the 1960s and the more than 20-year long Great Moderation in the US, starting in the late 1980s. Japan was trumpeted as "No. 1," confidently feeling that it "can say no" to the US and US Fed Chairman Alan Greenspan was hailed as the "Economic President." However, the Austrian school of economics forewarned about the housing bubble, expressing concerns about Greenspan's monetary policy, which had triggered excessive investment in housing by maintaining low interest rates despite a rise in the real equilibrium level of interest rate due to China's transition to a market economy. Why couldn't the Great Growth of Japan continue? Was Greenspan an Economic President indeed? If the Great Growth and the Great Moderation were genuine, where did the fuel that fed Japan's Lost Decade of the 1990s and the 2008 global economic crisis come from?

| Investor or speculator

If I do it, it's investment; if you do it, it's speculation. In fact, it is difficult to distinguish between speculation and investment. As a public official continuously monitoring the movement of money, the persistent question was where to draw the boundary between investment and speculation. When the real estate and stock markets heated up, we tried to find measures to control speculation, and when they cooled down, we looked for ways to boost investment. There was no clear wall between investment and speculation, but one criterion was clear: too much was as bad as too little. In other words, excess can be worse than scarcity. Human greed, like fire, can be a catalyst for development, but too much greed can become the root of a disaster.

US management guru Peter Drucker did not view profits as the ultimate purpose of a business. Rather he regarded profits as an essential component for innovation, which lubricates the true calling —creating customers. According to Drucker, buying low and selling high is a merchant's scope of activity. I believe one can draw definitions of investment and speculation from this.

Let us define investment as value–creating through entrepreneurship, and speculation as profit–seeking through greed. Investment and speculation share similarities in that they both involve risk–taking and wealth creation, but value is different from profits in that it entails social contribution. Let us also define a person who takes profits created by others as a rent–seeker.

Many assert that the Asian financial crisis and the global economic crisis were rooted in greedy speculation. Utilizing low–interest carry trade funds to invest in periphery nations and sharing any resulting profits is not harmful. Indeed, it can act as a driving force behind development at the same time. Even an invisible hand, if not managed well, can turn into instinctive greed. If the unmanaged financial capitalism was the root of the Great Depression of the 1930s, the unmanaged casino capitalism can be the wellspring of the 2008 global economic crisis. Stakes are required in casinos. How were the stakes created?

The seedbed of the 1997 Asian financial crisis was capital from Japan, the US, and the Eurozone that was borrowed at low interest rates and flowed rapidly in and out of Asian nations with higher interest rates. This carry trade was short-term and managed by neither the capital-exporting nations nor the capital-importing states. The speculative funds succumbed to greed, flowing, as they pleased, in and out of Asian financial markets, which had opened up under pressure from advanced economies. In Korea, the carry-trade funds were not only allowed to enter and exit freely, no taxes were imposed on speculative income.

| Greed and speculation

Bubbles, which set the stage for crises, are created by human greed and an oversupply of currency. Before the 1929 Great Depression, currency oversupply was an outcome of concerted government action. Since then, it has been caused by excessive fiscal deficits and current account and capital account imbalances. While inordinate fiscal and current account deficits bedeviled the US, excessive current account surplus and fiscal deficit vexed Japan.

The 1997 Asian financial crisis was rooted in currency appreciation caused by an excessive inflow of overseas borrowed capital and current account deficit. The crisis was fueled by bubbles in the real estate and stock markets, which had been created by the oversupplied currency, and highly leveraged financial structure of businesses. Some US$207 billion in foreign capital cascaded into Korea, Thailand, Indonesia, Malaysia, and the Philippines in 1997, supplying the oxygen for the bubble. Excessive money supply in Japan caused by its current account surplus and fiscal deficit created asset price bubble, and as the bubble exploded in the 1990s, US$86.7 billion of excess capital flowed elsewhere in Asia. .

The 2008 global economic crisis was the result of the biggest asset bubble in history exploding. That bubble was created by excessive derivatives and the speculative money that had escaped the Asian financial crisis. As of 2007, the size of total outstanding derivatives worldwide recorded US$596 trillion, which was ten times larger than the size of the world's market capitalization of US$61 trillion. Global foreign exchange transactions totaled US$803 trillion, which was 46 times larger than the world's annual export transactions of US$17 trillion. Hence, the estimated size of the bubble in 2008 exceeded US$1,000 trillion.

The financial bubble created by the enormous scale of excessive currency revolved separately from the real economy, while constantly disturbing it. While the 1997 Asian financial crisis was mainly rooted in Japan's yen-carry funds, the 2008 global economic crisis was principally rooted in Greenspan's Great Moderation. The size of the bubble was too large to be supported by the real economy. Compared with the size of the bubble, Asia's economy was too weak and the global economy was too unstable. When the stakes in a casino run out, the game has to come to an end.

Inevitable burst of bubble

The 2008 global economic crisis was the grand binge of bubbles of low interest capital created by Greenspan's Great Moderation. The funds that had exited from the Asian crisis gathered in New York, making the binge even more extravagant. The free flow of speculative money boomeranged back to center economies.

No one knew that the Great Growth, which propelled Japan's massive trade surpluses for more than 30 years, would pave the way to the nation's so-called "Lost Decade" in the 1990s, and that the US's Great Moderation, which allowed low interest rates to continue with no inflation for more than 20 years, would sow the subprime mortgage crisis. Together, they gave birth to a zero-interest rate, grand bubble era.

During the Great Growth period, Japan lowered interest rates to as low as 2.5% to overcome an economic downturn after the Plaza Accord of 1985, and stock prices rose 50-fold and Tokyo's real estate prices surged 200-fold. When the country raised interest rates to around 8% in 1990, the bubble burst and the Lost Decade began. To overcome the recession of the Lost Decade, the country opened the era of zero-interest rate in 1995. The US, to overcome the collapse of its IT bubble, lowered interest rates down to as low as 1.0% in 2001 and expanded low-interest loans to homebuyers with low credit. These loans became underlying assets of financial derivatives, which became underlying assets themselves of other derivatives. Speculative trades on these derivatives generated an enormous bubble, and this massive housing bubble ruptured when interest rates were raised to

5.25 % in 2006, resulting in the subprime mortgage crisis. To overcome the recession that ensued, the US also, following the example of Japan, opened the era of zero-interest rate in 2008. The bankruptcy of Lehman Brothers, one of the five largest investment banks in the US, on September 15, 2008 was a prelude to the massive bubble bursting, triggering worldwide financial panic.

The upheaval in 2008 occurred exactly as the Austrian school of economics had foreseen in 2005. Despite a rise in the real equilibrium level of interest rate due to China's transition into the market economy, the financial market in New York maintained low interest rates, pushing insurance companies that had sold financial products designed during the high-interest era into bankruptcy. Furthermore, embarrassing derivatives such as credit default swaps, which compensate buyers if countries default, were invented. Greece, lured by low interest rates, had a role in the bubble creation with its issuance of government bonds, and ended in a ruptured economy when the bubble burst.

Japan and the US created identical bubble-and-burst cycles, and when their zero-interest rates did not connect with the real economy, they became the fuel for another bubble. The US has injected more than US$3 trillion through quantitative easing and Japan is also releasing an unlimited amount of money. No one knows how far the global economic crisis and the money printing will go. There is no mechanism that can manage the bubble-creating energy. No one can tell how much of that energy will be created or the time frame. When the bubble finally bursts, both center and periphery nations will suffer even more.

03 Crises like Typhoons

The low-pressure vortex created by the midsummer heat in the equatorial region turns into a typhoon accompanied by strong winds and rains, and it hits Northeast Asia in early fall just before harvest. Referred to as hurricanes in the Caribbean Sea and cyclones in the Indian Ocean, typhoons are predictable but unavoidable. Crises, like typhoons, unfold with accelerating speed and leave many scars.

In the history of capitalism, the vortex of bubbles created by the hot energy of greed has panicked financial markets and dealt severe setbacks to economies. The energy of greed causes disasters repeatedly as a typhoon does. It is always sunny and peaceful on the eve of a typhoon, and when the typhoon passes, people perform an exorcism, or witch-hunts, amid the ruins, only to eventually forget what happened. Just as we can reduce disaster risks by fully preparing for and properly managing typhoons, we can also minimize risks of catastrophes if we rightly manage human avarice.

The Panic of 1825 in Britain, often referred to as the first modern financial crisis, occurred when mining investments in Peru, supported by capital from the Bank of England, collapsed, as did bond purchases in the imaginary republic of Poyais in Central America. This crisis spread to the European continent and shook the financial markets in Paris, Leipzig, and Vienna, striking a hard blow to their nation's economies. The crash of the New York Stock Exchange in October 1929 caused by rumors heralded the Great Depression of the 1930s, which stiffened financial markets, paralyzed industrial production, and cost the jobs of 15 million Americans. The economic ravages spread throughout the world, dealing massive blows to several countries, including Germany, France, and the UK. The depression did not end until the outbreak of World War II in 1939.

On the eve of a crisis, banks, investors, and businesses all enjoy an economic boom, but survival instinct kicks in when a critical point is crossed and the bubble bursts. The quest to survive causes tariff and currency wars, and beggar-my-neighbor policies, which seek gains regardless of negative consequences on other countries. Beggar-my-neighbor policies hurled nations toward World War II, but in the post-war era motivated the creation of the General Agreement on Tariffs and Trade (GATT) and the International Monetary Fund, the first global cooperation systems.

The crisis unfolded in the order of: tranquility before the typhoon, vortex of the typhoon, a survival game amidst the ruins, and repentance and oblivion. The functions of the IMF system were diluted substantially when the US stopped the gold convertibility in 1971. Under the circumstances, speculative capital triggered the Asian financial crisis in 1997 and then flocked to New York in 2008 for another binge. The GATT evolved into the World Trade Organization in 1995 through the Uruguay Round, halting tariff wars.

❘ Misjudgments by authorities

The ocean is calm and the sun is warm before a typhoon strikes. Fishermen unwittingly go out sea and lose their boat, and perhaps their lives, when they are surprised by the typhoon. This was what elapsed before the advent of accurate weather forecasts. We were in this situation during the 1997 Asian financial crisis, and the advanced economies who taught us then were no different when the 2008 crisis arrived on their doorstep. Although the IMF introduced an early warning system in 1995 to prepare nations for a crisis, on October 15, 1997, just before Asian financial contagion spread to Korea, the IMF Article IV consultation team announced that Korea's growth rate, inflation rate, and current account balance were strong and its economy was not in a crisis.

The 1997 currency crisis and the 2008 global economic crisis had different aspects and nature, but behaviors of policy makers before the crises were similar. In both cases, financial indicators were flashing danger and observers were issuing warnings, but officials either were unaware of the severity of the situation or did not hear or see enough. "Catch all the three rabbits," a reference to economic growth, inflation, and the current account balance targets, circulated among Korean authorities. It echoed their overconfidence in weathering the 1997 crisis. A decade later, "The impact on the broader economy and financial markets of the problems in the subprime market seems likely to be contained" was heard months before the 2008 meltdown roiled the global financial system. Indeed, the voices of the Korean and US authorities just before the two crises resembled each other too much as shown below.

Korea Voices before the 1997 Asian financial crisis

- "We can catch all the tree rabbits of the macroeconomy: 7–7.5% economic growth, 4.5% or lower inflation, and US$5 billion to US$6 billion current account deficit." (March 29, 1996, Government)
- "Of the three macroeconomic goals for this year, the growth and inflation targets are likely to be met, but the balance of payment target is not. Nonetheless, short–term measures treating symptoms such as foreign exchange rate controls are not appropriate." (May 23, 1996, Government)
- "Concerns were raised on the recent economic situation at the meeting of the senior secretaries at the Blue House, but it is our position that the economy is currently not in crisis." (June 29, 1996, Office of the President)
- "To show his appreciation for the accomplishment of meeting the seemingly unattainable inflation goal of 4.5% by the Price Policy Bureau employees, the Deputy Prime

Minister of Finance and Economy attended the Bureau's year-end party, drank several cups of *soju*, and even sang songs." (December 30, 1996, Newspaper report)

- "Just as the sun shone again after a raging snowstorm on New Year's Day, our economy will regain its vitality in the second half after a difficult start in this new year." (January 4, 1997, Government)
- "Sharp falls in the value of the won increased fluctuations in the foreign exchange market. However, the current exchange rates rightly reflect the current status of our economy." (January 16, 1997, Bank of Korea)

US Voices before the 2008 global economic crisis

- "The impact on the broader economy and financial markets of the problems in the subprime market seems likely to be contained." (May 2007, Fed Chairman Ben Bernanke)
- "I expect that financial markets will be driven less by the recent turmoil and more by broader economic conditions and, specifically, by the recovery of the housing sector." (May 2008, Secretary of the Treasury Henry Paulson)
- "Sure, there are trouble spots in the economy, as government takeover of mortgage giants Fannie Mae and Freddie Mac, and jitters about Wall Street firm Lehman Brothers, amply demonstrate. And unemployment figures are up a bit too. None of this is cause for depression or—exaggerated Depression comparisons." (September 14, 2008, Donald Luskin, *Washington Post*)

Korea was caught up in the currency crisis in the year after the highest government authorities assured that the country can catch all three of its targeted rabbits. In the US, on September 15, 2008, the day after stock market expert Luskin said that Lehman Brothers was not a cause for worry, the crisis exploded with the company filing for bankruptcy. It was a comedy-like tragedy.

There are always voices of wise men. People just can't hear them. Regarding Korea's currency crisis, Professor Rudiger Dornbusch at the Massachusetts Institute of Technology (MIT) on January 3, 1997 warned, "Immediate currency depreciation should help reduce large external deficits," adding that the Bank of Korea (BOK) has been playing the role of the "currency czar" for appreciation, which was inconceivable in an open economy. In October of the same year, Booz Allen Hamilton, a US consulting firm, likened Korea to a nut caught between China's low costs and Japan's technical excellence, saying, "the competitive nutcracker of Japan on one side and China on the other is putting enormous pressures to change on the economy." Without "making the irreversible changes," it warned, "plummeting fortunes eventually force change."

Regarding the global economic crisis, *The Economist* warned on June 30, 2005 about the looming crisis in advanced countries by saying, "The entry of China's army of cheap labour into the global economy has increased the worldwide return on capital. That, in turn, should imply an increase in the equilibrium level of real interest rates. But, instead, central banks are holding real rates at historically low levels. The result is a misallocation of capital, most obviously displayed at present in the shape of excessive mortgage borrowing and housing investment." When the real estate bubble in the US began to break in 2006, New York University Professor Nouriel Roubini pointed out in September, 2006 that this yet-to-materialize housing bust could "lead... to a systemic problem for the financial system."

Such warnings were raised as Fed Chairman Alan Greenspan had been continuously sowing the seeds of crisis through low interest rates and expansion of housing loans. On September 4, 1998, when the waves of the Asian financial crisis were rolling towards the US through Eastern Europe and Central and South America, Greenspan stated, "It is just not credible that the United States can remain an oasis of prosperity unaffected by a world that is experiencing greatly increased stress," and lowered the federal funds rate by 0.25 percentage point on September 29. On October 7, he said, "It's pretty obvious, I think, that the outlook for 1999 for the US economy has weakened measurably," and added, "We are clearly facing a set of forces that should be dampening demand going forward to an unknown extent. ... This is a time for monetary policy to be especially alert." However, the fact that the Fed's interest rate was kept in the 1% range after 2001 shows that there was no awareness of the low interest rate acting as fuel for bubble creation rather than for investment in the real economy.

Greenspan's Great Moderation elated everyone. The geniuses of Wall Street devised derivatives that diverted risks through financial innovation and received enormous paychecks. The supervisory authorities had no reason to create problems when everybody was happy, and the legislative authorities felt that the remaining regulations were a burden. The Great Moderation burst in 2008 after Greenspan retired. Why couldn't the authorities hear the voices of the wise men?

| Fearful tranquility

With harvest ahead in Northeast Asia before a typhoon, the sky is blue, the sun is warm, and the winds are fair. By a dispensation of nature, a typhoon turns northwards to resolve the imbalance between heat, which is excessive in the equatorial region, and deficient in the Arctic region. Likewise, when the energy, which is excessive in surplus countries and in shortage in deficit nations, reaches a critical point and bursts, it is a natural phenomenon of seeking balance.

In the 1960s, Japan's Great Growth period embarked on its more than 30-year run, compiling enormous current account surpluses. The Great Moderation in the US began in the late 1980s and lasted more than 20 years without inflation. Those periods were the fearful tranquility before the typhoon.

The prelude to the 1997 Asian financial crisis appeared as US$86.7 billion, which had been accumulated through Japan's Great Growth, flowed into Korea, Thailand, Indonesia, Malaysia, and the Philippines. As a result, the financial markets were upbeat, businesses went on an expansion spree, and high current account deficits accumulated. A massive bubble ensued. Albeit with differences in magnitude, the crisis-struck five Asian countries had similar difficulties such as excessive inflows of foreign capital, currency overvaluation, current account deficits, high debt ratio of businesses, and high levels of external debts.

The signs of the 2008 global economic crisis were the excessive expansion of the financial market caused by the Great Moderation of the US. The energy of the Great Moderation was the accumulation of current account surpluses in Japan, Germany, and China, and the credit expansion resulting from the accumulation of current account and fiscal deficits in the US. The pileup of surpluses forced capital exports, and the build-up of deficits forced capital imports. In terms of the scale of current account surpluses, Japan recorded US$136.2 billion in 2003, which surpassed 3% of GDP, Germany exceeded 5% of GDP in 2005 and peaked in 2007 at US$249.1 billion, or 7.5% of its GDP, and China recorded the highest point in 2008 at US$412.4 billion, or 9.1% of its GDP. On the other hand, the US current account deficit topped 3% of its GDP in the 2000s, peaking in 2006 at over US$802.6 billion, or 5.8% of GDP. A current account deficit exceeding 3% of GDP causes problems in sustainability.

The aggregated excess capital opened the era of low interest rates. The excess capital stockpiled in Japan opened the era of zero-interest rate in 1995, and the US ushered in a 1% interest rate era from 2001, moving onto a zero-interest era in 2008 with the outbreak of the global economic crisis In 2009, with the UK and Germany joining in the trend, a zero-interest era began in center countries for the first time in history.

The 1997 Asian financial crisis was a regional earthquake that shook five Asian countries, with its epicenter being Tokyo, and the 2008 global economic crisis was an earthquake that shocked the entire global village whose epicenter was New York. The only way for the enormous capital surpassing US$200 billion that exited Asia and gathered in New York to overcome the 1% low interest rate was to create bubbles. When capital does not connect to the real economy, it only creates bubbles, generating the energy for a crisis. The Great Growth of Japan and the Great Moderation of the US opened the era of low interest rates with the entry of China into the market economy as the backdrop, and made central banks in many countries cooperate in the creation of bubbles.

Nothing is free in economics. Aggregation of free things manifests in bubbles created by excessive spending and speculation. Signs of a crisis exist, but preparing for the crisis is not easy in reality. Political populism focused on price stabilization and economic stimulus has the side effect of fostering a crisis.

❙ Tariff and currency wars: Beggar-my-neighbor

When hit by a disaster, people go into survival mode. Since the 18th century, economic crises have brought about enormous disasters, and nations have tried to escape from them by exporting the recessions to neighboring countries rather than working on fundamental solutions.

Boom-and-bust cycle recurs with regularity. Reckless expansion of credit gives rise to wild speculation, which creates a bubble. The inevitable implosion ignites bank runs, which leads to a credit crunch. That, in turn, causes defaults and bankruptcies, eventually resulting in a recession. In response, nations loosen monetary reins. The resultant depreciation of their currency provokes currency wars and accompanying tariff wars with trade partners, or beggar-my-neighbor policies. Such policies deepen recession conditions such as massive unemployment in both center and periphery countries, sometimes turning the economic wars into military warfare.

The US Smoot-Hawley Tariff Act ignited the fiercest tariff war. To protect domestic industries and contain unemployment in the face of the Great Depression, the US raised its tariff rates to almost 60%, the highest tariff in history. The UK, France, Germany, and other European states responded by hiking their tariff rates. The Smoot-Hawley Tariff Act slashed US trade volume by more than 60%, and also reduced international trade volume by around 60%. The recession in Germany resulted from the decrease in international trade volume gave birth to the Nazi regime of Adolf Hitler, leading to World War II in 1939. Were they victims of the "666 curse"?

The Plaza Accord of 1985 was arguably the most aggressive currency gambit. When inflation rates surpassed 10% due to skyrocketing crude oil price caused by the oil shocks in 1973 and 1979, the US aggressively hiked interest rates to 18%. The hawkish policy upended the US manufacturing sector, leading to double-digit unemployment rates. To overcome the situation, the US pushed for currency realignment through the Plaza Accord and the exchange rate of the dollar against the yen fell to 120 yen from 250 yen. Japan responded by lowering interest rates.

This led to stock and real estate bubbles of the late 1980s and when the bubbles burst, Japan was thrown into its Lost Decade. In 1997, eight financial institutions in Japan, including banks and securities and insurance companies, went bust, and stock prices plummeted by 21.19%. The country's current account balance dropped to below US$100 billion in 1996 and 1997, and for the first time, the economy recorded negative growth for two years, starting in 1998. The Plaza Accord was a retribution for Japan's accumulation of excessive current account surpluses.

The US Federal Reserve's quantitative easing of more than US$3 trillion to overcome the economic slump after the 2008 crisis, and the Shinzo Abe administration's unlimited monetary easing to decisively lift Japan from its decades of economic malaise probably will be seen as the most intense currency war. The IMF has maintained a neutral stance on currency wars. Against this backdrop, the G-20 system was established and a new gold standard is being proposed. There was no tariff war during the global economic crisis as countries were not allowed to arbitrarily set up tariff or non-tariff barriers under the WTO system.

I Birth of IMF and GATT

Beggar-my-neighbor policies put nations on a path to co-destruction as witnessed in the Smoot-Hawley Tariff Act during the Great Depression. To avoid such policies, the IMF and GATT were established in 1945 and 1948, respectively.

During my time as a government official, I received considerable assistance from the IMF in the development of Korea's fiscal and financial areas, and participated in the Uruguay Round for the development of the GATT. In 1997, I worked very hard to arrange the IMF bailout loan to Korea. While participating in the IMF and GATT related activities, I felt that under a system led by center countries, the functions of the IMF and GATT would be incapacitated without the active leadership and compromise of center economies. Periphery nations attempted to actively cooperate, embracing the circumstances of the existing international order.

Established in 1995, the WTO went beyond the GATT, which was mainly applied to trade in goods, to cover trade in services and intellectual property rights. Mandated to abolish non-tariff barriers and mediate trade disputes, the organization evolved into a more powerful international body that governs international trade. Although center countries spearheaded the establishment of the WTO, periphery countries had their opinions reflected by actively participating in the process. No country possesses veto power, and although the US and European countries fill most of the organization's roster, participation by periphery nations is guaranteed.

While the international cooperation system in the real economy developed into the WTO, the international financial cooperation has been steered by the IMF. There have been no major reforms in its initial tasks: international monetary cooperation, expansion of trade, and promotion of employment and income in member countries. The Bretton Woods system suffered significant damage when the gold standard system collapsed after the US terminated convertibility of the US dollar to gold in 1971. The US still holds veto power and the IMF operations are still led by the Group of Seven (G-7), which includes the US, Japan, and European nations.

Although the IMF played a leading role in resolving the 1997 Asian financial crisis, critics said the IMF's bailout terms over-represented the interests of creditor nations. The IMF did not play a decisive role during the 2008 global economic crisis and with the growth of the emerging economies, the influence of the G-7, the leading trust of the IMF, faced limitations.

The G-20 system, born against this backdrop, reached agreements during the 2010 G-20 Seoul Summit on institutional reforms, including increasing board seats for emerging countries while reducing those of European countries. Agreements were also made on the principles on government intervention in the foreign exchange market and adjustment of quotas for newly emerging countries and underrepresented nations. However, there were no fundamental discussions on global economic imbalance and international monetary order such as the global currency standard system and the role of key currency countries

It will be difficult to find fundamental solutions to global imbalance and the distortion of international financial order by speculative money if there are no reforms in the global currency standard system and the role of key currency countries. Consolidated development of the roles of the IMF and the Bank for International Settlements is also necessary. One concern is that capital provided by quantitative easing of the US and Japan may lead to another enormous asset bubble.

CHAPTER 2

1997
ASIAN
FINANCIAL
CRISIS

04   Liquidity Mismatch

The 1997 Asian financial crisis can be likened to the region catching a cold from the sneeze of Japan's Lost Decade. The flu that first appeared in Thailand moved north to infect other countries, including Korea, and the East Asian economy crumbled helplessly—except for countries that had nothing to crumble!

The root cause of the 1997 Asian financial crisis was a total of US$207.3 billion of bank loans—US$86.7 billion from Japan, US$22 billion from the US, and US$98.6 billion from the EU—that flowed into Korea, Thailand, Indonesia, Malaysia, and the Philippines. This enormous inflow appeared in the form of bubbles in capital flows, current account balance, corporate debt ratio, and external debts. Due to the inflow of foreign capital, the Asian financial market was buoyant, companies were expanding their businesses, and accumulated current account deficits manifested as bubbles.

Korea built up current account deficits of US$38 billion due to currency appreciation caused by the short-term capital of US$58 billion that flowed into the country in three years preceding the 1997 crisis. Debt ratio of corporations that made investments with foreign-borrowed money reached almost 400%. External liabilities as of 1997 were US$161.6 billion, 31% of GDP, and short-term borrowings amounted to US$58.3 billion. To varying degrees, Thailand, Indonesia, Malaysia, and the Philippines also faced the same kind of problems, including excessive inflows of foreign capital, currency overvaluation, current account deficits, high corporate debt ratio, and high external debts.

With regard to the causes of the 1997 Asian financial crisis, a historical view claims that it broke out in the process of integrating the Eastern world's crony capitalism and secrecy society into the Western world's market capitalism and transparency society following the establishment of the WTO system. Another view says that the crisis occurred as Southeast Asian countries that had been pursuing export-led economic growth suddenly lost their competitiveness with China's entry into the market economy and accumulated outsized current account deficits.

From a statistical point of view, the cause of the Asian financial crisis was sudden outflows of short-term capital amidst a situation where currency was appreciated and current account deficits were piled up due to the prior inflows of excessive short-term money. Compared with the 1996, currency depreciated substantially and current account balance turned into surplus in 1998. This comparison between 1996 and 1998, before and after the crisis, reveals that currency appreciation and the build-up of current account deficits were the roots of the crisis.

In Korea, with a slew of bankruptcies of large companies, including Kia Motors in 1997, US$37.5 billion of short-term borrowings ebbed away. Japan, the largest creditor, withdrew US$13 billion, 60% of its short-term loans of US$21.8 billion. The sudden outflow of Japan's short-term yen-carry funds was the primary reason behind a collapse in the value of the won. Excessive inflows and outflows of speculative capital were bigger problems than economic fundamentals.

| Typhoon from Southeast Asia

The Asian financial crisis began with the collapse of the Thai baht on July 2, 1997, the day after the handover of Hong Kong to China. The day also marked the beginning of a different type of ordeal for the global economy that it had never experienced since the inception of the Bretton Woods System in 1944.

The crisis in Thailand spread to Indonesia and then headed north, triggering a series of redemptions and a 23.3% drop in the Hong Kong Stock Exchange between October 20 and October 24. In November, the crisis arrived in Korea. The contagion effect was fast and strong. China narrowly avoided the typhoon with a fixed exchange rate and foreign reserves of US$140 billion, but its economic growth rate dropped to below 8% for the first time. Malaysia confronted squarely the crisis through capital control, but suffered many wounds. The yen-carry funds of US$86.7

billion that flowed out through the sneeze of Japan's Lost Decade were big enough to make the whole Asia catch a cold.

The Asian financial crisis was different in many ways from the foreign debt crisis of South America in the 1980s. The former was caused by weakness in private enterprises and maturity mismatch caused by using short-term borrowings to obtain long-term funds. The latter was caused by the accumulation of foreign debts in the public sector and misuse of capital, or inefficient investment of foreign loans. Asia had maintained relatively sound rates of economic growth, savings, unemployment, and inflation, but confidence vanished when sudden withdrawals of capital by foreign investors ignited its financial crisis. In contrast, South America's economic fundamentals were poor and defaults on its debts raised the curtain on its crisis.

The crisis of 1997 can be referred to as a financial crisis in that its direct cause was maturity mismatch of short-term liquidity and sudden outflows of short-term money.

| Capital flood and currency appreciation

The 1997 Asian financial crisis and the 2008 global economic crisis told me that if current account balance is not sound, the economy itself is sick. When supply increases, prices fall. That is one of the basic principles of economics. During the 1997 Asian financial crisis, the exchange rate moved in accordance with the inflows and outflows of foreign capital regardless of economic fundamentals. Losing external balance is bound to bring about a crisis in a small open economy that lacks technologies and resources.

The root causes of the Asian financial crisis were currency overvaluation and current account deficits. This is demonstrated by the comparison of the value of currencies to the US dollar and current account before and after the crisis. From 1996 to 1998, the Korean won depreciated 43.1% from 844.2 won to 1,207.8 won, shifting the current account deficit of US$23.8 billion to a surplus of US$40 billion. In Thailand, the baht depreciated 43.3% from 25.61 baht to 36.69 baht, and its current account deficit of US$14.3 billion turned into a surplus of US$14.2 billion. Meanwhile, Indonesia's current account deficit of US$7.6 billion changed into a surplus of US$4 billion when the rupiah depreciated a whopping 236.8% from 2,383 rupiah to 8,025 rupiah. The same situation happened in other countries.

Due to the inflow of excessive foreign capital, currencies continued to appreciate despite the accumulation of current account deficits. This created a vicious circle where appreciated currency expanded current account deficits, which further increased the demand for overseas borrowings. In three years preceding 1996, the inflow of foreign capital increased by US$97.6 billion in Korea, US$55.1 billion in Thailand, and US$39.7 billion in Indonesia. The short-term foreign debt ratio was 48.5% in Korea, 39.5% in Thailand, and 25.0% in Indonesia. The effort to maintain currency value in 1997 was not the cause but a means to prevent the outflow of foreign capital.

Sudden outflow of foreign money

The direct cause of the Asian financial crisis was the dash-in and rush-out of short-term carry trade from advanced economies. Low interest short-term funds that dashed in from Japan, the US, and Europe were used for high interest long-term loans in Asia, resulting in a maturity mismatch. Corporate debt ratios skyrocketed as companies made excessive investments with the borrowed money, current account deficits rapidly increased due to excessive imports of capital goods, and short-term carry funds lit the detonation cord in the securities and real estate markets. Then, one day, the weakness of the Asian economy was exposed, and short-term funds began to rush out, causing the bubble to burst.

Korea, Thailand, Indonesia, Malaysia, and the Philippines suffered the brunt of the Asian financial crisis. They had explosively borrowed low-interest short-term funds from Japan, Europe, and the US and used them to finance long-term loans. When the money flowed out precipitately, their financial markets were devastated. The interest rate of the short-term money market decreased in Japan from 5.56% in 1991 to 0.56% in 1996, opening the era of zero-interest rate, and the figure slightly rose in the US and the UK from 4.09% and 4.31% in 1991 to 5.58% and 5.63% in 1996, respectively. Short-term borrowings for three years before the financial crisis until 1996 increased dramatically in the crisis-hit countries: from US$12.2 billion to US$70.2 billion in Korea, from US$22.6 billion to US$42.6 billion in Thailand, and from US$17.9 billion to US$32.2 billion in Indonesia. This tsunami of short-term borrowings rushed out during the two years, in 1997 and 1998 —US$37.5 billion from Korea, US$12.9 billion from Thailand, and US$12.1 billion from Indonesia. Since discount rates for commercial bills in Asia at that time were around 12% for Korea and 15% for Thailand and Indonesia, the demand for short-term funds from the US and Japan was in fact infinite, and the temptation of low interest rates was far bigger than the risk of maturity mismatch. For Asians, the abrupt outflow of short-term carry funds was a typhoon that could not be controlled by any means, and an unprecedented situation that could not have been imagined in the past.

I made arduous efforts amid this whirlpool of events. I visited HSBC, Barclay's Bank, Standard Chartered Bank in London, and ABM AMRO in Amsterdam in April of 1997 to ask for continued transactions, and promised the government's guarantees for the banks with liquidity problems. In July, I went to Credit Suisse and Swiss Bank in Zurich to request continued business with Korea. During a Foreign Banker's Group meeting in Seoul held in September, I requested the representatives to refrain from withdrawing money precipitately, emphasizing, "A friend in need is a friend indeed."

When Hong Kong financial market stiffened after the great collapse of its stock market on October 23, ways to borrow short-term money were practically blocked. None of the preventive measures worked; they couldn't stop the rush-out tide of short-term foreign funds amounting to US$37.5 billion. The withdrawal of US$13 billion by Japan, the largest lender of short-term money, had the greatest impact.

Forced change: IMF program

As US consulting firm Booz Allen Hamilton pointed out in 1997 that Korea was like a nut in a "nutcracker" of China's low costs and Japan's technical excellence and without "making the irreversible changes," the situation will "eventually force change." Korea was forced to change after all, when it agreed to the IMF bailout. Before Korea, Thailand and Indonesia were also forced to change. While negotiating the IMF bailout funds as Vice Minister of Finance in 1997, I embraced the thought that everything was our fault, accepted the forced changes, and strived to turn the crisis into an opportunity.

The IMF bailouts during the 1997 Asian financial crisis included US$17.2 billion for Thailand, US$43 billion for Indonesia, and US$58.35 billion for Korea, totaling US$118.55 billion. Combined with US$1.37 billion for the Philippines in 1998, the figure rose to US$119.92 billion. Out of such funds, US$22 billion for Indonesia and US$23.35 billion for Korea were contributed by Japan and Europe as a second line of defense.

Albeit with country-specific differences, policy programs implemented as prerequisites for the IMF bailouts largely consisted of four key areas: 1. downward adjustment of macroeconomic policy goals; 2. implementation of tight financial and fiscal policies; 3. financial and corporate restructuring; and 4. expansion of trade and capital liberalization. With the IMF acting as a channel, Japan led the program in Thailand and the US headed the one in Korea. Indonesia suffered severely with the resignation of President Suharto, who had been in power for

33 years.

Thailand applied for bailout funds on July 28, 1997 and received US$17.2 billion (US$4 billion from the IMF, US$1.5 billion from the IBRD, US$1.2 billion from the ADB, US$4 billion from Japan, US$1 billion from Australia, China, Hong Kong, Singapore, and Malaysia, each, and US$500 million from Korea, Indonesia, and Brunei, each) on August 3. The main contents of the policy program included: adjustment of growth rate to 4% and inflation to 9%, financial austerity for cutting off domestic bailout funds, fiscal tightening by cutting 1 trillion baht in spending and raising value-added tax (VAT) by 10%, closures of 56 short-term finance companies and restructuring of the financial industry, expansion of foreign shares in financial institutions by more than 25%, and prohibition of the government subsidies for public services.

Indonesia applied for bailout funds on October 8 and received US$43 billion (US$10.14 billion from the IMF, US$4.5 billion from the IBRD, US$4.2 billion from the ADB, US$7 billion from Japan, US$5 billion from Singapore, US$3 billion from the US, and US$1 billion from Malaysia and Australia, and so forth) on October 31. The policy program was mainly about adjustment of growth rate to 3% and inflation to 9%, fiscal prudence to achieve a budget surplus of 1% of GDP, shutdown of 16 banks and restructuring of the financial sector, privatization and abolition of monopoly, and abolition of fuel cost subsidies. This initial agreement was considerably adjusted through additional negotiations in 1998.

Korea applied for bailout loans on November 21 and received

US$58.3 billion (US$21 billion from the IMF, US$10 billion from the IBRD, US$4 billion from the ADB, US$10 billion from Japan, US$5 billion from the US, US$5 billion from France, Germany, the UK, and Italy, and US$1 billion from Austria and Canada, each), which was the largest amount in the shortest period of time, on December 3. The key contents of the policy program included: 1. adjustment of current account surplus to 1% of GDP, inflation rate to 5%, and growth rate to 3%; 2. flexible management of exchange rates and interest rates, and financial austerity; 3. fiscal tightening through cutting expenditures by 1.5% of GDP and increasing VAT coverage; 4. restructuring of the financial industry, including closure of five regional banks and 22 merchant banks, and the establishment of an consolidated supervisory body; 5. trade liberalization by abolishing the import approval system, and capital liberalization by raising the ceiling on aggregate foreign ownership of stocks to 50%; 6. improvement of corporate transparency and a reduction in debt ratio; and 7. enhanced flexibility in the labor market.

The Philippines received US$1.37 billion of IMF bailout on March 27, 1998 and Malaysia could barely overcome the crisis without applying for IMF bailout loans by pegging the ringgit to the US dollar, controlling capital, raising interest rates, and employing fiscal austerity measures.

Singapore and Hong Kong rode the wave of abrupt capital flows as the financial centers of Asia, and Taiwan and China, with foreign exchange reserves of US$90 billion and US$104.3 billion, respectively, avoided the crisis without much injury. The financial crisis that swept Asia moved to Russia, Eastern Europe, and Central and South America before calming down for a while. No center country realized that the capital that exited Asia could become the embers for another crisis.

Assured about and relieved at the IMF bailouts and support funds of center countries, banks of center economies joined in a rapid flight. Around December 3, when the IMF rescue package for Korea of US$58.3 billion was agreed, Japanese banks went ahead with an intensive withdrawal of US$7 billion, causing the risk of a moratorium despite the IMF bailout. I was completely taken aback by this situation. In fact, the IMF bailout transferred the debts of private banks in periphery nations into government debts, allowing private banks in center economies to withdraw loans through public funds of the periphery governments. The US$13 billion that was withdrawn by Japan was larger than US$10 billion committed by the country. The IMF became the lender of last resort for speculative money, and center countries became the supporters of their own banks. We were in a situation where it was unclear who was providing bailout funds and financial support to whom. First came the malady, and then the remedy, and again the malady. The IMF beat the bush and speculative capital caught the birds. Japanese banks, the biggest lenders to the three Asian countries —Thailand, Indonesia, and Korea —were reassured by the bailouts, and completed their withdrawals under the protection of the IMF.

Wounds of crisis

Asian people suffered unimaginable pain due to the Asian financial crisis. More threatening than that was the tsunami of an enormous amount of short-term carry funds of Japan with almost zero interest rate. People on Wall Street viewed the 50% appreciation of the yen following the Plaza Accord of 1985 as punishment of Japan for using its massive trade surpluses earned through the weak yen for the past 30 years to accumulate national wealth by exporting dollars, not importing goods. The result was Japan exporting the wounds from the Plaza Accord to its Asian neighbors, damaging them again, as it did during the Pacific War.

After speculative money swept across the region, the Korean economy fell off the cliff. The freefall included massive unemployment and banks and buildings sold at giveaway prices. Economic growth rates sharply dropped in 1998 to -5.7% in Korea, -10.8% in Thailand, and -13.1% in Indonesia, while unemployment soared to 7.0%, 3.4%, and 5.5%, respectively. During the crisis, the number of people who lost jobs reached 1.06 million in Korea, 0.85 million in Thailand, and 1.79 million in Indonesia. Stock prices dropped by 61% in Korea, 53% in Thailand, and 64% in Malaysia, and they also fell by 43% and 45% in Hong Kong and Singapore, respectively. Banks and businesses went bust or were sold overseas for their scrap value, and buildings were also sold away. In Korea, more than 20,000 companies disappeared, and six banks and 22 merchant banks were also gone with the wind. Malaysia and the Philippines also suffered greatly and city-states with well-developed financial markets such as Hong Kong and Singapore dodged the crisis. This was the first disaster that appeared after the opening of the global village.

| Asian cooperation: Chiang Mai Initiative

Amid the turmoil of the Asian financial crisis, the first Association of Southeast Asian Nations plus Three (ASEAN+3) Finance Ministers Meeting was held in Kuala Lumpur on December 2, 1997. In commemoration of the 30th anniversary of the ASEAN, three countries—South Korea, China, and Japan—were officially invited, with the US, Australia, Hong Kong, the IMF, and the IBRD also specially participating in the event. The agenda of the conference included the causes of the crisis and regional financial cooperation. At the meeting I explained Korea's efforts to overcome the crisis, saying that it was a difficult pill to swallow, but it might be a blessing in disguise. I had busy time there, cooperating with Japan, the US, the IMF, and the IBRD.

At the opening ceremony, Prime Minister Mahathir bin Mohamad of Malaysia strongly blamed hedge funds for being the cause of the Asian financial crisis. At the joint IMF-IBRD Annual Meeting in Hong Kong on September 20 of the same year, he also insisted that foreign exchange transactions in the international financial markets were abnormal and should be stopped, singling out George Soros as the person who caused the collapse of the Malaysian ringgit. Before that, he claimed that financial market opening was for rogue speculators, and that the world of international speculators was a jungle where cruel beasts were roaming around with nothing to fear. Prime Minister Mahathir's remarks reflected the extreme views of Asians.

With regard to Prime Minister Mahathir's criticism, IMF Managing Director Michel Camdessus defended hedge funds, saying they had a positive influence on global movement of capital based on market functions, and that they were not the main cause of the crisis, given their small scale compared with institutional investors such as pension funds. US Assistant Secretary of the Treasury Timothy Geithner held the same stance. IBRD Vice President Joseph Stiglitz ascribed the cause of the Asian financial crisis to the confidence collapse of the financial market rather than to macroeconomic conditions, and suggested the improvement of transparency in the financial market and the strengthening of supervision and prudential regulations as a means to restore confidence. His emphasis on pursuing growth-oriented policies rather than traditional fiscal and financial tightening in macro policies implied opposition to the IMF's austerity policies.

Financial Secretary Donald Tsang of Hong Kong proposed an initiative to issue regional long-term bonds to improve the situation where more than US$600 billion of foreign reserves in Asia, which had been invested in offshore long-term bonds, were flowing back to the region in the form of short-term borrowings. ASEAN countries and I supported his plan.

Views on regional cooperation measures to prevent the

recurrence of crises in Asia differed from those of Japan. When the bailout package of US$17.2 billion for Thailand was announced on August 3, 1997, Vice Minister of Finance Eisuke Sakakibara of Japan said that his country would play an important role in Asia corresponding to its economic scale. To back the commitment, Japanese Finance Minister Hiroshi Mitsuzuka proposed the creation of an Asian Monetary Fund (AMF) at the IMF Annual Meeting held in Hong Kong on September 20 with US$100 billion in funding. The US and IMF strongly opposed the idea while China reserved its judgment and many Asian countries didn't show active support. The proposal fell to the wayside. An abrupt withdrawal of funds by Japanese banks dimmed the glow of Japan's AMF proposal and Miyazawa initiative aimed at providing US$30 billion of aid to Asia. I thought that Japan's AMF proposal was a good alternative, but was confused about Japan's truth intention behind the precipitate withdrawal of money.

Discussions on the regional cooperation measures in Asia materialized as the Chiang Mai Initiative (CMI) and Asian Bond Market Initiative (ABMI). At the ASEAN+3 Finance Ministers Meeting held in Chiang Mai, Thailand on May 6, 2000, an agreement was reached on the CMI, which was aimed at signing currency swap arrangements among member states to prevent crises; and the ABMI proposed by South Korea was endorsed at the ASEAN+3 Finance Ministers Meeting held in Manila, the Philippines, on August 7, 2003, with the aim to utilize foreign reserves, which were being predominantly invested in the US government bonds, in the regional bond market.

After taking office as Minister of Finance, I attended the ASEAN+3 Finance Ministers Meeting held alongside with the ADB Annual Meeting in Madrid, Spain, on May 4, 2008 and proposed a measure to further develop the CMI from bilateral currency swap arrangements to a multilateral cooperative fund and expand it to US$120 billion. In addition, to vitalize the ABMI, an agreement was reached on my proposal of Credit Guarantee and Investment Mechanism. Before attending this meeting, I chaired the Trilateral Finance Ministers Meeting among Korea, China, and Japan and consulted with Chinese Finance Minister Xie Xuren and Japanese Finance Minister Fukushiro Nukaga to share the contribution to the CMI cooperation fund by the ratio of 80:20 between the Plus Three countries and the ASEAN and adjusted the sharing ratio among Korea, China, and Japan to 2:4:4. Since China and Japan were competitors, Korea's mediating role was important. Next year, it was fixed that Korea would bear 16%, US$19.2 billion, and China and Japan, each, would bear 32%, US$38.4 billion.

Although the proposal on the AMF fell through due to the opposition of the US and the IMF, the CMI and the ABMI functioned as alternatives. I expect the initiatives to be developed into a regional cooperative mechanism that can help Asia to resolve crises on its own.

05

Korean Economy
in a Nutcracker

In a report released just before the 1997 crisis, Booz Allen Hamilton, a US consulting firm, ascribed the economic slowdown of Korea to its high cost–low efficiency structure. "Today, the competitive nutcracker of Japan on one side and China on the other is putting enormous pressures to change on the economy," it claimed. Without "making the irreversible changes," it warned, "plummeting fortunes eventually force change." *The Wall Street Journal* pointed to the leadership vacuum. "The commodity Korea needs most is leadership—and that is something in even shorter supply than dollars these days," it said.

When these observations were made, the economy was already sliding into a crisis and was forced to change by the IMF. We erred in too many things. Forced changes left painful scars on us. They, however, could be disguised blessing. The changes were part of our regrettable history on one hand, but left us with many lessons to learn on the other.

| Pre-crisis missteps

In retrospect, the behavior and statements of policy makers in 1996 were a display of complacency, flawed leadership, and failure to follow through on announcements.

In 1996, the Korean government confidently claimed that it could catch "three rabbits," namely 7.5% economic growth, 4.5% inflation, and US$6 billion current account surplus, in the first half of the year. The government also said that it was not appropriate to use foreign exchange rates to maintain a trade surplus, insisting the currency policy was only a short-term tool designed to treat symptoms. The presidential Blue House pushed restructuring programs, advocating raising national competitiveness by more than 10% with "excruciating efforts" in the second half. For its part, the Bank of Korea said that the country's current account deficit would not exceed US$7.9 billion if exports grew in the second half of the year. Taking a step further, it took a short position in currency forwards against the dollar for the first time in its history to keep the won from weakening. That later was judged "a serious misstep."

No one paid attention to the toxic mixture of 8% flat tariff rate and overvalued currency. Coupled with "excruciating effort" by the Blue House and the central bank's "misstep" the Korean government's effort to catch "three rabbits" was pursued when the won's exchange rates reached a point driving exporters out of business and sharply increased the country's current account deficit to a new high at US$23.8 billion, four times larger than the government's forecast. We missed the biggest "rabbit," played "excruciating" havoc with the economy, and rushed toward a crisis in the following year.

The following quotes from the government and the Bank of Korea (BOK) officials, analysts from the Korea Development Institute (KDI), a government think tank, and other economic experts display their misreading of the brewing crisis conditions.

- "We can catch all the tree rabbits of the macroeconomy: 7–7.5% economic growth, 4.5% or lower inflation, and US$5–6 billion current account deficit." (March 29, 1996, Government)
- "Thanks to the stable (3%–range) growth of the global economy this year, exports and imports are forecast to grow 14.3% and 11.1%, respectively, recording a US$6.5 billion current account deficit." (April 18, 1996, KDI)
- "After reaching US$7.4 billion in the first half, the balance of payment deficit is likely to grow slower on sluggish imports growth in the second half to reach US$7.9 billion by the end of the year." (May 18, 1996, BOK)
- "Of the three macroeconomic goals for this year, the growth and inflation targets are likely to be met, but the balance of payment target is not. Nonetheless, short–term measures treating symptoms such as foreign exchange rate controls are not appropriate." (May 23, 1996, Government)
- "Concerns were raised on the recent economic situation at the meeting of the senior secretaries at the Blue House, but it is our position that the economy is currently not in crisis." (June 29, 1996, Office of the President)

- "The economic policy will be focused on bringing stability to the livelihoods of the working people. If the won continues to weaken, the current account balance will improve by the year's end." (August 8, 1996, Government)
- "Let's pour all our energy into the campaign of raising the national competitiveness by 10% as it is like an all-out war to resolve the problem of high cost-low efficiency structure. Let's improve the competitiveness by cutting cost by 10%, by raising efficiency by 10%, or by both of them." (September 23, 1996, Office of the President)
- "Just as the sun shone again after a raging snowstorm on New Year's Day, our economy will regain its vitality in the second half after a difficult start in this new year." (January 4, 1997, Government)
- "Sharp falls in the value of the won increased fluctuations in the foreign exchange market. However, the current exchange rates rightly reflect the current status of our economy." (January 16, 1997, BOK)
- "At the end of January, the Ministry of Trade, Industry and Energy expressed its opinion to the Ministry of Finance and Economy that the won/dollar exchange rate needs to continue to rise to improve the balance of payment." (January 31, 1997, Government)
- "The Bank of Korea adopted a tough stance in taking a short position in currency forwards against the dollar for the first time to cope with the steep depreciation of the won. The won has weakened 2.9% and the yen has depreciated as much as 5.6% to the dollar over January and February in

1997." (February 12, 1997, Newspaper report)

When the policymakers were misjudging the situation, the economy was slipping into to a crisis. Except for figures on growth and prices, data on the current account balance, external liabilities, and corporations' financial structure were dismal. The following 1997 saw Korea's large corporations go bankrupt one after another. Non-performing loans (NPL) at financial institutions increased. The country's credit ratings fell, and foreign lenders suspended their loans to local financial institutions. The ills facing the Korean economy before it was hit by the full fury of the Asian contagion were seen in five conditions.

First, productivity growth stagnated, but wage, interest rates, and rent continuously rose throughout the 1990s. From 1987 to 1996, the economy grew 8.6% on an annual average, but wages jumped 9.1%. As of 1996, Korea's average interest rate was 11.9%, which translated into a financial cost to the country that was four times and two times higher than Japan's and Taiwan's, respectively. The price of plant land in Korea was also four times more expensive than in the US and Japan as of 1995.

Second, the price competitiveness of Korean products plunged at home and abroad due to the policy mix of 8% flat tariff rate and the overvalued won. The current account deficit exploded from US$3.8 billion in 1994 to US$23 billion in 1996 with the won strengthening 2.3% in 1994 and 1.8% in 1995. In addition, as the 8% flat tariff rate, unseen in other economies, was introduced in 1993, imports of consumer goods surged, and local manufacturers of consumer goods such as textiles and shoes lost their market at home because of weakened price competitiveness. Some of them went bust and others moved production abroad. Exports and investments contracted sharply, but imports and domestic consumption expanded.

Third, local firms heavily borrowed short-term money to fund projects requiring long term to recover initial investments. Therefore, the more they grew, the softer their financial base became. In 1996, the debt-to-equity ratio of the manufacturing sector was 317.1% and 382.0% among the 30 largest conglomerates, figures higher than the US's 159%, Japan's 206%, and Taiwan's 85%. In addition, most of the debt carried by Korean firms was offshore. The accumulated amount of external liabilities of the Korean economy reached US$144.8 billion and the short-term debt, US$70.2 billion, representing 48.5% of the total. The so-called "Miracle of the Han River" postwar development already had become "the mountains of debt of the Han River" by 1996.

Fourth, local financial institutions extended loans to companies based on their size and physical collaterals, thereby failing to check their reckless growths. Without proper knowledge and experience in credit screening, local financial institutions extended excess credit during boom times and curtailed credit supply during a slowdown. This ineptitude created a vicious circle. Companies in distress prompted a pullback in credit, which led to bankruptcies and losses to banks that had extended loans. The cash flow of these financial institutions also became unstable because they had used short-term borrowings for longer-term business loans..

Fifth, financial supervision did not progress in accordance with financial deregulation, opening, and globalization. Short-term debt which had to be regulated was deregulated; and long-term debt which had to be deregulated was regulated. This was a serious misstep taken by policy makers. Without an effective financial supervision in place, non-performing loans increased, undermining the economy's creditworthiness. Separated government agencies supervised the financial industry and they displayed an inability to prevent financial disasters affecting multiple financial institutions or manage a crisis. For example, about 60 financial institutions were involved in the fall of Hanbo Steel, and about 100, in the collapse of Kia Motors. However, they did not have a mechanism to integrate their data or to coordinate their response efforts. Meanwhile, Korea's short-term foreign debt rose sharply, a consequence of reckless offshore borrowing by 24 merchant banks.

| Nut in nutcracker

The root causes of the 1997 foreign exchange crisis were excess foreign capital, overvalued won, and large current account deficit externally, and underdeveloped technology, heavily-indebted companies, and overly-lent banks internally.

Contrary to the confident claim by the Korean government that they could catch "three rabbits," foreign analysts declared, "The government-led economic miracle of Korea was over." In a report titled "Revitalizing the Korean Economy toward the 21st Century," Booz Allen Hamilton painted a grim picture of the pre-1996 Korean economy. "Today, the competitive nutcracker of Japan on one side and China on the other is putting enormous pressures to change on the economy. There is currently a stalemate of many words, without deeds," it claimed. Without "making the irreversible changes," the report said, "plummeting fortunes eventually force change." Main points of the report are as follows.

First, Korea has achieved enormous success over the last 30 years, rising to become the 11th-largest in the world. This outstanding economic success was achieved through a government-guided framework. But the economic miracle has ended. Korea now finds itself in the nutcracker between advanced nations, like Japan, and rapidly developing ones, like China. Korean enterprises face too many unnecessary costs such as high cost of financing, a lack of access to sophisticated financial instruments, inflexible labor conditions, and widespread and costly bureaucratic intervention. The Korean economy has lost its vitality. The knowledge gap between Korean businesses and leading global companies is significant in both managerial and technical areas. Korea's success model, discouraging foreign direct investment (FDI) and earning few industrial friends worldwide, makes it difficult to bridge this gap. Unless Korea escapes the pressures from emerging economies like China equipped with low production costs and advanced economies like Japan with technological advantages, and successfully innovate to regain its competitiveness, it will soon be caught by a myriad of emerging economies, face sharp and massive restructuring, and eventually collapse.

Second, there is currently a stalemate of many opinions, without deeds. There is a raft of analyses about Korea's economic ill and prescriptions but almost no effective action has been taken. This inaction reflects four underlying problems: disagreement over the nature and severity of the economic problems facing Korea; lack of broadly shared vision on economic objectives and the path to them; avoidance of transition issues; and numerous self-interest groups who felt they would be the main casualties of proposed reforms. Some of the few more fundamental actions that have been attempted such as labor reform have ended up being neutered in their passage into law. There is widespread concern that any move to deregulate the financial industry and reorganize the manufacturing sector could trigger a landslide of bankruptcies, delaying the necessary moves. The measures which have been taken to limit *chaebol* dominance of the domestic economy are driving them offshore, accelerating the hollowing out, but not curing the causes of the weakness of the domestic economy. The immature state of Korea's democratic processes has led to an electorate with a low level of trust in the political and business leaders. In light of the economic opportunity and potential for decline facing Korea, today's policy paralysis is increasingly costly and dangerous.

Third, the vision is for Korea to become an advanced, industrialized entrepreneurial economy, without government intervention, acting as a nerve center of Northeast Asia by 2020 and bringing to bear the best of global managerial and technical knowledge. If Korea stands alone in competing against its neighboring economic giants Japan and China, it still risks falling behind. Thus, it must leverage to the maximum extent possible the business and technical knowledge of the rest of the world. It is imperative for Korea to become market-led, knowledge-based, and entrepreneurial to achieve a new economic paradigm. The new economic paradigm implies a new social contract for Korea: a different set of relationships among the government, enterprises, and individuals. With the new social contract, individuals will assume responsibility for his or her own employment, healthcare, and education; enterprises provide employment; and the government will ensure a high quality of life to individuals and an attractive economic environment to enterprises.

Fourth, to realize this vision, the government should adopt a three-pronged strategy: 1. light the fuse to ignite necessary changes; 2. institutionalize the full range of changes; and 3. complete and re-focus the transition. In lighting the fuse, the backbone of the systematic impediments should be broken by restructuring the economic functions of the government, liberalizing the corporate finance markets, and making real changes to gain labor flexibility. To institutionalize changes, Korea has to become a knowledge-based competitor; facilitate the transition to become an entrepreneurial society; establish infrastructure for a regional nerve-center by modifying its educational system and building the physical and knowledge infrastructure; and accelerate its global connections with leading countries to achieve competitive parity with Japan and to maintain the current lead over China. In the third phase, the key task will be to manage the completion of these programs to revitalize the Korean economy.

Fifth, the agenda for lighting the fuse will involve establishing a new body with sufficient authority and independence. The agenda for institutionalizing the changes is widening deregulation, completing educational reforms, stimulating more venture start-ups, developing regional airports and port infrastructure, and identifying one or two advanced countries as core global partners. The agenda for completing the transition is to take stock of the progress and to launch a new set of programs.

The political commitment to see this through and the agreement on the new economic paradigm and the new social contract will be crucial. Otherwise, plummeting fortunes eventually force change.

As warned by the Booz Allen Hamilton consulting firm, the Miracle on the Han River was over, the Korean economy fell into a crisis, and we were forced to conduct reforms. The report was released in October 1997 when the economy was already moving toward the crisis. I sometimes wish it would have been released just one year earlier. If anything can go wrong, it will go wrong.

| Overvalued won and flat tariff rate

In 1996, sluggish exports and mounting current account deficit placed downward pressure on the Korean economy. Increased consumption was barely sustaining economic growth and import growth was keeping inflation at bay. The main culprit behind the widening current account deficit was the worst policy mix of overvalued won and 8% flat tariff rate. Critical to price competitiveness are wage rates internally and foreign exchange rates and tariff rates externally. Changes in the country's current account balance after 1994 demonstrates that its high cost-low efficiency structure, a root cause of the 1997 currency crisis, was closely related with the 8% flat tariff system. In other words, the Korean economy was heading toward a crisis due to external imbalances created by internal balances.

Among the "three rabbits," the Korean economy almost caught the two, growing 6.8% and logging a 4.9% inflation rate in 1996. The current account deficit, however, amounted to US$23.8 billion, four times larger than the government estimate. Export growth plunged to 4.1% in 1996 after rising to 30.0% in the year before from 13.9% in 1994, while growth in facilities investment steadily shrank from 23.9% in 1994 to 18.1% in 1995 and 9.1% in 1996. Meanwhile, during the same period, import growth stayed relatively higher, recording 22.1%, 32.0%, and 11.3%, respectively. Private consumption also rose 8.2% in 1994, 9.6% in 1995, and 7.1% in the next year. These show economic growth around that time was led by domestic demand and inflation was contained by overvalued won and expansion in imports.

Sharp decline in price competitiveness was one of the critical factors that forced the Korean economy to into a crisis. The decline was attributable to the introduction of the 8% flat tariff rate in 1993 as well as the appreciation of the won starting from

1994. This is verified by various economic indicators as is shown below.

First, the won began rising from 1994, making a vivid contrast to the sharp deterioration in the current account balance. The won/dollar exchange rate dropped from 807.2 won in 1993 to 788.7 won in 1994 and then to 774.7 won in the year after. This represented appreciations of the won by 2.3% in 1994 and 1.8% in 1995. The rate reversed to 844.2 won in the next year, for an 8.2% loss in exchange rate. During the three-year period from 1994 when the won began rising, imports jumped 21.8% on an annual average whereas exports grew only 18.1%, which fell further to 14.3% if the effect of the booming chip industry was excluded. In the meantime, the country's travel account deficit surged 75.1% on an annual average over the same period. A stronger won was like a double-edged sword, suppressing exports on one hand while lifting imports on the other.

On the won's rise, the current account balance turned red after recording a surplus of US$2 billion in 1993. Deficit more than doubled from US$4.4 billion in 1994 to US$9.7 billion in 1995 and then surged to US$23.8 billion in 1996. At that time, Japan was running a surplus of about US$100 billion in its current account. The won/yen exchange rate calculated by their relative value against the greenback has a greater influence on Korean exporters' price competitiveness than the won/dollar exchange rate does because Korean exporters were competing with Japan in numerous sectors. In 1996, the yen/dollar exchange rate was 115.7 yen, meaning that the yen's relative value to the won was lower than 1 to 8. This significantly hurt Korean products' competitiveness overseas. Consequently, Korea's exports and investment dwindled, but imports and domestic consumption soared. The export environments were fairly good in 1996 — the OECD member countries registered 3.0% in their GDP growth, the US, 3.6%, Japan, 3.5%, and the EU, 1.7% — and the world's trade volume increased 4.2%.

Besides, the application of the 8% flat tariff rate in 1993 helped boost imports and aggravated price competitiveness of consumer goods made by local firms. Until 1988, the average tariff rate for 2,188 import items was 18.1%. The rate, however, was lowered to 12.7% in the next year. The rate system was then converted to a linear one of 8% in 1993. At that time, tariff rate was 16% for clothing and 30% for running shoes in Japan; 28.6% and 15%, respectively in the US; and 13.8% and 8%, respectively in the EU. Meanwhile, the rate for steel was zero in Japan; 4.1% in the US; and 5.5% in the EU. Flat rate based on average is not an option for tariff rate decision due to different competitive environments for different goods and industries. In general, countries apply higher rates for consumer and finished goods as well as for imports in sectors in which their local industries have low-price competitiveness. In the same formula, they maintain low rates for raw materials and investment goods, and for sectors in which local firms keep strong price competitiveness. No country except Korea has shifted the tariff rate system from multiple rates with an average of 18.1% to a linear 8% rate in only five years to prevent trade friction. The move was too drastic.

For three years from 1994, imports grew 21.8% on an annual average, outpacing exports growth for the same period by as much as 5.7 percentage points. This attests to the fact that the flat tariff rate, along with the appreciation of the won, rapidly aggravated the country's current account balance. Over the period, imports of expensive consumer goods exploded. In 1994, imports of fur clothing, lobster, sedan, and perfume soared 167.0%, 161.5%, 161.4%, and 108.8%, respectively. Imports of whiskey, wine, and color television also jumped 68.5%, 37.2%, and 25.2%, respectively. Such rapid gains continued throughout 1995 before losing steam in 1997.

I believe the combination of a strong won and 8% flat tariff rate was the worst policy combination ever seen in history. It ultimately plunged the Korean economy into a crisis. It was told that in 1996 the Ministry of Finance celebrated its containment of inflation, one of the "three rabbits," it had promised to catch. Low inflation was something to deplore, not celebrate. It is not an achievement of administrative efforts. Rather it is a consequence of tight monetary policy, currency appreciation, low tariff rates, imports growth, and low public utility rates. In the end, the price management bureau within the ministry, which had literally managed prices, was abolished. Governments of advanced countries did not have such a function.

A small open economy cannot but face a crisis if its current account deficit goes above a certain level. Then, external balance should take a priority over internal balance despite criticism when they conflict. Internal balance is represented by low inflation, a fundamental task of central banks, and a value to which politicians pay attention to win votes. This is why governments of countries deal with foreign currency exchanges directly, rather than vesting it in their central banks.

Cracked nut:
Deterioration in current account balance

Cracked by China and Japan, the Korean economy saw the fissure widen in 1996. In the 1990s, it experienced rise in production factor prices and stalled productivity growth, which, together with the stronger won and a low, flat tariff rate, pummeled the country's external competitiveness. This in turn aggravated the current account balance and the resultant accumulation in current account deficit limited the country's ability to repay its offshore debt.

A closer look reveals that the economy lost much of its competitiveness already in 1996. First, it grew 8.6% on an annual average from 1987 to 1996, while wages rose 9.1% during the same period. With the interest rate reaching 11.2% in 1996, Korea's financial cost was four times more expensive than in Japan and two times, than in Taiwan. The price of factory land was four times more expensive than in the US and Japan in 1994. The won/dollar exchange rate gained 4.27% from 1994 to 1995, significantly lowering the relative ratio of the yen to the won to 1 to 10 or below. The competitiveness of Korean products competing with Japanese goods in overseas markets plunged accordingly. Moreover, the average tariff rate of 18.1% which had covered 2,188 items since 1988 was suddenly adjusted to a flat 8% in 1993.

Second, the current account deficit surged to US$23.8 billion in 1996. The deficit exploded from US$14.5 billion in 1994 to US$26.2 billion in the next year and to US$38.2 billion in 1996, excluding the profit earned by the then-booming chip industry. Local firms already struggling with marginalized price advantage lost their home market and suffered setbacks in trade as their exports price competitiveness waned further. Without enjoying opportunities to restructure themselves, some eventually went bankrupt and others had to relocate their factories overseas.

Third, Korea was near default. In 1996, the country's foreign reserves totaled US$33.2 billion, representing mere 47.3% of its short-term foreign debt of US$70.2 billion with the net foreign debt reaching US$41.4 billion. The proportion of the current account deficit of the GDP precipitously rose to 4.2% in 1996 from 1.0% two years earlier. In most cases, a current account deficit exceeding 3% of GDP risks a nation's ability to obtain loans from foreign banks and signals impending sovereign debt default. For instance, facing a situation where its current account deficit accounted for 2.9% of the GDP, the US pushed down the yen's exchange rate to its currency from 250 yen through the 1985 Plaza Accord. The yen/dollar exchange rate continued to tumble thereafter to below 90 yen at its low in 1995. Korea's US$38 billion current account deficit accumulated over the three years until 1996 was too large in relation to its economic size. Its US$161.6 billion in external debt, 31.4% of its GDP in 1997, was too heavy, too, given that the country had very little public debt.

Last, individual companies were near default, too. Manufacturers were making little or no profit in order to service their large and expensive debt. In 1996, the manufacturing sector's debt-to-equity ratio was 317.1% and the average interest rate, 11.2%. In addition, their operating profit to interest payment ratio was 112.1% and the financial cost to revenue ratio was 5.8%, which were too high as well. Against this backdrop, their net profit was squeezed to 0.5% or even below. Korea's debt-to-equity ratio in 1995 was excessively high in comparison with 159.7% of the US, 206.3% of Japan, and 85.7% of Taiwan. The ratio was particularly troubling at 396.2% in the manufacturing sector in 1997, presumably one of the highest in the world. In other words, Korean companies were struggling just to service their debt and using up nearly all of their operating profit to do so.

In 1996, Korea slipped into a crisis and was near default in external competitiveness, current account balance, national ability to repay foreign debt, and corporate ability to repay foreign debt. The IMF recommends a country to hold foreign reserves equal to three months of payments. At that time, Korea's average monthly payment was about US$12 billion, meaning that it needed to reserve a minimum of US$36 billion. Its foreign reserve, however, was US$33.2 billion.

Foreign exchange rates and tariff rates are critical to exports, imports, and wages and at that time were the only means to control them. Foreign exchange rate in particular is also a means to compensate for losses caused by wages hikes and the resultant weakening of price competitiveness. Situations would have been different if the won depreciated by 5% every year. Strengthening of the won coupled with the high cost-low efficiency economic structure was like pouring oil onto a fire. In 1996, exports should have been lifted on a weaker won at the expense of inflation and on a higher tariff rate at the expense of imports. A small open economy is bound to face a crisis if it fails to strike a balance in external payments. Policy makers confidently pledging to catch "three rabbits" despite worsening economic conditions and current account balance in particular, left us in sorrow; and the BOK's attempts to put a ceiling on the won/dollar exchange rate drove us into despair.

Failure in customs management

Witnessing the current account deficit snowballing, I twice attempted to replace the flat tariff rate system with a multiple one: the first was when I was the Assistant Minister for Tax and Customs at the Ministry of Finance in 1995 and the second, the Commissioner of the Customs Service in 1996. The two attempts, however, failed to get any support from the ministry heads.

In 1995, I submitted a proposal to the finance minister to set tariff rates for raw materials and agricultural products at the level of Japan's and the rates for finished goods at the US level. This was in accordance with an international standard of applying higher rates on consumer goods and finished goods, low rates on raw materials and capital goods, and medium rates on the rest. However, the minister, who had led the introduction of the 8% flat rate plan when he was a lower level official, dismissed the proposal. In the next year, as the Commissioner of the Customs Service, I suggested to the new finance minister to apply different tariff rates for 1,524 items based on the opinions of the chiefs of customs offices nationwide. The proposal was turned down once again by the minister who was arguing to catch "three rabbits." Much effort was exerted, but it bore no fruit after all.

A system of multiple tariff rates averaging 18.1% for 2,188 items was replaced with a flat rate of 8%, the level of advanced countries in 1993 to stave off trade friction. The new linear rate system had two problems. First, it did not reflect specific conditions of different industries and different items and second, the figure had to be 12%, the weighted average of price differences of items between Korea and export destinations, not the simple average of 8% calculated by the Korea Development Bank (KDB). Assume Country A and Country B have the same three import items. Country A applies a uniform 8% tariff rate on the imports but Country B applies rates of 6%, 8%, and 10% to the three items, respectively. The average rate of each country is thus 8%. However the influence the actual rate has on the countries' home markets is critically different from market to market. That is, Country A may be more protected or less protected than Country B in a certain market. At that time, Japan had its tariff rate up to 30% on running shoes and the US, up to 15%. For steel, Japan's rate was zero but the US rate was 4.1%.

Tariff rates need to be negotiated very specifically, for example to tenths or hundredths, according to the specific environments of each industry. Japan maintained a 40% tariff rate on imported sweets which competed with its traditional confectionary produced in Kyoto even though its average tariff rate was a meager 1.6%. In addition, price differences between Korea and foreign countries, the basis for calculating the average rate, change over time and "average" is conceptual, not real. The conversion to the linear rate system was something beyond a necessary move to avoid trade friction; it disarmed the country at trade negotiations. The price was dear. Many local firms lost competitiveness even in the home market. Previously, in the 1980s, Chile introduced a flat tariff rate system on the advice of those who subscribed to the Chicago school of economics, but abolished it as its economy plunged thereafter.

After the failed attempt to move the tariff system back to multiple rates in 1996, exports contracted and imports surged. Anyone could make a fortune by importing goods and selling them in the local market. The trade deficit snowballed to US$7.7 billion in just the first half, of the year, nearing the annual target of US$8 billion. The country's ten largest companies accounted for 90% of the deficit. The local consumer goods industry came under attack from both from premium goods imported from advanced countries and cheaper products manufactured in developing countries. General trade companies, which had been created to promote exports and develop raw materials, transformed themselves into aggressive importers when facing harsh conditions for exports. They imported everything that could fetch a hefty profit, from cars, urinals, cosmetics, and golf gear to toothpaste and snacks and then sold them without careful consideration using their abundant capital and well-established network. Their methods accelerated the country's move into a crisis.

| Steps to improve competitiveness

I was appointed as the Vice Minister of Trade, Industry and Energy on Christmas Eve, 1996, when the Ministry was promoting the 300 Action Plans for Trade, Industry, and Energy to address the country's high cost-low efficiency industrial structure. Apart from it, the sense of crisis was mounting in the ministry, which had been leading the country's export-driven high-growth strategy for the previous 30 years. After running a US$3.5 billion deficit in its goods account in 1994, a turn from a US$3 billion surplus in the year before, the deficit skyrocketed to US$16.7 billion in 1996, sending warning signs on the trade account balance. The Ministry believed several big companies like Hanbo Steel, Kia Motors, and SsangYong Motor were on the brink of bankruptcy, and they actually went bankrupt or entered reorganization in the next year one by one.

To stop the trade deficit from increasing further, I dealt with urgent needs first—foreign exchange rates, interest rates, and capital flows—before implementing the 300 action plans.

The first need was to raise the won/dollar exchange rate to 920 won or higher. The BOK stepped into the market to curb the weakening of the won in line with the government's price stabilization policy as the won/dollar exchange rate rose to 840 won at the end of 1996 and then took a short position in currency forwards against the dollar as the rate continued to rise to 870 won in 1997.

At that time, Korea was rapidly losing its competitiveness in its main sectors of exports such as cars, electronic goods, ships, and steel products as the won strengthened in relation with the yen, whose exchange rate to the dollar fast rising to 120 yen or higher. According to a survey conducted by the Trade Ministry and the Korea International Trade Association, exporters could continue their business on a stable footing if the won/dollar exchange rate stayed around 920 won, but had to exclusively focus on the local market or relocate their factories overseas if the rate slid below 910 won.

Based on the results, I insisted to the Ministry of Finance that the won/dollar exchange rate had to continue to rise above 920 won, a threshold for exporters in choosing whether to continue business or not. Korean products lose their competitiveness significantly when the won's relative ratio to the yen falls below 10 to 1. It was therefore inevitable for Korea to run such a large current account deficit given that the relative ratio stayed below 1 to 8. The won/dollar exchange rate had to be 1,100 won or higher in light of the yen/dollar exchange rate at that time. The Ministry disagreed with me, though. A weaker won would help improve the trade balance temporarily, but spark inflation and push up the costs of foreign-currency borrowings, having negative impact on exports in longer-term, it argued. To my despair, the attempt to raise the won's exchange rates ended in vain even though it was an urgent need.

In January 1997, Rudiger Dornbusch, a professor at MIT

and Jeffrey Sachs, a professor at Harvard University advised the Korean government to depreciate its currency, arguing that exchange rate intervention would be the only solution. The MIT professor even criticized the BOK for its acting like a currency czar, which was inconceivable in an open economy. In 1994, a number of Americans suddenly appeared in apartment complexes in Seoul as private English language tutors. This proved that they felt they could earn more money in Korea than in the US thanks to the overvaluation of the won around that time. In 1996, Korea's current account deficit totaled US$23.8 billion, representing 4.2% of its GDP with the figure jumping to US$38.2 if the profits of local chipmakers were excluded.

The second need was about interest rates and capital flows. I compiled a report on interest rate cuts and flexible monetary management with interest rate management as the basic policy tool in order to deal with chronic shortages of capital and high-running interest rates. The report titled, "Pending Issues for Financial Reform in View of Real Economy" was submitted to the Commission for Financial Reform launched at the initiative of the Office of the President. The report contained 11 specific tasks, including interest rate cuts and facilitation of capital supply, improvement in credit management, improvement in exchange rate and trade financing systems, expansion of bottom-up supply of capital, fostering of regional, small-sized financial institutions, and long-term capital supply for facilities investment.

The third need was to dissuade large trading firms from importing goods recklessly. I convened trade balance management meetings, which were attended by director generals from relevant government agencies. We discussed solutions to improve the trade balance based on the monthly trade statistics compiled by item, region, and company by the Customs Service, and asked trading firms to use their sense of morality to limit excessive imports, which was the main culprit in the economy's descent into a chaos. The meeting was part of the last-ditch efforts we made to stave off a crisis.

The 300 action plans referred to above included tasks in the areas of trade, industry, and energy as well as a shift to multiple tariff rates.

About 60 tasks were identified to reduce the trade deficit: 1) 10 to increase capital supply for exports such as expansion of trade bills and export advances, 2) 12 to strengthen support for offshore marketing such as backing companies' participation in overseas trade exhibitions, 3) 13 to improve trade-related institutions, including more deregulation of exports and imports and increase in tariff refund, 4) 11 to minimize factors encouraging imports, including expansion of demand for Korean-made machinery and shortening of the period of consumer goods imports conducted on a deferred payment basis, 5) 8 to promote sound spending such as imposing special tax on luxury goods purchases, and 6) other tasks to strengthen control over shelf life of imported foods, apply tougher punishments to acts of breaching on place of origin rules, and so on.

In the area of industry, 150 tasks were identified to boost the competitiveness by 10%: 1) 27 to reduce production factor costs, including monetary expansion and rate cuts, increased supply of capital for facilities investment, and reorganization of the basic tariff rate system, 2) 47 to boost productivity such as resumption of the temporary capital investment tax credit, reorganization of customs duty exemption, increased tax support for technology developments, and fostering of start-ups, 3) 25 to advance the country's industrial structure, including approval of borrowing in foreign currency and overseas financing for purchases of Korean-made machinery, a rescue fund for smaller firms, and commercial bill insurance, and 4) others to increase the use of Korean-made semiconductor equipment, support technology development for auto parts, remove the ceiling on advances for ship exports and so on.

As for energy-saving, 50 tasks were set up: 1) 11 to lay the foundation for energy saving, including reasonable adjustment of prices, backing of investments into energy saving facilities, promotion of technology development, 2) 28 by source of demand such as implementation of energy saving plans at work places with heavy consumption of energy, promotion of cogeneration, and promotion of district heating system, and 3) 11, including lowering of the standard for the octane rating of gasoline, distribution of anthracite, and efficient use of generation facilities.

The report was very detailed and weighty —it contained status descriptions, issues, foreign examples, possible solutions, expected results, and execution schedules. Officials were assigned to each of the tasks. Minister Ahn Gwang-gu promoted the plans with full energy, checking every detail personally.

However, he resigned in March 1997 to take responsibility for the bankruptcy of Hanbo Steel as the head of the relevant ministry and I was appointed Vice Minister of Finance. Consequently, carefully formulated policies were abandoned, which was regrettable.

06 | 1997 Foreign Exchange Crisis in Korea

The Korean government calls the crisis it experienced in 1997 a "foreign exchange crisis," but the IMF calls it an "economic crisis." The difference is due to differing views on the nature of the crisis. The former believed the crisis was caused by a liquidity crunch stemming from low foreign reserves while the IMF blamed a structural problem in the Korean economy. Both views were right.

Mismatched maturities and collapsed confidence in financial institutions were direct causes of the crisis that swept across Asia in 1997. The trigger was the burst of the bubble created by eagerness for economic growth. The crisis started in Southeast Asia and spread to Hong Kong and Taiwan due to successive redemptions driven by contagion effects. The crisis also spread to Korea and the rest of Northeast Asia.

Meanwhile, the Korean economy was stuck in several dilemmas: the widespread "too-big-to-fail" myth; a flat tariff rate and explosive growth of imports; overvalued currency and mounting current account deficit; and over large short-term debt and sharp flows of funds financed through carry trade. We were in the so-called nutcracker, pressured by China and Japan, while a lot of rhetoric for changes failed to lead to real action. We failed to make changes by ourselves, but were eventually forced to do so by the IMF.

The Korean government pledged it would catch "three rabbits" in 1996. However, the US$28.3 billion current account deficit representing 4.2% of the country's GDP was insurmountable. Different government agencies had different perceptions of the crisis facing the country since none of them ever experienced one. The sense of crisis was high in the Customs Service and the Ministry of Trade, Industry and Energy but not in the Ministry of Finance and the BOK. Their judgments about exchange rates and tariff rates also differed. As the won/dollar exchange rate rose to 840 won at the end of 1996, the central bank stepped into the market to stop further depreciation. When it increased to 870 won at the beginning of the next year, the bank took a short position against the dollar. In the meantime, the Office of the President initiated financial industry reforms through the Presidential Commission for Financial Reform, and the Ministry of Finance was committed to the resolution of the bankruptcy process of Hanbo Steel. No one paid attention to our overvalued currency and flat tariff rate.

Economic health indicator: Current account balance

I was appointed to the Vice Minister of Finance post on March 7, 1997. What I found there was a lack of understanding of the severity of the current account deficit and negligence of the worst policy mix of 8% flat tariff rate and the overvalued won. The whole ministry was focused on programs to raise the national competitiveness by 10%, financial reforms, and other restructuring measures. These were ill-timed and wrong in terms of direction. The economy was not that crucial to politicians when the presidential election was coming up. Only a few news outlets reported on the "rumor of an imminent chaos" from time to time.

In my inauguration speech, I shared my understanding of the state of the Korean economy with the ministry officials. I explained that the first priority would be placed on the improvement of the current account deficit and the tasks to do so were to raise exchange rates and adjust the tariff rate. The details are as follows.

『An economy with a current account deficit is not healthy no matter how positive other economic indicators are. The top priority for us is to improve the current account balance. The only way to do so is to raise the national competitiveness. What determines the success in raising the national competitiveness is price competitiveness affected by foreign exchange and tariff rates in the short term, higher quality in the mid-term, and technology in the long-term.

Despite the current account deficit, the won has been strengthened and stays relatively strong to the yen. With these in place, we cannot improve price competitiveness, external competitiveness, and the current account balance. No other country in the world has an 8% flat tariff rate. Quality and technology development policies are also need to be revisited.

The World Trade Organization system implies economies without borders. In the past, higher taxes ensured higher revenues. In the future, however, revenues will not increase as much as tax rates rise. In light of the current high interest rates, high wages, and high rents, enterprises will have no other option but to leave the country or close down their business if they have to deal with even high tax rates.

Obsession with the past dogmas on currency, interest rates, and foreign exchange rates will make our economic problems more difficult to solve. Think about why the dinosaurs, the Soviet Union boasting about its strong military and the once impregnable Roman Empire disappeared. We, the most powerful ministry, will also suffer the same fate unless we make changes and overcome the dilemmas.

The country's current account deficit soared to US$23.8 billion last year. You my colleagues are the people who have to solve this problem. We are such people who have developed the country from one of the poorest agricultural economy on earth to the world's tenth largest trader in only one generation.』

I began by receiving a brief from Director of the Foreign Exchange Market Division on foreign exchange rates and foreign reserves, which were standing at 863 won and US$29.7 billion. I asked him to prepare daily reports on them and put a yellow note under the desk glass, which read, "Check daily and ceaselessly!" To me, it was like a yellow card to the Korean economy.

| Crisis prevention measures

I worked day and night without a day off throughout 1997. There were a myriad of challenges such as resolutions of serial bankruptcies of large enterprises, management of financial market stability, management of balance of payment deficit, restructuring of the financial sector, and realignment of financial supervisory systems. As international flows of capital hardened, management of foreign reserves and overseas borrowing became higher priorities.

To deal with myriad problems, we disclosed 39 programs on 14 occasions: 7 to restructure the financial sector; 13 to stabilize financial markets; 15 to stabilize foreign exchange markets; and 4 to deal with other economic problems. Sometimes, I feared a crisis, other times, I expected otherwise. I did all I could to stabilize jittery financial and foreign exchange markets. However, to recover confidence and stop capital outflows were insurmountable challenges.

First, we focused on financial restructuring. With the

Presidential Committee for Financial Reform being launched in the beginning of 1997, attempts were made to revise 20 financial laws. They included the Act on the Establishment of the Financial Supervisory Body, the Bank of Korea Act, the Banking Act, the Deposit Insurance Act, the Securities and Exchange Act, the Insurance Business Act, the Act on the Structural Improvement of the Financial Industry, and the Act on Non-Performing Loan Resolution Fund. Seven, including the Act on Non-Performing Loan Resolution Fund were passed by the National Assembly in July, and the remaining 13, in December on a recommendation by the IMF. There were some disputes with the BOK over the establishment of an integrated financial supervisory body. Still, the passage was meaningful in that it ended the 30-year long controversy over the independence of the central bank and the establishment of an integrated supervisory body.

Second, we used all possible tools to stabilize financial markets. They included: 1. creation of the 20 trillion won fund for NPL resolution, 2. a rescue fund for smaller firms affected by the bankruptcies of large enterprises, 3. introduction of bankruptcy protection arrangements to provide opportunities for negotiations between creditors and debtors, 4. bankruptcy protection for Kia Motors, 5. liquidation of failing commercial banks, merchant banks, and credit unions, 6. provision of 2 trillion won in special loans to Korea First Bank and merchant banks by the BOK, 7. 800 billion won in government funding to Korea First Bank, 8. guarantee of full deposit insurance coverage for three years, 9. higher limit on stock savings for workers, 10. separate taxation on 10% of dividends paid to long-term holders, and 11. higher limit on equity investments by the National Pension Service.

Third, measures used to stabilize the foreign exchange market included the following : 1. adjustment of foreign exchange rates to reflect actual conditions of the economy, 2. expansion of the limit on overseas borrowings by banks, 3. expansion of the limit on equity investment by foreigners, 4. liberalization of deferred‐payment imports by small and medium firms, 5. liberalization of issuance of foreign currency denominated securities, 6. government payment guarantee for foreign debt held by financial institutions, 7. elimination of the limit on export advances, 8. opening of the government, public, and corporate bonds markets, 9. liberalization of commercial loans and cash loans, 10. wider foreign exchange rate fluctuation band, and 11. higher limit to US$2 billion on swaps by foreign banks.

The collapses of Hanbo Steel in January 1997 and Kia Motors in July in the same year significantly undermined Korea's international creditworthiness. Against this backdrop, we required financial institutions and enterprises to disclose the details of bad loans and create consolidated financial statements in an effort to enhance their transparency. A total of 11 market stabilization measures were announced after the fall of Hanbo in January, but the problem increased in severity. After August 25, the government announced three package plans that involved using all the available tools to regain market stability. However, stock prices tumbled further and foreign investors accelerated their withdrawals of funds whenever an announcement was made.

At the same time, we took various other steps to fix the country's high cost-low efficiency structure. Among them were programs to facilitate creation of small and medium firms and reorganize existing ones; budget planning with a goal of one-digit growth in spending; mid- to long-term plans to improve Korea's economic fundamentals; and shift to multiple tariff rates.

Important measures are as follows: 1. adjustment of tariff rates for 257 items such as textiles and shoes from 8% to higher levels; 2. exemption of venture start-ups from investigation into sources of capital and tax preferences, including 20% income tax deduction for investment into venture firms; 3. stringent budget planning with a 4% growth in spending; and 4. pursuit of "the National Agendas toward an Open Market Economy." The major agendas were redefining government roles and functions, advancing corporate governance and promoting competition, achieving higher labor flexibility, promoting the Northeast Asia logistics hub plan, achieving technology innovation, and developing information technology.

Aside from such efforts explained above, we continued our efforts to address imminent problems without resorting to the IMF. Special envoys and other high-ranking government officials visited financial institutions in the US, Japan, and the EU after April 1997 to facilitate the supply of funds from overseas. In October, provision of back-up facility was discussed with foreign banks but to no avail.

Financial institutions were on the brink of bankruptcies due to a foreign currency crunch. Thus, the government inevitably supplied funds to help them settle international payments, sharply depleting its usable foreign reserves. S&P and other credit rating agencies downgraded their ratings of Korea. On November 5, Bloomberg added salt into wounds by wrongly reporting that Korea had foreign liabilities of US$110 billion and of it US$80 billion would mature before the end of the year. Foreign banks accelerated their withdrawals regardless of maturities. Korea barreled toward an inevitable default without an outside help.

| Kia Motors: Too big to fail

In early 1997, I received a report at the Trade Ministry that not only Hanbo Steel but Kia Steel was on the verge of default, and SsangYong Motor wouldn't last long, either. If Kia Steel went bankrupt, it would put insurmountable pressure on Kia Motors which provided joint surety for it, the report said. The ministry's officials concluded that the situation would spin out of control unless decisive action was taken. With this in mind, I hurriedly prepared response plans right after being moved to the Finance Ministry.

While staying in New York as a financial attaché, I realized promissory notes, collective bankruptcy, and joint surety were irrational and not available in the US. The practice of using promissory notes for payments could force otherwise financially sound subcontractors to default one by one in a chain reaction. Through the collective default policy of banks, a default at a bank's branch could have triggered defaults at the rest of the branches while the joint surety system spread the risk of a default from one affiliate to other affiliates in the same business group, forcing them into collective bankruptcies. When a rumor of a default circulated, merchant banks which lent money without collateral pulled their money and then other banks followed. As Mark Twain said, they gave companies an umbrella when the sun was shining, but took it back once it began to rain.

Hanbo Steel defaulted in January. The President wanted to clear up the problems without additional defaults of large enterprises. Against this backdrop, the Bankruptcy Protection Arrangement were first introduced in April, modeled on the US' bankruptcy system. The goal was to help creditor banks and companies on the brink of collapse freely come to a compromise through negotiations and seek mutual benefits. The arrangements were also intended to promote stable operations at companies by keeping banks from withdrawing their funds competitively. In addition, the government created a 3.5 trillion won fund to resolve NPLs held by banks earlier rather than later.

Kia Motors, with sales revenue of 12.1 trillion won and debt of 9.7 trillion won, entered bankruptcy protection on July 15. The two main creditor banks, Korea First Bank and Korea Development Bank, had demanded Chairman of Kia to resign and the union to accept a restructuring program as the pre-conditions. The company, however, refused to do so for two months after it escaped the risk of default. With the presidential election fast approaching, not only the opposition party but the ruling party and the government did not want to see Kia go bust and be under court receivership. Kia sought to secure rescue funds from the protection arrangements without having its executives resign.

Kia Motors dragged its feet for three months and finally decided to go under court receivership on October 22. It seemed that the company depended on being treated as "too-big-to-fail," and hoped to survive past the upcoming election and then find ways to keep management intact with a new administration. During the three months, we witnessed the country's sovereign credit ratings plunge. Trusting to the "too-big-to-fail" fallacy lit the fuse of a crisis. The Kia Chairman stood before court the next year.

| Escaping trap of flat tariff rate

The flat tariff rate was the only thing in our tax system that undermined the country's national competitiveness; it significantly aggravated the current account balance. Escaping the trap was thus one of the most important tasks. I tried twice to do so: first when I was the Assistant Minister for Tax and Customs of the Finance Ministry in 1995 and second when I was the Commissioner of the Customs Service in the next year, but to no avail. At the third attempt made after I was became the Vice Minister of Finance in 1997, I finally succeeded in reintroducing multiple tariff rates.

Consequently, tariff rates were lowered for raw materials

whereas those for finished products were uplifted following the precedents of advanced countries. This way, companies' external competitiveness improved while the average tariff rate was lowered. The principle was to match the rates for raw materials and agricultural products to Japan's and the rates for finished goods to the US' to prevent possible trade friction with Japan and the US. Potential friction with other countries was left for individual negotiations. Basic tariff rates were raised for industries such as shoemaking and textile which were facing lowered competitiveness so that they could compete on a level playing field. Particular attention was paid to small and medium firms which had already lost much of their competitiveness. Rates for 257 items out of 2,871 in total were adjusted first in favor of them. It was agreed to adjust rates for the remaining of about 2,000 items step by step, depending on the circumstances of each industry.

The adjustment of tariff rates reinforced the country's tax system. When it came to fiscal soundness and corporate competitiveness, we had no problem. As a junior-level official, I led the initiative to introduce a 10% flat value-added tax in 1977. The tax has been very productive since then: it accounted for about 35% of domestic tax revenue and still represents about 30% of it. The IMF praised it as the best tax system in the world. The tax policy stops individuals and corporations from evading their income tax by functioning as a cross checker at every stage of transactions. Korea was rather concerned about fiscal surplus, not fiscal deficit. The fiscal soundness achieved thanks to such tax schemes was one of the most powerful engines for Korea to overcome the currency crisis in 1997. Since the crisis, Korea has been ranked higher among the OECD member countries in terms of national sovereign debt level.

Heightened tariff rates for some items did not trigger trade friction. The adjustment came after most enterprises had shifted their operations overseas or shut down due to falling price competitiveness caused by the flat tariff rate, without having an opportunity to restructure or shift to other sectors.

The 8% flat tariff rate was the result of flawed judgment and the Korean economy paid a dear price. Unfortunately, the tariff rate scheme was fixed only after two failed attempts. Meanwhile, those responsible for the damage ironically went on their way to adapt well to the times.

▎Overcoming trap of overvalued won

The won's exchange rate against the dollar was 863 won and foreign reserves stood at US$29.7 billion when I arrived at the Ministry of Finance. The most urgent tasks were to lift the exchange rate to 920 won, a point below which exporters would give up selling products overseas; build up foreign reserves to US$36 billion, equivalent to three months' international payments in the current account; and raise the reserves further to US$50 billion as an emergency buffer. I ordered working-level officials to push up the exchange rate to 920 won or higher as quickly as possible, meet the US$36 billion foreign reserve target by end-March, and secure an extra reserve by end-June. Reports were made on a daily basis on the levels of exchange rate and foreign reserves. To monitor the foreign exchange market, hotlines were opened between responsible government officials and large companies that frequently made foreign currency transactions.

According to the Ministry's survey conducted together with the Ministry of Trade, Industry and Energy, the Customs Service, and trading enterprises, manufacturers were not able to break even unless the won/dollar exchange rate surpassed the 900 won level in the first half of 1997. In light of the weight of domestic demand and raw materials in the country's GDP, the lowest optimal exchange rate was estimated at 920 won. As of 1996, the country's monthly current account payments based on imports stood at US$12 billion and rose to US$15.1 billion, including non-trade payments. According to the recommendation by the IMF to hold reserves for three months' payments, the amount of reserves we needed was US$36 billion based on imports and US$45.3 billion, including non-trade payments.

After rising from 863 won at end-February to 897 won at end-March, the won/dollar exchange rate stayed in the 890 won range until May, then fell below 890 won in June. The BOK curbed increases to hold the rate below 890 won, the Maginot Line established by the central bank. I called to the BOK board director for international finance to ask him not to intervene in the currency market, to help the rate surpass 900 won. "890 won is the Maginot Line," the director replied, adding that the point was the appropriate real effective exchange rate and sharp fluctuations in exchange rates were not desirable. His response made no sense to me given that the current account deficit reached the unbearable level. However, it was a hard sale persuading the central bank due to the strained relationship after the revision of the Bank of Korea Act in May. I could only express my view on exchange rates and foreign reserves with sincerity once again.

I ordered to the Ministry officials to continue to increase the exchange rate to 920 won in cooperation with the BOK. In early August, the rate rose above 890 won as withdrawals by foreign banks accelerated, and then exceeded 900 won at end-August. The rate finally broke the 920 won target on October 23, the day when Hong Kong stocks plunged 10.4%, as the crisis spread northward from Southeast Asia.

On November 19 when the Korean government announced that it would not seek an IMF bailout, the won/dollar exchange rate went over 1,000 won for the first time. The rate further rose to above 1,100 won two days later when it requested IMF aid and 1,200 won on December 3 when a letter of intent was signed between the Korean government and the IMF. After exceeding 1,700 won on December 15, the rate peaked at 1,964.80 won on December 24 and then closed the year at 1,415.20 won.

During the first half of 1997, tremendous effort was made not to spend even a single dollar to block the rise in the won's exchange rates and pile up foreign reserves as much as possible. We abolished the limit on banks' mid- to long-term borrowings and the limit on businesses' overseas issuance of equity-linked securities, and allowed foreign-invested companies' foreign currency borrowings for operating capital. As a result, foreign reserves expanded to US$31.9 billion in May and US$33.3 billion at end-June. Nonetheless, US$50 billion in reserves was a far-fetched goal as banks were already feeling the pinch in borrowing offshore as the country's sovereign ratings deteriorated after the fall of Hanbo Steel.

After peaking at US$33.6 billion in July, foreign reserves reversed, falling to US$24.4 billion by the end of November. In particular, usable reserves—foreign reserves minus domestic banks' deposits in their foreign branches—nosedived to US$7.2 billion. In October, we found ourselves in a catch-22. With foreign borrowings cut off, spikes in exchange rates fueled currency speculation and foreign capital outflows. We should have pushed up the exchange rate as quickly as possible to 920 won, the break-even point of exporters, and then kept it at that level to turn the current account to a surplus as well as to ward off currency speculation. However, we spent too much time lifting the rates, during which speculators gained profits, and foreign reserves were drained. There was nothing left for us to do from November to shun an imminent crisis.

The Korean government failed to properly use its powerful tool of foreign exchange rates and accumulated a US$23.8 billion deficit in its current account in 1996. Behind the failure were unshackled flows of short-term funds. The BOK also failed to break from the dogmas of interest rates and prices: it left interest rates unchecked while taking a short position against the dollar to head off hikes in foreign exchange rates in a wrong judgment. It is understandable that as a central bank, it aspires to achieve price stability and thus wants to appreciate the won.

Nevertheless, its move at that time was a serious misstep. The conflict between the Finance Ministry and the BOK over the revision of financial supervisory system made the necessary cooperation even more difficult. Unless things are all right and crisis is nothing of concern, the control of exchange rates should not be trusted with a central bank nor with the market.

The biggest culprit of the crisis was the overvalued won. The current account balance is a composite health index of an economy and exchange rate constitutes a country's sovereign rights to protect its national economy. A weaker currency and capital outflows may be double-edged swords in a crisis; but, it is inevitable to depreciate the currency to improve the current account balance since exchange rate is one of the most critical variables which have tremendous impacts on exports, imports, and wages. I have a personal experience from which I realized control of exchange rates was an exercise of sovereign rights seeing that Japan was forced to double the yen's value to the dollar on September 22, 1985 in an event named the Plaza Accord.

I Fuse of a crisis: Merchant banks

Korea, Thailand, and Indonesia were the most affected countries by the Asian financial crisis. Until 1996, banks in these countries extended long-term loans at high interest rates with short-term money they borrowed at low interest rates from advanced countries and Japan in particular. Against this backdrop, sudden withdrawals of funds by these advanced countries' lenders devastated the Asian financial markets in 1997.

Interest rates of short-term money were very low in 1996. The rate of certificate of deposit (CD) was 5.58% in the US and 0.56% in Japan. Between 1991 and 1996, Korea's short-term borrowings rose 594.5% from US$11.2 billion to US$70.2 billion with the country's 91-day CD rate remaining at 12.63%. This boomed the demand for short-term borrowings from Japan and the US. The lure of low interest rates much outstripped the risk of maturity mismatches.

As of 1996, the country's short-term borrowings stood at US$70.2 billion, representing 48% of its total external liabilities of US$144.8 billion. Local financial institutions' overseas borrowings amounted to US$122.7 billion, including offshore financing and borrowings by their foreign branches, and short-term debt reached US$78.0 billion, accounting for 64% of the total. External liabilities held by merchant banks were estimated at US$20 billion with short-term debt reaching US$12.9 billion or 65% of the total. These institutions were obliged by law to lend their foreign-borrowed money in 1-year or longer loans for facilities investment only. This meant that there were maturity mismatches between borrowing and lending of the US$78 billion funds. Against this backdrop, an outflow of US$37.5 billion in 1997 dealt a fatal blow to the Korean economy. In particular, merchant banks were forced into a situation where they were no longer able to borrow money or roll over existing debt regardless of maturity in 1997. At the end of 1996, lending extended by local financial institutions amounted to 163.7 trillion won. Discount bills, trade bills, overdrafts, and other short-term debt instruments with maturity of less than 1 year accounted for 21.5% (35.2 trillion won) and longer-than-1-year debt, the remaining 88.5%.

There were 30 merchant banks in Korea in 1997. After the financial market liberalization of 1982, the number of short-term finance companies mainly involved in discounting of short-term bills rose to 32. The top eight market leaders among these companies were transformed into commercial banks or securities firms in 1992. Of the rest, nine regional short-term finance companies were converted into merchant banks in 1994 and the remaining 15 followed suit in the following year. This conversion increased the total number of merchant banks to 30, including six existing ones. The 24 short-term finance company-turned merchant banks had no prior experience in foreign exchange. They recklessly borrowed short-term money with easy lending standards at low interest rates and lent it on a long-term basis in search of higher profits with scarce knowledge of the risks entailed. In 1996, 90-day CDs paid 0.56% and its prime rate was 1.63% in Japan, and the same facility paid 5.58% and the prime rate was 8.25% in the US. CDs with shorter maturities offered lower yields. In Korea, CD yields were much bigger with 91-day CDs paying 12.63% and the average interest rate of corporate lending was 10.98%. Unlike Japan or the US, CDs with shorter maturities offered higher yields.

Merchant banks absurdly provided lease financing for bowling alley equipment with their short-term debt, sparking bowling booms even in small neighborhoods in provinces at the expense of the country's current account balance. They competitively jumped into international financial markets. They even bought junk bonds from Thailand, Indonesia, and Russia with short-term money, and could not pull their money back when the crisis hit those countries.

As the country's sovereign ratings were downgraded in the wake of the fall of Hanbo Steel, Korea's merchant banks faced a situation where they had to survive day by day with ultra short-term money with maturities of less than one week. The default of Kia Motors almost suffocated them; they had to resort to overnight lending. A report during that time described them as a herd of people in every nook and cranny of the financial market in Hong Kong looking for money regardless of cost, amount, and maturity.

The Capital Market Division, the Industrial Financing Division, the Securities Division, and the International Financing Division of the Ministry of Finance conducted supervision of merchant banks by function. The governing laws were also varied such as the Banking Act, the Securities and Exchange Act, the Securities Investment Trust Business Act, the Short-Term Financing Business Act, the Equipment Rental Business Act, the Foreign Exchange Control Act, and the Foreign Capital Inducement Act. Inspection was trusted with the auditors' office of the Ministry, the Office of Bank Supervision of the BOK, the Securities Supervisory Board, and the Credit Management Fund. Systematic and comprehensive supervision was not existent nor was integrated information.

Merchant banks were on the brink of default on their foreign debt in August when capital outflows accelerated upon Kia's filing for bankruptcy protection. The government provided US$1.5 billion from foreign reserves for 12 of them whose foreign currencies dried up. With large enterprises defaulting on their debt one after another in October, the BOK gave a special 1 trillion won loan to Korea First Bank, the main creditor of Kia Motors, and another 1 trillion won to 16 merchant banks experiencing severe shortages of capital. These were the first central bank's loans to merchant banks.

Without crisis experience, we neglected the importance of managing short- and long-term foreign borrowings. With little knowledge of the risk of short-term debt, we made a critical mistake of deregulating financial institutions to borrow short-term money at lower interest rates. We should have tightened supervision after loosening financial regulations. The IMF described this as an act of confusing regulation with supervision, pointing that we loosened them all together.

After seeing the reckless behavior of merchant banks, foreign credit rating agencies downgraded Korea's ratings to the bottom and foreign lenders cut off their supply of short-term money to local banks. The 24 former short-term finance companies were finally driven out of the market, but only after devastating the local financial markets. Hence, we were ensnarled in a US$78 billion short-term debt trap and the fuse of a crisis was lit.

| Sharp withdrawals of short-term funds

Short-term funds with low interest rates swamped Korea's financial markets like tsunami until 1996, and fled the country when a crisis hit it in the next year. Of US$62.9 billion short-term money financed through carry trade, as much as US$37.5 billion were pulled back in only one year, wreaking havoc with the economy. Such sharp outflows of capital were like a typhoon that could not be handled with anything, and unimaginable to most in the country which had never experienced something similar since the opening of financial markets to the outside world.

Local financial institutions had to pay higher costs for their foreign debt and found it difficult to take out new loans from March 1997. Foreign lenders began pulling their loans from August. At the end of 1996, 13 local banks owed US$94.5 billion to foreign lenders with US$62.9 billion being short-term. Of them, US$37.5 billion was withdrawn in 1997. Japan which represented the largest share of Korea's short-term foreign debt pulled US$13 billion or 60% of its US$21.8 billion short-term lending. The EU withdrew US$7.6 billion or 45% of the US$17.3 billion, and the US, US$2.1 billion or 38% of the US$5.6 billion. Japan's move was so much faster and larger that we could not manage appropriately.

At that time, short-term debt offered 12.63% in Korea. That was 7 percentage points higher than the US' 5.58% and 12 percentage points up from Japan's 0.56%. This wide gap fueled the near six-fold explosive growth in short-term money flowing into Korea from US$11.2 billion in 1991 to US$66.5 billion in 1996, the year before the currency crisis swept Korea. No one could imagine short-term money funded through the yen carry trade to be pulled back in such short time.

We did all we could do to stave off sharp withdrawals of funds. I explained Korea's efforts to improve its current account balance and restructure its financial sector at the annual meeting of the European Bank for Reconstruction and Development held in London in April 1997. I asked HSBC, Barclays, and Standard Chartered Bank, all of whom had many transactions with Korean banks, not to suspend their lending while promising the Korean government's payment guarantee for local banks suffering from a liquidity squeeze. HSBC Chairman Willie Purves, a Korean War veteran, recounted the UK's experience of receiving emergency liquidity support facilities from the IMF and pointed to three factors pushing foreign banks to cut their supply of short-term funds: first, they were concerned about Korea's militant labor unions; second, they had doubts about Korean companies' transparency, seeing the massive default and bribing scandal of Hanbo Steel; and third, worries over the unpredictability of North Korea lingered. Days at London were long and gloomy. In a meeting with Chairman of ABN AMRO Jan Kalff in Amsterdam, I repeated what I had told to other bankers in London. His response was not positive, too.

On the way to Geneva to attend the meeting of the UN Economic and Social Council, I visited Credit Suisse and Swiss Bank in Zurich in July and asked for continued relationships with Korea. It was before the financial crisis materialized in

Southeast Asia and signs of a default of Kia Motors emerged. Korea's foreign reserves increased to US$33.3 billion and borrowing costs turned to edge down at the end of June. The atmosphere turned a little upbeat in meetings in Zurich. The spread of short-term borrowings by commercial banks soared from 38 basis points at end-March to 61 basis points at end-May before tumbling to 50 basis points in July. I became confident we could overcome the difficulties if exchange rates surpassed 900 won and foreign reserves were increased to US$36 billion. Until then, Swiss banks remained positive about retaining back-up facility to help Korean banks. However, as the fall of Kia Motors was announced and Thailand fell victim to a crisis at the end of July, Swiss banks became concerned and market conditions began to sour again.

I explained the Korean government's diverse efforts to stabilize its financial markets at the meeting of the Foreign Bankers' Group on September 11. "Korea was the only country recognized for full repayment of foreign debt at the World Debt Congress in New York in 1985," I emphasized, calling for the bankers to refrain from pulling money drastically. "A friend in need is a friend indeed. We will never forget today" I added. However, Japanese bankers were unwavering in their position that they had to pull their money back, citing orders from their headquarters to meet the capital adequacy ratio of 8% set by the Bank for International Settlements (BIS) prior to the settlement scheduled at end-September. Japan's situations were not much better than ours—eight banks, trust funds, securities firms, and insurers went into default in 1997 alone.

We implemented 14 sets of measures to stabilize financial markets and shun drastic withdrawals from March. Despite these efforts, short-term borrowings were practically cut off after the Hong Kong financial markets experienced a squeeze in the wake of the plunge in the Hong Kong Stock Exchange on October 23, 1997. Bloomberg reported on November 5 that Korea's foreign reserves stood at only US$15 billion and US$80 billion short-term debt out of its total US$110 billion external liabilities would mature before the end of the year. This exaggerated report sent things out of control. Among the US$37.5 billion which left Korea in 1997, Japan withdrew US$13 billion. In particular, it pulled US$1.3 billion in the first two weeks after the Bloomberg report and another US$7 billion thereafter until the end of the year.

I had known Vice Minister of Finance of Japan Eisuke Sakakibara since working in the International Finance Bureau in the Ministry of Finance. I called him on November 21, the day when we applied for an IMF help. I asked him to provide a bridge loan of US$10 billion until the IMF bailout was provided. He answered that Japan would provide support in due course in the framework of IMF, and consultation with the US was important. I once again asked him to persuade Japanese banks to refrain from pulling their funds too quickly at the ASEAN+6 Finance Ministers' meeting in Kuala Lumpur on December 2, the day before signing the IMF bailout deal. He said the Japanese government could not stop the banks from doing so since they were also going into default one after another. Collection of funds by Japanese lenders was particularly intensive around

December 3 — they pulled US$7 billion around the time of agreement on the US$58.3 billion IMF help. This raised even the possibility of national moratorium. In a last-ditch effort, I sent a letter to Vice Minister Sakakibara on December 19, which read as follows:

「I would like to request your kind consideration on recent hesitation by the Japanese banks to roll over short-term debts of Korean financial institutions due this month, which gives us great concern since its size is comparatively larger than borrowings from banks in other regions. The thing that worries us more is the fact that Japanese banks are accelerated the withdrawal of their loans to Korean banks since December 10, 1997, which could jeopardize the stability of the foreign exchange situation of Korea leading to the difficulties in implementing the IMF package as envisaged.」

The three attempts to get help from Japan resulted in nothing. I only felt ashamed in an unforgettable way. Japan also saw eight of its banks, securities firms, and insurers go bankrupt and its stock market plunge 21.19% in 1997, a time during the Lost Decade. Nonetheless, Japan was accountable for a large part of the Asian financial crisis. The Plaza Accord of 1985 was a consequence of retaliation against Japan's excessive current account surplus, which led to the Lost Decade. The behavior displayed before the crisis amounted to transferring the pain to neighbors. There was no friend in need. Japan lent us its umbrella when the sun was shining and took it away quickly when it rained.

| Failed financial reforms

President Kim Young Sam announced he would pursue financial reforms in the New Year's address in 1997. He said all 20 financial laws, including the ones regarding the establishment of a financial supervisory body and the BOK would be revised and, for this, a presidential committee would be established with private-sector experts, including a businessman as chairman. The decision was a strong move taken when there was only one year left before the end of his term in office. But it deepened the lame duck period of the president.

In 1997, supervision of local financial firms was not conducted in a proper manner and their capital structure was bad. They lacked external competitiveness and had poor lending practices. Specifically, progress in financial regulation and supervision was not in step with the trends towards financial deregulation, opening, and globalization. Heavy dependence of enterprises on debt led to bad loans mounting in financial institutions, further aggravating their capital structure. This in turn downgraded their credit ratings and deteriorated their external competitiveness. The long-held practice of requiring material collateral for loans did not function as a brake on irrational pursuit of growth. There were about 60 financial institutions involved in lending to Hanbo Steel and about 100, to Kia Motors, but no system was there for integrated information and supervision. Worse, 24 merchant banks recklessly borrowed money from overseas, ballooning the country's short-term debt in foreign currency so quickly. The focus of the financial reform plan was placed on the central bank act and the act on one integrated financial supervisory body, which were modeled on the laws governing the US' Federal Reserve System and the Office of the Comptroller of the Currency. I directly worked with junior officials to formulate the revisions.

The main objectives in the revised law on the BOK were as follows: 1. establish the Central Bank Act to replace the Bank of Korea Act; 2. establish the Monetary Policy Committee, and the BOK, a special corporation to execute the decisions of the Committee; 3. have the Committee Chairman appointed by the President after deliberation at the State Council meeting assume the post of the BOK Governor concurrently; 4. grant the Minister of Finance the rights to suggest bills to the Committee and to request re-examination of decisions, and the Vice Minister the right to attend and speak at the Committee meetings; and 5. trust the job of foreign currency exchanges with the Ministry of Finance and have it have consultations with the central bank when necessary.

The main points of the revision to the act on financial supervisory body were as follows: 1. establish a single financial supervisory agency under the Ministry of Finance, which would govern the supervision of all financial institutions; 2. trust the rights to legislate laws on financial supervision and authorize a financial institution to the ministry; 3. set up the interim Financial Supervisory Commission to control three legally private supervisory organizations for banks, securities firms, and insurance companies; 4. incorporate the organizations into the Financial Supervisory Commission after three years; and 5. establish an integrated organization which would provide insurance for deposits at all financial institutions.

During consultations with the Presidential Committee for Financial Reform and the ruling party, it was agreed to modify the Central Bank Act to the Central Bank of Korea Act and to take the banking supervision authority from the BOK and set up the Financial Supervisory Agency at a later time. It was also agreed to establish the Financial Supervisory Commission and the Financial Supervisory Service, a legally private organization, as interim agencies. The modified bills were submitted to the National Assembly.

According to the final draft of reform bills in June, the BOK's Office of Bank Supervision was to be abolished. Then the bank employees threatened to go on strike and even challenged the BOK governor, who had agreed to abolish the Office to step down, calling him a "traitor." With the prospect of a crisis looming large, the internal dispute made it difficult for the bank to cooperate with the Ministry of Finance, driving a wedge in their relationship. Another conflict in the relationship occurred when the BOK adhered to 890 won as the ceiling of the won's exchange rate to the dollar. "The government's argument has no ground that it is urgent for the National Assembly to pass the financial reform bills, including the one seeking integration of financial supervisory agencies," claimed senior officials of the Bank in a statement. These actions deepened the divide between the BOK and the finance ministry when cooperation was needed more than ever to complete the reforms. Former BOK governors conducted an anti-reform demonstration in front of the National Assembly building and the demonstration was reported worldwide.

Of the 20 bills, seven less controversial laws, including the Act on Non-Performing Loan Resolution Fund were passed during an extraordinary session of the National Assembly in July. The remaining 13 bills were submitted to the Assembly at end-August, but the sub-committee meeting to examine them was convened as late as in November after going through hearings at end-September and submission to the Finance Committee at end-October. Members of the political circle were obsessed with the presidential election coming in December. Lawmakers from both the opposition and the ruling parties said it was premature to pass the bills or passage needed to be postponed no matter how strongly the government stressed the urgency of passage to maintain the country's credit ratings. Members of the ruling New Korea Party who did not regard it helpful to win more votes paid no attention to the bills, and even demanded the president leave the party.

The disputes were very influential in the decision by foreign credit rating agencies to downgrade the country's ratings. Also, it disclosed to the world that Korea was all talk, but no action, and a country with no leadership.

The opposition party lawmakers did not attend the finance committee meeting held on November 17 while the ruling party was reluctant to pass the bills unilaterally. The regular session was over on the next day with the prospect of a crisis looming large and the bills drifting to nowhere. On the same day, I left Seoul in the morning to attend the Korea-China Economic Vice Ministers meeting in the afternoon. I had to cancel the remaining schedule and return to Korea the next day upon hearing that Deputy Prime Minister and Minister of Finance Kang Kyung-Shik had been dismissed. The reason was not clear but I assumed it was political. Replacing the person in charge of crisis management added confusion as the country was struggling to weather the economic turmoil.

From mid-August, I never passed a day without checking foreign exchange rates and foreign reserves. I spent most of my time in the National Assembly to push through the budget for 1998 and financial reform bills from November. A sub-committee of the Finance Committee started deliberation of tax laws and financial reform bills on November 3 and the Special Committee on Budget initiated deliberation of each ministry's budget plan seven days later. I had to attend the three sub-committee meetings on budget, tax laws, and financial reform bills, which all proceeded in parallel. I wished I had three of me to attend them all. However, all these efforts ended in vain and the economy became a lame duck. We decided to announce that the country would apply for IMF aid on November 19.

Efforts coming to naught

The Asian financial crisis, which ignited in Thailand and

Indonesia in July 1997, spread to Hong Kong and Taiwan in October and then to Korean in November as investors rushed to redeem their loans. Like Southeast Asian countries, Korea had dash-in and rush-out short-term money financed through carry trade, which converted cheap short-term money in advanced countries into expensive long-term loans in Asian economies.

Local financial institutions extended long-term loans with debt they borrowed from overseas on a short-term basis, resulting in mismatched maturities. Local corporations made excessive investments and imported capital goods with borrowed money, drastically boosting deficits in the country's current account. The short-term carry trade funds also sparked a boom in the local stock exchange. Against this backdrop, heavy debtors defaulted on their debt one after another and bad loans mounted in financial institutions. They saw their confidence collapse and foreign investors rushed out of the country with their money. This was how the bubble-and-burst cycle played out in Korea.

In 1996, Korea's external liabilities stood at US$144.8 billion with short-term debt reaching US$70.2 billion, and its current account deficit amounted to US$23.8 billion. The debt-to-equity ratio was 317% in the manufacturing sector and it was even higher at 382% among the 30 largest business conglomerations. Upon the successive defaults by large enterprises, foreign investors aggressively collected their money back, which totaled US$37.5 billion in 1997 alone.

During the 1997 crisis, successive defaults of large companies prompted non-bank financial institutions to withdraw their funds indiscriminately. Non-performing loans piled up in financial institutions, severely undermining their credit worthiness. This in turn caused foreign creditors to pull their money back. The liquidity crunch proceeded as follows.

First, Hanbo Steel failed to repay their debt upon maturity, which was followed by Kia Motors and other large enterprises. The series of defaults exposed the limits of leveraged business operations such as obsession with external growth, excessive amount of short-term debt, and reckless entry into areas where they lacked expertise.

Second, upon the serial defaults, non-bank financial institutions which largely extended collateral-free loans, rushed to collect their money, further aggravating a liquidity squeeze in the financial market. For instance in 1997, merchant banks withdrew 6.4 trillion won, representing about 25% of their total purchases of discounted bills. This implies that not only ailing companies but firms with a sound financial base were forced to default on their debt.

Third, as corporate defaults continued, the amount of NPLs in financial institutions soared to 38.2 trillion won by the end of November in 1997 and their credit ratings tumbled consequently. Overseas borrowing costs precipitously rose to a point which it is actually impossible to take out new loans. Afterwards, Moody's cut Korea's credit rating by six notches from A1 to Ba1 and S&P, by as much as ten from AA- to B+. The spread of the KDB's 10-year bonds skyrocketed more than ten times from 60 basis points at end-1996 to 650 basis points in December 1997, suffocating additional inflows of funds.

Fourth, foreign banks swiftly joined the ranks of taking their money out of the country. The default of Kia Motors verified their suspicion that Korean companies' financial statements lacked the transparency demanded by international standards. Then, they refused to roll over loans to local financial institutions after August 1997. From October, even foreign investors began aggressively pulling their money from the stock market.

On November 5, Bloomberg reported Korea had only US$15 billion in foreign reserves while its US$80 billion short-term debt out of the total external liabilities of US$110 billion would mature before the end of the year. The report sent things out of control. IMF Managing Director Michel Camdessus made a secret visit to Korea through the cargo terminal of Gimpo International Airport on November 16, being aware that awareness of his visit would impact the economy, and met with Finance Minister Kang Kyung-Shik in Intercontinental Hotel in Seoul. Minister Kang asked for emergency liquidity support facilities and they agreed on the provision of US$30 billion.

All of the efforts and pains ended in vain. We applied for an IMF help on November 21 in the end. We could not stand the sudden, massive outflows of US$37.5 billion or as much as 60% of the total short-term foreign debt held by financial institutions. The economy slipped into a recession, massive layoffs ensued, and local banks were sold to foreign buyers at dirt cheap prices. As the Vice Minister of Finance, I stood against the turmoil caused to the Korean society with all the dedication and effort. This experience left scars on one hand as well as lessons on the other. I cannot forget the days in 1997.

07

Forced Changes: IMF Bailout

In 1997, Booz Allen Hamilton compared Korea to a nut placed in a "nutcracker" with China's low costs and Japan's technical excellence applying the pressure. The US consulting firm warned that without "irreversible changes," the situation would "eventually force change." Soon the changes were really forced upon Korea by foreign powers. Interpreting the situation, *The Wall Street Journal* pointed out, "the commodity Korea needs most is leadership — and that is something in even shorter supply than dollars these days." Indeed, we suffered from a leadership vacuum.

As the Asian financial crisis crippled Korea in 1997, I took on the role of negotiating with the IMF for bailout funding. Although foreign powers were dictating the structural changes, I needed to demonstrate leadership with deeds to save Korea from being trapped in the nutcracker for a long time. It was a vital role that could decide the fate of the country and it demanded nerves knowing I would be judged by history.

Our basic negotiating stance was to turn the forced changes into spontaneous action. We were willing to embrace the opinions of the IMF and the US based on the premise that everything was our mistake. We made the restoration of external confidence and the improvement of international balance of payments the highest priorities. If hardship is unavoidable, it is best to actively respond to it. This was the lesson I learned from my past negotiations with the IMF on fiscal and financial policies and negotiations with the US on opening up the financial market when I was a junior official. In some ways, the changes being demanded were a blessing in disguise. We had to show leadership to turn it into reality.

One cannot survive competition with a closed mind in the global age. As a result of adopting a closed-door policy at the dawn of the 20th century, we suffered the pain of losing the sovereignty of our nation. With China acting as the world's factory and Japan displaying the highest level of manufacturing prowess in Northeast Asia, which was becoming the center of the world economy, Korea had reached a crossroads not knowing where to go. But we knew that failure to escape the nutcracker effect would have doomed Korea.

| Requesting IMF help

After Thailand applied for the IMF rescue package on July 28, 1997, and Indonesia applied on October 8, Korea became the third country to request bailout funds, on November 21. Minister of Finance Kang Kyung-Shik was supposed to announce the bailout request on November 19, but there was three days of hesitation because he was being replaced.

Lim Chang-yuel, the new minister, was inaugurated at 3 p.m. on November 19 and he announced "Comprehensive Measures for Financial Market Stability and Financial Industry Restructuring" at 6 p.m. The main contents included: widening the foreign exchange rate fluctuation range from 2.25% to 10%; increasing the funds for the resolution of NPLs from 3.5 trillion won to 10 trillion won; raising the scope of a guarantee of principal and interest of deposits from 20 million won to the whole amount for three years; suspending foreign exchange activity of bankrupt merchant banks; and enforcing management improvement and conducting acquisitions, mergers, or closures of nonviable banks, merchant banks, and credit unions.

The measures, which were originally scheduled to be announced by Minister Kang on November 19, changed in several items: the limit on the foreign exchange fluctuation range was lowered to 10% from 15%; the decision to request the IMF bailout was deleted; and a plan to issue government bonds or pursue BOK-led syndicated loans among central banks was added. Minister Lim stated, "We can restore confidence of the international financial market through these stabilization measures, and if the international financial circles cooperate accordingly, we can resolve the currency crisis without the IMF's financial support." He added, "If Korea, which is the world's 11th largest trading partner, goes wrong, the US and Japan will also face problems."

In the evening of that day, Minister Lim met with working-level officials of the Ministry of Finance and the BOK at the Renaissance Hotel. Having worked as an Alternate Executive Director at the IMF and the IBRD, he recommended reconsidering the decision to go to the IMF because the IMF rescue package would be accompanied with demands for aggressive restructuring and belt-tightening. This was the reason why the original plan to apply for the IMF bailout was replaced with the plan to issue government bonds and pursue syndicated loans among central banks. Discussions were made on the syndicated loans, issuance of government bonds, back-up facility, and so forth. The meeting ended after midnight without a clear-cut conclusion.

The next day, Kim Young-sub, the newly appointed Senior Presidential Secretary for Economic Affairs, delivered a message from President Kim Young Sam. It said that the request for the bailout needed to be announced as soon as possible as agreed with the IMF. However, Minister Lim still wanted to reconsider the matter. In the afternoon, IMF First Deputy Managing Director Stanley Fisher and US Assistant Secretary of the Treasury Timothy Geithner arrived in Korea. They had come for necessary preparations, believing that Korea would have announced its request for an IMF bailout on November 19, following the agreement with IMF Managing Director Michel Camdessus on November 16. It was quite natural for the US Assistant Treasury Secretary to come with the IMF Deputy Managing Director since the US participated in back-up loans as well as IMF-led financial support, and it was also natural that they came promptly since it was a matter of urgency. But upon arrival, they found that the situation had changed.

In the evening, Minister Lim, BOK Governor Lee Kyung-shik, Mr. Fisher, and Mr. Geithner met at Metropolitan Club of the Lotte Hotel to discuss the bailout, but they did not reach a definite conclusion. The IMF and the US obviously wanted to proceed as agreed earlier. Senior Secretary Kim Young-sub thought that turning to the IMF was unavoidable, and I shared his view. If a bailout could have been avoided, we would have done so, but if it wasn't, the best thing would be to commit as soon as possible.

In the morning of November 21, the inevitability of turning to the IMF for bailout was discussed at an emergency meeting chaired by President Kim Young Sam at the Office of the President. Minister Lim, after meeting Mr. Fisher for the second time, told a press conference in the afternoon that day, "To resolve liquidity shortage problem, if necessary, we will cooperate with the IMF, and also with our allies, including Japan. We have not requested the bailout yet, and we will draw a final conclusion on whether we will apply for it or not within two to three days."

That afternoon, I telephoned Vice Minister of Finance Eisuke Sakakibara of Japan, who was in charge of international finance. I had known him since the time when I was the Director General of the International Finance Bureau. I asked for a bridge loan of US$10 billion through swaps between central banks until we could receive the bailout funds from the IMF. For the first time, I had this ominous feeling that Korea might face a sovereign default; Japanese banks began to further accelerate their withdrawal of capital from the previous day. He answered that the support would be provided through the due process within the framework of the IMF. He added that reaching a consensus with the US would be crucial.

Considering what Vice Minister Sakakibara said and the visit of Mr. Fisher and Mr. Geithner to Korea, it was evident that the IMF, the US, and Japan already had decided their position on how to respond to Korea's currency crisis. I reported my telephone call to Minister Lim and said that there was no other way than to receive the IMF bailout funds at the earliest possible date. Minister Lim then called Japanese Finance Minister Hiroshi Mitsuzuka and received the same answer.

On Friday, November 21, 1997, at 10:15 p.m., Minister Lim Chang-yuel announced the request for liquidity support from the IMF. The main thrust of his statement was the following:

Accepting the recommendations of many allies and the IMF that it is necessary for Korea to resolve the financial hardship by working with the IMF, we decided to apply for the IMF bailout funds. We are expecting US$20 billion from the IMF to put out the most urgent fire. The IMF is expected to dispatch a working-level negotiation team to Korea early next week to start detailed negotiations with our government, and we think it would take three to four weeks until the fund is provided. We expect our international creditworthiness to be improved if we receive the IMF bailout funds, dispelling fears in the market, which will eventually resolve the liquidity shortage we are facing now at the earliest possible date. Since we anticipate considerable difficulties in economic management, including restrictions in macroeconomic and fiscal management and acceleration of restructuring in the financial industry, we need active cooperation from the public.

Short-term capital continued to be withdrawn from Korea even after the announcement, and the three days of indecision had substantially damaged foreign investors' confidence.

The Wall Street Journal Asia article under the headline "Seoul Swallows IMF's Medicine: But If Left with a Bitter Taste" said that Korea once treated the IMF negotiations team as the "stooge" of the US Treasury, and that the IMF's efforts in Korea have involved a "messy clash" of "proud institutions." The article described Minister Lim as a "strong nationalist who could stand up to IMF leadership," and also described Korean officials, in particular, the new finance minister, as "embodying the 'Korea knows better' school of thought." At that time, our image shown to the IMF people was too negative.

Strategies of negotiation with IMF

As the head of our negotiations team, I dealt with the terms for the IMF bailout and the accompanying economic program. The appointment of a vice minister as the team leader and chief negotiator with the director of the IMF's Asia and Pacific Department showed how much significance was given to the task. I organized the team into seven groups led by the ministry's directors for more effective negotiations. Their areas of concern were general management, macroeconomy, fiscal policies, supply and demand of foreign currencies, currency/interest rate/exchange rate, financial structure, and industrial policies. After the seven groups prepared negotiating strategies, we decided the scale of the bailout and positions on key requisites for the funding in consultations with relevant authorities. Macroeconomic and fiscal policies, financial reform, exchange rate policies, and industrial and labor policies were included in the key conditions for the financial aid.

Our basic priorities were the restoration of international investors' confidence and the improvement of international balance of payments. I brought a global perspective to the table, based on my experience of negotiating with the IMF on fiscal and financial policies and with the US on the financial market opening when I was a working-level official. We referred to the cases of Indonesia, Mexico, and Thailand and produced "Strategies for Negotiating the IMF Stand-by Arrangement." The main points of the strategies were as follows:

Basic objectives: 1. turn the IMF economic program into "Korean Program" so that we lead and the IMF cooperate; 2. request a large enough bailout fund to restore foreign investors' confidence; 3. decide conditions for the bailout based on our circumstances and within the framework of our policy direction; and 4. devise implementation plans for financial reform bills, which were pending at the National Assembly, and "Comprehensive Measures for Financial Market Stability and Financial Industry Restructuring" announced on

November 19.

Methods: 1. seek a package settlement regarding the scale of the fund and conditionality; 2. introduce a phased implementation system on a yearly basis for policies that could have great impact on the economy to buffer such impacts; 3. proceed with the negotiations based on faithful provision of data and trust; and 4. exclude private business sector from the negotiations.

Strategies for the key conditions: 1. decide financing gap at a level that can assuage the international financial market and heavily front-load the IMF funding; 2. prioritize macroeconomic goals to improve international balance of payments over the next three years; 3. implement educational policies and infrastructure construction as planned in view of our fiscal soundness to avoid extreme austerity; 4. restructure the financial industry, with emphasis on mergers and acquisitions based on the OECD schedule; 5. accept a demand for a tight monetary policy and high interest rate and phase in reforms in the foreign exchange market; and 6. decide industrial and labor policy depending on IMF suggestions.

Timing: we wanted the negotiations schedule to be accelerated, given that our foreign exchange situation was continuously getting worse even after the bailout request had been made. Bailout negotiations typically take three to four weeks to complete. But for this negotiation, we set a goal of reaching a working-level agreement by December 5, within 10 days, assuming the negotiations would start on November 24. Given approval on the agreement by the IMF executive board, we thought Korea could receive the first disbursement by the following Monday, December 8. For this purpose, it was decided that the finance minister would participate in the ASEAN +6 Finance Ministers Meeting to be held in Kuala Lumpur on November 30 and have contact with the US and Japan to receive their cooperation.

Bailout size: The scale of the requested fund was to be more than US$50 billion. Foreign exchange reserves as of November 26 totaled US$24.2 billion, but the amount of usable reserves was only US$9.3 billion. Additional foreign currency requirements were estimated to be over US$56 billion in total—US$10 billion for short-term debts coming due, US$36 billion for adequate foreign exchange reserves, and US$10 billion for other usages, including payment for forward exchange. External liabilities amounted to US$119.7 billion.

IMF economic program

In the afternoon of November 23, two days after the government made an official request for the bailout, an IMF team working on the financial sector led by Assistant Director Tomás Baliño arrived in Seoul, and on November 26, the director of the IMF's Asia and Pacific Department Hubert Neiss, the leading negotiator, also arrived in Korea.

The IMF team brought a draft titled, "Main Measures of the Economic Program to be Supported by a Stand-by Arrangement with the IMF," which was prepared in Washington D.C. The goal of the program was an early return of foreign investors' confidence.

The draft contained 10 measures. They were: 1. set macro-economic goals of reducing the current account deficit to 0.5% of GDP, containing inflation at or below 5%, and adjusting real GDP growth to 2–3%; 2. immediately introduce tightened monetary policies and allow a rise in interest rates and exchange rates; 3. maintain a fiscal surplus of 0.2% of GDP by increasing VAT coverage and widening the corporate tax base; 4. expedite financial sector reform bills by passing a revised Bank of Korea Act and the Act on the Establishment of the Financial Supervisory Body at the National Assembly before the end of 1997; 5. liquidate insolvent financial institutions based on clear principles and accelerate the disposal of NPLs; introduce a limited deposit insurance scheme; and adjust capital adequacy ratio of banks to meet the BIS 8% minimum requirement; 6. enhance trade liberalization by eliminating export-related subsidies and abolishing the import diversification program; 7. accelerate capital account liberalization by eliminating restrictions on foreign ownership of domestic equities and foreign direct investment; 8. improve corporate governance by enhancing transparency of corporate balance sheets through external audits based on international standards, by obliging business conglomerates to prepare consolidated financial statements, by reducing the high debt-to-equity ratio of corporations, and by preventing government intervention in bank lending decisions; 9. reform the labor market by strengthening the capacity of Employment Insurance system as well as improving labor market flexibility; and 10. provide financial information through regular publications of data on foreign exchange reserves, forward exchange, NPLs, capital adequacy, ownership structures, and affiliations.

The key features of the document were the establishment of a consolidated financial supervisory agency, liquidation of insolvent financial institutions, a complete opening of the stock market, and improvement of corporate transparency. Elimination of the import diversification program, which was a matter of interest to Japan, was also included.

Regarding the scale of funding, it was agreed that an enough funding would be provided after due diligence on the status of foreign exchange reserves and debt maturities.

The IMF's economic program agreed in principle with our own thinking since it was based on policies we already had announced. Abolition of the import diversification program also had already been decided. We determined to fix details through due diligence on specific circumstances and statistics. The working groups proceeded with negotiations on particular items, and I directly negotiated with IMF's chief negotiator Hubert Neiss on major issues, including the scale of the fund and the Act on the Establishment of the Financial Supervisory Body.

Mr. Neiss was from Austria and he was a quiet and nice person. He said two important things to me: to resolve the current economic crisis, Korea should persuade not the IMF but the international financial market, which was the place where the crisis occurred; and even if Korea and the IMF reach a consensus, the agreement would not pass at the executive board without the consent of the US and Japan. In other words, Korea needed to focus on convincing the international financial market, the US, and Japan, not the IMF. I decided to trust him and the IMF. I also acknowledged the efforts of the US and Japan to preserve their domestic banks' loans. I started from the premise that all the problems originated from our policy failure and we had to pay the price.

| Presidents' talk: Finish in one day

On Friday, November 28, at 3 p.m., I received a telephone call from President Kim Young Sam. Minister Lim was on a business trip to Japan to meet Japan's Finance Minister Hiroshi Mitsuzuka at that time. The conversation, recorded in my business log, was as follows:

"I got a call from President Clinton, and our situation is worse than we thought. The government has no idea. The negotiations should be finished within today. We heard that the US can give the money only when we finalize all the necessary procedures by next Monday."

"I will try to make it within today. I will do my best not to cause worries."

A summary record of the telephone conversation between the two Presidents below shows that President Clinton was very specific and stern.

『President Clinton said he had heard that Korea was in extremely dire financial state, and it could face a default as early as next weekend. He said the only practical way that Korea could choose was to reach a consensus with the IMF on an economic and financial program that was necessary to restore confidence and announce it in a few days, before Monday at the latest. If Korea prepares a powerful economic program, the US is ready to support through a package in cooperation with other countries, with the IMF, the IBRD, and the ADB leading the process. President Clinton heard that the financial authorities in Korea had asked the US and Japan for provisional financial support in the form of bridge loans for the next three weeks, during which Korea would come up with its program with the IMF. President Clinton and all of his aides believe that bridge loans would have no effect. A short-term bridge loan would run out in a few days. It would only delay decisions essential for restoring confidence. The loan should not be separated from the IMF program. If it is separated, money will run out in a few days. Everyone will lose money and Korea will not get any help. We must deal with this problem as soon as possible. Treasury Secretary will contact Korea's Deputy Prime Minister to explain an action plan on this matter after this call.』

At that moment, Minister Lim was in Tokyo consulting with Japan's Finance Minister Hiroshi Mitsuzuka on getting a bridge loan. After their meeting, the spokesperson of Japan's Ministry of Finance said:

『When the negotiation between the IMF and Korea is finalized, Japan will be also poised to support Korea along with the IMF. We will discuss the scale of the IMF's funding with relevant countries within the framework of the international support led by the IMF. We hope that Korea will reach a consensus with the IMF on the framework and principles of the assistance as soon as possible.』

It was evident that the IMF reached a consensus in principle with the US and Japan on their stance after the agreement on financial support between the former minister Kang Kyung-Shik and Managing Director Michel Camdessus on November 16. It was essential for the IMF to have prior consensus with the US, the real power broker in deciding the financial support, and Japan, which would provide the largest amount for the back-up loan. The US and Japan had no choice but to actively engage in the process to protect their own banks who had provided massive loans to Korea. We were going in the opposite direction from where the IMF, the US, and Japan were heading, accelerating the fall of confidence of the international financial market as a result. Regarding the situation at that time, *The Washington Post* reported that there were discussions within the US government on letting Korea fail and pay the price for economic mismanagement. The summary of the article is as follows.

『The US government and the international financial club are displeased with the Korean government's continuous requests for a faster bailout schedule while delaying IMF demands, including financial reform, after applying for the IMF funding. Treasury Secretary Robert E. Rubin's "tough love" message was much louder: he insisted that even with their help, Seoul should get religion about the need for far-reaching reform. The fate of South Korea, on the brink of default, changed when state Secretary Madeleine Albright and Defense Secretary William Cohen expressed strong concerns about the possibility of unrest and crisis on the Korean Peninsula if South Korea went bankrupt, and international banks in Seoul considered giving the South Koreans some breathing room by granting extensions on the billions of dollars of short-term debt. At a White House meeting where Albright and Cohen were participating, Rubin said the US would agree to a package of accelerated U.S. loans to South Korea, based on the expectation that the banks would come through and the South Korean authorities would step up their moves to revamp the economy. On December 24 an additional US$10 billion infusion of cash to Korea by the Group of Seven major industrial nations (G-7) along with the IMF's bailout was announced.」

| Consensus on economic program

After receiving the telephone call from President Kim on November 28, I closed my eyes and prayed silently. With the right to make a final decision not granted to me, it was impossible to finalize the negotiations within a day. I told myself, "Let's go to the Hilton Hotel and negotiate through the night!" There was no way but to do whatever I can do as a man and wait for God's will. I went to the hotel in preparation for around-the-clock talks the next two days.

I called Mr. Neiss and told him that I and my team would be at the hotel that evening to hammer out undecided matters. I met with him and told him about the President Kim's call, and we agreed to have the final negotiations the next day after organizing our stance on undecided matters that night.

At a late night meeting with director generals and directors, I listed the undecided matters and we worked on solutions. There were five undetermined matters, which included issues on macroeconomic indicators, a revised Bank of Korea Act, audits on financial institutions, cancellation of capital in banks, and abolition of Interest Limitation Act. Through a working-group meeting that lasted until 4 a.m. on November 29, we organized our positions on the undecided matters. Our decisions were: 1. accept GDP growth rate of 3% on the condition of flexible management; 2. decline to submit a revised Bank of Korea Act by fully explaining discussions and legislative progress; 3. change the wording of "international firms" to "internationally recognized firm" because stipulating accounting firms that conduct audits of financial institutions as "international firms" can make the country lose its face; and 4. accept the cancellation of capital in banks and abolition of the Interest Limitation Act, which had been strongly demanded by the IMF.

At 8 a.m. I convened a meeting of assistant ministers at the Hilton Hotel and checked our proposals on undecided matters again. At 10 a.m. I met with Mr. Neiss and concluded the negotiations on the aforementioned five matters. All of our positions were accepted and at 11:30 a.m. I joined a State Council meeting chaired by President Kim to report that basic terms had been reached and that the specifics of an agreement would be finalized that day. In the afternoon, I briefed Minister Lim, who had returned from Japan, and finished consulting the heads of relevant government ministries at 5 p.m. Two hours later, I informed the President about the agreed upon IMF economic program.

The final meeting to wrap up the negotiations began at 11 p.m. and we reached an agreement on the memorandum on the basic policy program at 1:30 a.m. on November 30. Basic policies on macroeconomic management and financial restructuring contained in the IMF's draft were agreed without major changes. Items for the capital market opening and the maintenance of the real-name system in financial account were added.

The Memorandum on Economic Program was the same as the IMF draft except for some minor changes. The main points called for: 1. adjusting the growth rate to 3%, containing inflation at or below 5%, and implementing tightened monetary and fiscal policies; 2. accelerating the disposal of NPLs and restructuring financial institutions; 3. passing financial sector reform bills before the end of 1997; 4. establishing a timetable to meet the Basel Core Principles; 5. increasing the ceiling on aggregate foreign stock ownership from 26% to 50%, and to 55%; 6. providing consolidated financial statements and strengthening corporate disclosure rules; and 7. strengthening the capacity of the new Employment Insurance system and taking steps to improve labor market flexibility. This memorandum was attached to the Letter of Intent for requesting a stand-by arrangement from the IMF.

Since the working groups of both sides disagreed on high interest rates and cancellation of capital, I directly consulted with the working group of the IMF and we reached an agreement.

In regards to the interest rate, the IMF said we should make it more advantageous to hold the won than the US dollar to prevent hoarding of the dollar. It warned that failure to prevent hoarding would cost Korea a massive amount of foreign capital. Based on this argument, the IMF insisted on the necessity of a temporary high interest rate until currency speculation sentiment abated. Under the IMF's interpretation, if the won depreciated by 40%, the interest rate of the won should be over 40%. Otherwise, people would hoard the dollar.

The IMF pointed out that during the currency crisis in Mexico, the interest rate increased to as high as 73% to prevent currency speculation. Our working group doubted that level was possible in Korea, citing the nation's Interest Limitation Act, which placed a ceiling of 40%. However, I embraced the IMF's opinion. Afterwards, domestic criticism arose over the high interest rate. But it was needed to keep currency speculators at bay and was intended to be temporary. The policy mistake was keeping the rate high even after currency speculation had subsided.

Next, regarding retirement of stock, the IMF insisted that cancellation of the whole capital met the global standards. However, Korea's Banking Act required a minimum capital of 100 billion won and our working group argued that the minimum should remain intact to protect business rights and minority shareholders.

The IMF said global loss-sharing standards recommended that 1. the entire loss of stocks, subordinated bonds, straight bonds, and secured bonds should be written off in that order; 2. immediately after the write-offs, nationalization should be implemented and new management should be organized; and 3. employees would be laid off in case of need. I accepted the global standard and wrapped up the negotiations.

A detailed timetable for the IMF economic program was prepared before Christmas of 1997. On January 13, 1998, the Interest Limitation Act was abolished and the Banking Act was also revised.

| Side letter: Tough negotiations

After finalizing working-level negotiations on the IMF bailout program within three days at the behest of the presidents of Korea and the US, I went home in the early hours of November 30, anticipating a 10:50 a.m. flight to Kuala Lumpur to join the ASEAN+6 Finance Ministers Meeting. A telephone message from Richard Christenson, Acting US Ambassador to Korea, was waiting for me. He wanted me to return his call because of an urgent matter regardless of the time. When I called him around 3 a.m., he suggested a meeting with US Under Secretary David Lipton, who was arriving in Seoul later in the morning. I explained that I had a flight to Kuala Lumpur but the ambassador said even a short meeting would be alright. I agreed to meet at a coffee shop of the Intercontinental Hotel at 8:50 a.m. and went to bed.

I met Under Secretary Lipton as scheduled, explained how the negotiations unfolded and the areas of agreement. He made no special comment. Pressed for time, I had to leave after 15 minutes. I did not know the exact purpose behind the meeting.

During December 1-2, 1997, I stayed at Renaissance Hotel in Kuala Lumpur where the ASEAN+6 Finance Ministers Meeting was held. The purpose of my trip that time was to explain Korea's effort to overcome the crisis and discuss measures for financial cooperation with the IMF, the IBRD, the US, Japan, and China.

During the meeting, IMF Managing Director Camdessus pointed out that the situation in Korea was "sudden, most acute, and painful," and that the growth would resume if all necessary actions were taken, adding that a consensus would be reached within 24 hours. He also stated that besides the primary support from the US and Japan, European countries were also expected to provide a second line of defense to Korea.

I explained that Korea's restructuring effort would be a "difficult pill to swallow, but a blessing in disguise" and Assistant Treasury Secretary Geithner emphasized the necessity for bold and expeditious actions. After the ministers' meeting, at a joint press conference attended by more than 300 foreign correspondents on December 2, Malaysia's Finance Minister Datuk Seri Anwar bin Ibrahim issued a joint statement consisting of 15 items. Many of the reporters' questions dealt with the currency crisis in Korea and I explained the policy program. I also had an interview with the UK's Reuters news agency on the crisis.

In Kuala Lumpur, I had long days, taking time out of my busy schedule to meet IMF Managing Director Camdessus, Senior Vice President of the World Bank Stiglitz, US Assistant Treasury Secretary Geithner, Japanese Vice Minister of Finance Sakakibara, and First Vice Minister of Finance of China Liu Jibin. Meeting with representatives from many countries, I realized, under the Kuala Lumpur sky, the prosaic truth that if a country has no power, it is given a cold shoulder. It was arduous and sad overseas business trip. I asked for support related to the IMF bailout and had consultations on financial cooperation. I discussed important matters with Japan and the US, which I describe in detail below.

On December 1, I asked Vice Minister Sakakibara to persuade Japanese banks to refrain from the precipitate withdrawal of their funds, but he said that the Japanese government could not stop the banks since they were also going into default one after another. He promised a second line of defense package in cooperation with the US and Europe and also assured Japan's active support at the IMF executive board He said that although the scale of financial support from Japan was undecided, it would be larger than that of the US, and that the total amount of the funding would exceed US$50 billion, which would consist of support from international organizations—US$20 billion from the IMF, US$10 billion from the IBRD, and US$4 billion from the ADB —and US$20 billion as the second line of defense in the form of bilateral assistance. I could sense that Japan had already had close consultations with the IMF.

On the same day, I met Assistant Treasury Secretary Geithner and noted that a provisional agreement was reached on the memorandum with the IMF right before my departure from Korea. He said additional negotiations were under way on new issues that had emerged. The US was very concerned about the contents of the agreement between Korea and the IMF, and called for a much stronger program. The immediate closure of 11 insolvent merchant banks was a prerequisite for IMF support. New demands in capital liberalization were more than what we promised to the OECD. They included allowing foreign financial institutions to participate in mergers and acquisitions of domestic banks, permitting limitless foreign ownership of domestic stocks and bonds, and eliminating limitations on foreign direct investment. Mr. Geithner also mentioned applying a higher penalty rate for liquidity support by the central bank and maintaining high interest rate. He stated that closing, restructuring, and recapitalizing were necessary for Korea First Bank and Seoul Bank. He also mentioned that direct soft loans to enterprises should end, reform of corporate governance and labor market rigidity should be promised, and political commitment to the IMF program should also be made. Lastly, he emphasized the US' demand for "clear, concrete, and upfront action" by Korea. The situation took on a completely different complexion.

I immediately informed Seoul about my meetings with Vice

Minister Sakakibara and Assistant Treasury Secretary Geithner. The substance of those talks was far different from the tentative agreement between Korea and the IMF, and new negotiations began on the US objectives. Back in Seoul, negotiations on such additional demands were already under way upon the arrival of Under Secretary Lipton. I left Kuala Lumpur at 11 p.m. on December 2 with Mr. Camdessus, who was due to sign the stand-by arrangement in Seoul. We arrived at the Gimpo Airport at 7 a.m. on December 3 and I heard how the situation had changed considerably. Via the IMF negotiations team, Under Secretary Lipton had demanded a side letter containing new requirements and compliance letters and public statements from presidential candidates in Korea to ensure the implementation of the IMF agreement.

The new requirements to be included in the side letter were an immediate closure of insolvent banks and merchant banks, a sharp increase in the call rate, and a complete opening of the capital market. I assumed that this action was taken with the intention to nail down Korea's policy in advance due to Treasury Secretary Rubin's distrust in Korea.

The backdrop to the compliance letter demand was presidential candidate Kim Dae-jung's election campaign comment that he would "renegotiate with the IMF" if elected. Foreign news media called his remark "unbelievable" and said Koreans' reaction to the crisis was emotional and radical for declaring their plight "the IMF crisis" and complaining their economic sovereignty was being lost and put under IMF trusteeship. Such views were not rational, considering the IMF was coming to the rescue with tens of billions of dollars, the foreign press said.

The final version of the agreed side letter was not disclosed at that time. It consisted of two parts: Prior Actions, which were to be taken before the IMF executive board approved the stand-by agreement, and Banking Reforms that could create jitters if made public.

The Prior Actions mainly included: 1. bringing the call rate to 25% by December 5; 2. applying a penalty rate of 400 basis points above the London interbank offered rate (LIBOR) if the BOK injects foreign exchange to domestic banks; 3. increasing the ceiling on aggregate foreigners' ownership of listed Korean shares from 26% to 50% by end-1997, and to 55% by end-1998, and allowing hostile takeover; and 4. permitting foreign financial institutions to participate in mergers and acquisitions of domestic financial institutions.

The main points of the Banking Reforms included: 1. requiring merchant banks to submit rehabilitation and restructuring plans; 2. requiring Korea First Bank and Seoul Bank to meet the BIS 8% capital adequacy ratio; 3. requiring other commercial banks to provide a resolution plan of NPLs and financial institutions to submit rehabilitation plans; 4. authorizing subsidized public assistance to banking institutions only after absorbing losses by current shareholders and non-guaranteed creditors; and 5. preparing an action program to strengthen financial supervision and regulation. In addition, to ensure proper monitoring of the economic program, the opening of a resident representative office of the IMF was requested.

Later, the side letter was implemented as agreed with the

IMF. Much of the contents in the side letter already had been reviewed or was in the comprehensive measures for financial market stability which had been laid out by former Finance Minister Kang Kyung-Shik on three occasions in the previous three months. The only difference was in approach. The working group from the IMF demanded an immediate closing of two banks in distress—Korea First Bank and Seoul Bank—and 12 failed merchant banks. We preferred a phased approach based on available procedures for mergers and acquisition to mitigate the shock to the financial market. From the time when the BOK began to provide special loans of 1 trillion won to Korea First Bank and each merchant bank, I thought that bank closures would be a more viable option since reviving the institutions would have cost more than shutting them down. Merchant banks were the trigger for the currency crisis and they soon disappeared.

Distrust for Korea by the IMF and the US lurked behind the requirement of clearly specifying the date of actions and the names of merchant banks subjected to closure. The root causes of distrust were the broken promise with Mr. Camdessus and the request made to Japan for a bridge loan after we had applied for the IMF bailout. I believe that it was against the same backdrop that President Clinton opposed the bridge loan. Of course, Kim Dae-jung's comment that he would renegotiate with the IMF if elected president also soured the atmosphere.

Birth of consolidated supervisory body

The most important part of the IMF economic program was the creation of a consolidated financial supervisory body and a new central bank. The program ended the conflicts between the Ministry of Finance and the BOK, which continued for half a century from 1948 after the establishment of the Korean government. The endless war of attrition surrounding the BOK, which was created by a foreign power, the US Federal Reserve Board, was extinguished by another foreign power, the IMF.

The root cause of the conflict was a report, "Banking Reform in South Korea," also known as the Bloomfield Report. It was written by Arthur I. Bloomfield, Chief Economist of the Balance of Payments Division at Federal Reserve Bank of New York in 1950. The report recommended a central bank modeled after the US Federal Reserve Bank, which was organized much like corporations, with combined aspects of the Board of Governors of the Federal Reserve System, a federal agency that belongs to the Congress, and the Office of the Comptroller of the Currency within the US Treasury Department. The BOK established based on this model caused many legal problems from the beginning.

After the establishment of the government, there were divergences of opinion between the Ministry of Finance and the Bank of Chosun (the old name of the central bank) surrounding the founding of the BOK. This prompted President Rhee Syngman to invite US experts—one of them was Mr. Bloomfield—to examine the process of creating the bank. Most high officials at the Finance Bureau under the

Japanese Government General of Korea were Japanese. After Korea's independence, people in the Bank of Chosun led the enactment process of the 1950 Bank of Korea Act, resulting in severe distortions in decisions regarding the Monetary Policy Committee, the Office of Bank Supervision, and the right to examine the bank's business.

On November 24, 1997, the ruling and opposition party members agreed to open a special, post-election session to deal with nine financial reform bills to satisfy the IMF's demand for passage before the end of the year, a precondition to the bailout. Kim Dae-jung was elected president on December 18, and the special session was held on December 22 to deal with financial reform bills, which included a revision of the Bank of Korea Act and the Act on the Establishment of the Financial Supervisory Body. On the opening day of the special session, a sub-committee of the Finance Committee held an afternoon meeting to revise the Bank of Korea Act. It placed the Monetary Policy Committee inside the BOK with the BOK Governor chairing the panel and gave the Minister of Finance the power to veto decisions of the Monetary Policy Committee.

On Christmas Eve, the revision of the long contested Bank of Korea Act was passed by the Finance Committee along with the other reform measures. The title of the Act was also changed from the Central Bank of Korea Act to the Bank of Korea Act, the original version. On December 29, all financial reform bills were passed by the Finance Committee and, in the evening, also by the regular session of the National Assembly.

The BOK's attempt to win both the chairmanship of the

Monetary Policy Committee and the banking supervision authority by claiming "independence of the central bank" amid the pro-democracy movement of 1988 failed. The Ministry of Finance's counterattack in 1995 attempted to separate the banking supervisory authority from the bank ended finally.

The government's approach to the Bank of Korea Act changed from defense to an all-out assault in 1997. It rode public cries to reform the bank's supervision system following the bankruptcies of Hanbo Steel and Kia Motors. The effort was led by the Office of the President to correct the distorted truth, but at the last moment, on November 18, the bill went into limbo again due to political calculations right before the presidential election. The arrival of the IMF amid the 1997 crisis gave rise to a new central bank and a consolidated financial supervisory body, leaving the originally drafted idea of the single government agency in abeyance!

The National Assembly finally passed the Bank of Korea Act, the Act on the Establishment of the Financial Supervisory Body, and 11 other financial reform bills on December 29, in its plenary session, five days after the Finance Committee's approval. We had finally corrected the central bank system, which had been distorted 50 years earlier. Still, it saddened me to see the change happening under pressure from a foreign power. Sympathy and sense of shame toward political circles that were absorbed in calculating votes before the presidential election washed over me. Outside, cold winds howled through the winter night.

Record bailout: US$58.3 billion

With the Memorandum on the Economic Program signed on December 3, Korea could escape from the sense of crisis which was surging like waves by receiving a total of US$58.3 billion of bailout —US$35 billion consisting of US$21 billion from the IMF, US$10 billion from the IBRD, and US$4 billion from the ADB plus the second line of defense package worth US$20 billion from the US, Japan, and other countries. The scale of funding was larger than the initially requested US$56 billion.

At 4 p.m. on December 3, we reached a final agreement with the IMF and at 7:30 p.m. Minister Lim Chang-yuel and BOK Governor Lee Kyung Shik signed a Letter of Intent requesting a US$21 billion IMF bailout at the Central Government Complex in Seoul. IMF Managing Director Camdessus was present and a joint statement was issued. The Memorandum on Economic Program, which was the conditionality for the bailout, and a classified Side Letter were attached to the Letter of Intent. The letter consisted of five points.

1. A request for a three-year stand-by arrangement from the IMF in an amount equivalent to special drawing rights (SDR) 15.5 billion (US$21 billion) to support an economic program that would be implemented over the next three years to overcome Korea's financial crisis, thereby restoring market confidence and returning the economy to a path of sustainable growth;
2. Strong Prior Actions to demonstrate Korea's seriousness in strictly implementing its policy commitments, full specification of the program through continuous consultation with the IMF,

and regular review of the program for three years to follow; 3. Comprehensive policy package to deal with insolvent financial institutions, further liberalize the Korean economy, and improve corporate governance; 4. Forgoing some subsequent drawing when the situation stabilizes as expected and making advanced redemption as soon as conditions permit; 5. Firm commitment to the policies outlined in the memorandum.

Mr. Camdessus, in an exceptional act to restore confidence in Korea, immediately issued a statement, promising that the three-year stand-by loan of US$21 billion (SDR 15.5 billion) would be presented to the IMF executive board that weekend. At the same time, he announced that financial support of US$10 billion from the IBRD and US$4 billion from the ADB had also been promised, which increased the aggregate amount to US$35 billion. He added that the US$20 billion second line of defense would be also provided from the US, Japan, the UK, Germany, France, Australia, and Canada for unexpected circumstances, making the total amount of financial aid reach US$55 billion.

Within 13 days after we requested for the IMF bailout, US$55 billion was pledged. Korea wrote a new record in the history of the IMF by receiving the largest amount of support within the shortest period of time. On December 4, the IMF executive board passed the stand-by arrangement. The next day, initial disbursement of US$5.57 billion (SDR 4.1 billion) was made, and three more disbursals followed up until January 8, 1998, amounting to US$11.14 billion (SDR 8.2 billion). Further disbursements depended on circumstances. On December 5, the negotiations teams of the IBRD and the ADB arrived in Korea and talks on capital assistance of US$14 billion were concluded.

Christmas of 1997 marked a clear turning point for Korea to escape from the crisis as an announcement was made on that day regarding US-led financial aid worth US$10 billion from G-7 countries. This was the result of US Treasury Secretary Rubin withdrawing his "tough love" on condition that Korea would execute reforms and international banks cooperate.

The final scale of preliminary supports from the allies was decided at US$23.35 billion: US$10 billion from Japan; US$5 billion from the US; US$5 billion from France, Germany, the UK, and Italy; US$1.25 billion from the Netherlands, Belgium, Sweden, and Switzerland; US$1 billion from Australia and Canada, each; and US$100 million from New Zealand, totaling US58.35 billion combined with other funds.

| Negotiation for debt rollover

The exchange rate was not stabilized and foreign currency continued to flow out even after the agreement was reached on the US$55 billion IMF-led bailout on December 3, 1997. Foreign banks, relieved after the agreement, joined in a rapid flight, driving Korea towards a moratorium.

The exchange rate exceeded 1,000 won level (1,012.80 won) for the first time on November 19 when we announced that we were not going to the IMF. It surpassed 1,100 won level (1,139.00 won) on November 21 when the bailout request was announced, and on December 3 when we signed the Letter of Intent, it exceeded 1,200 won (1,240.60 won), and continued to rise until it surpassed 1,700 won (1,737.60 won) on December 15.

Foreign exchange reserves had shrank since August due to the acceleration of capital withdrawal of foreign banks. After peaking at US$33.6 billion at the end of July, the reserves plummeted, reaching US$24.4 billion (US$7.2 billion of usable reserves) at the end of November. Although the first IMF money of US$5.57 billion was disbursed on December 5, the capital withdrawal continued, and foreign exchange reserves continued to fall. It seemed that if the trend did not abate, the remaining usable reserves of US$7.2 billion could not be preserved. I thought we could escape the crisis by requesting for the IMF bailout, but I still had an uneasy feeling.

Korea's credit rating also fell by three steps on December 10, putting Korean bonds in the "junk" grade category.

On December 10, Stephen Long, head of Citibank's Asia Pacific Group, came to see me from Hong Kong. He delivered a message from New York-based Citigroup's Chairman John Reed: "We are ready to totally commit to Korea." The bank had also shown this kind of commitment during the 1973 oil shock. Mr. Long added that Citibank would actively come forward for the maturity extension of Korea's foreign debts. I asked him to deliver my appreciation to Mr. Reed and expressed willingness to actively support operations of foreign banks, including raising the maximum currency swap of the bank's Seoul branch. I had known Mr. Reed since 1985, when I worked as a financial attaché in New York, and we met several times more when I was negotiating with the US on the financial market opening as the

Director General of the International Finance Bureau. I could see he had a passion for business in Korea. The message of support, the first one amid a situation where we were besieged on all sides, gave me a great courage.

The failure of the KDB to issue a US$2 billion Yankee bond in New York on December 13 came as a great shock. At that time, issuance of foreign bonds of the KDB and the Export–Import Bank of Korea was the only way to supplement foreign exchange reserves. But American investors had taken on a callous attitude towards Korea's restructuring effort after presidential election rhetoric contained a renegotiation with the IMF. They demanded a 500 basis points spread and the bank gave up. There was a news report that described the KDB's effort to issue a Yankee bond as madness. With issuance of bonds by any Korean bank nearly impossible, we announced on December 15 to issue a US$10 billion government bond denominated in foreign currency within the year. The US investment bankers Goldman Sachs and Salomon Smith Barney were quick to express their willingness to take charge of the bond issuance, but it was impossible to finish the procedure within the year. I didn't know where we had made mistakes.

On December 18, after voting for the presidential election, I went to my office. The weather was cloudy and bleak. I prepared a report on the status of the crisis and measures for the foreign exchange reserves to submit to the new president. The situation was deteriorating and I could not find the right answer. As the sun went down, a strong sense of anxiety about the next day washed over me. I called Robert Wilson, general manager of the

Citibank in Seoul and talked about maturity extension proposed by Mr. Long, a week earlier. Then, I called Michael Brown, general manager in Seoul for the First National Bank of Chicago. He was the first person who predicted a currency crisis in Korea in August, and said the prevailing expectation was a won/dollar rate of 1,200 won in three months. At that time, the exchange rate was at 900 won level, and I didn't pay heed to his advice, but in early December it exceeded 1,200 won. I asked what went wrong because the situation had continued to worsen even after the promise of the IMF's bailout was announced. He said what we were doing was in the wrong order.

He said that trying to raise US$10 billion in new money through long-term bonds without rolling over the old money first was the wrong sequence. Capital kept flowing out because there were no measures to extend the maturity of the old money, Mr. Brown observed. He stated there was no use procuring US$10 billion when another US$10 billion was going out, adding, "Most foreign banks were quite liquid and were having trouble finding a safe place to invest." I asked for a solution, and his answer was simple. He said we first had to roll over the maturity of the short-term debt, and then we should pursue a syndicated loan that only involved banks with which we had a longtime business relationship. Lastly, Mr. Brown said we should issue long-term bonds first through private placement centered on underwriters who had business relationship with Korea and then through public offering. He noted that the interest rate will increase even when the public offering succeeds. As a way to extend the maturity of short-term borrowings, he suggested the government guarantee or transforming debts into BOK borrowings.

After an hour-long phone conversation, I realized exactly what was wrong and what we should do to correct it. To discuss the issue, I made a lunch appointment on the following day with representatives of major foreign banks at Bankers Club in central Seoul. In the morning of December 19, general manager Mr. Brown sent me a fax that contained our conversation.

I went to Hotel Shilla to meet the finance minister who was in a preliminary negotiation with the representatives of Goldman Sachs and Salomon Smith Barney on the issuance of a US$10 billion bond and told him that we had been handling the situation the wrong way. I also reported on my plan to meet the managers of major foreign banks the next day to discuss the rollover of short-term debts. The issuance of a US$10 billion bond had been announced already and an issuance in January was being prepared. I promised that I would take charge of pushing the extension of the maturity of our short-term foreign debts together with Director of the Financial Policy Division. Around midnight, news reports said that it seemed certain that Kim Dae-jung was likely to be the new president.

On December 19, Friday, I had a lunch with general manager Robert Wilson and general manager Michael Brown at the Bankers Club to discuss measures to extend the maturity of short-term debts in detail. They said that branch offices of foreign banks wanted to maintain the existing business relationships since they were having trouble finding a safe place to invest their fund. They said transforming the debts into borrowings of Bank of Korea will cut off such relationships, so they preferred the sovereign guarantee. The two managers said they would actively support the effort to roll over the debts. The government guarantee on banks already had been announced on August 25.

In the afternoon, I had a meeting with general manager Robert Wilson, who was also chairman of the Foreign Bankers Group (FBG). Mr. Brown and other general managers of major foreign banks such as the Chase Manhattan Bank, the Bank of America, and the Bank of Tokyo–Mitsubishi were present. We reached a basic agreement on the rollover through the government guarantee or by transforming it into the debt of the BOK. The manager of the Bank of Tokyo–Mitsubishi remained quiet.

The bank executives said that the negotiations on maturity extension could be misunderstood as moratorium so it should proceed in utmost secrecy. They stated that they had to report the basic outline to their headquarters by December 20, finish working–level consultations by December 23, and get the approval from the headquarters by December 24, prior to the start of Christmas holidays. Otherwise, it will be carried over to the next year, making the situation more difficult to deal with. They noted they could reach a detailed agreement only when they knew the exact status of Korea's external liabilities and maturity status of short–term loans from foreign banks. They said to successfully roll over short–term debts, all the major banks should participate, especially Japanese banks. On December 19, as concerns on moratorium was being raised due to the extensive withdrawal of US$7 billion by Japanese banks around December 3, when the US$58.3 billion IMF bailout was agreed, I drafted a desperate, last-ditch letter to Vice Minister Sakakibara of Japan asking for help in stemming the abrupt withdrawal of money by Japanese banks.

After FBG meeting, I met with the executives in charge of international finance of major banks, including the BOK and the KDB. We decided to choose the government guarantee since the BOK was not engaged in foreign borrowing business. We categorized the short-term foreign debts by bank and by period in cooperation with the BOK. At that time, there was no such data. On Sunday, December 21, I met again with Mr. Stephen Long at Hotel Shilla with Minister Lim Chang-yuel. Citibank promised to play an active role regarding the debt rollover. That night, Goldman Sachs and Salomon Smith Barney were chosen to be lead managers and they prepared a prospectus, the core procedure to issue a US$10 billion bond.

On Monday, December 22, we compiled data on the external liabilities and short-term foreign debts maturing in 1998 by month and by bank. As of December 20, short-term borrowings amounted to US$80.2 billion, 52.4% of a total of US$153 billion Korean external liabilities that included offshore borrowings of Korean banks and borrowings by overseas branches of Korean banks, and 24.5% of the short-term borrowings, which was US$37.4 billion, was those of domestic financial institutions. Since there was a misunderstanding about the definition of external liability among foreign countries, we recalculated gross external liabilities based on the working-level agreement with the IMF. We added the overseas borrowings of Korean banks and their foreign branches to the external debt as defined by the IBRD, and excluded borrowings of overseas branches and subsidiaries of Korean enterprises.

The calculations categorized by bank showed that short-term foreign borrowings that were subject to debt rollover in 1998 was US$23.7 billion in total—US$6.5 billion from Japanese banks, US$3 billion from US banks, US$1.3 billion from British banks, US$2.8 billion from German banks, US$1.6 billion from French banks, and US$8.4 billion from others. Providing the government guarantee on US$12.2 billion coming due between December 18 and December 31, 1997 was technically difficult. "The status of maturity on short-term foreign borrowings—by bank" prepared at that time was the first dataset showing short-term foreign debt status by country, bank, and month.

On December 22, I briefed Mr. Neiss on the negotiations involving maturity extension. He expressed his support, saying that it was an absolutely necessary action. In the evening, I met with the representatives of major foreign banks, including Mr. Wilson and Mr. Brown at the Korea Federation of Banks building and showed them the dataset and made a prior adjustment regarding the method to extend maturity. We decided to deal with the debt maturing within 1997 on our own and extend the debt maturing in 1998. We concluded that a rollover was necessary for at least two-thirds of US$35.9 billion, which was borrowed through the money market on a short-term basis.

On December 23, foreign banks participated in the FBG meeting held at Chosun Hotel and agreed on the maturity extension through the government guarantee. The scale of

Korea's external liabilities as well as the maturity status of short-term borrowings from foreign banks was explained. The data on the maturity status was classified since disclosure could cause problems. The bankers agreed to get the approval from their headquarters by December 24. A basic agreement on maturity extension was reached. The Washington Post reported that foreign banks, from the moment when the crisis was approaching Korea, already concluded that rollover was more advantageous than letting the country default. The managers of US banks, who held the smallest amount of short-term bonds, led the process, while Japanese banks, the largest creditors, concentrated on capital withdrawal and didn't actively engage in maturity extension. Japan promised to contribute US$10 billion, but its banks pulled out US$13 billion from Korea.

On December 24, US Treasury Secretary Robert Rubin announced that the IMF and G-7 countries would move up the schedule for financial assistance to provide US$10 billion by early January. Based on the basic agreement on the maturity extension in Seoul, IMF Deputy Managing Director Stanley Fisher had a meeting in New York for debt rollover with major US creditor banks on December 29, and the venue for the consultation to finalize the issue of debt rollover moved to New York.

| Agreement in New York

After reporting about the currency crisis to the committee

on emergency economic planning of the newly elected Kim Dae-jung administration on January 6, 1998, I was supposed to go on a business trip to participate in the negotiation to be held in New York from January 21. In the middle of preparing for the trip, I was given the short notice by the minister that Assistant Minister Chung Duck-Koo would go instead of me. On December 18, 1997, when Kim Dae-jung was elected president, ushering in the first opposition administration, I thought the time had come to end my public service career. It seemed that there was nothing that I could do under the leftist government, and the wind from the change in power was blowing hard in public offices. After Christmas, no role was left for me except to substitute for the minister at meetings.

I climbed up a hill behind my office building and prayed God to give me fortitude to step down if this was not the right time. I accepted everything as a will of God. As a Vice Minister of Finance, I had limitations, but I had put my heart and soul to get through the crisis since taking my post in March, 1997. I wanted to finalize the negotiations for maturity extension myself because I thought that it would be my last service for the country.

I called in the negotiation team before they departed to New York for the negotiations. I explained the progress so far and said, "We are standing on the edge of a precipice, but now we are holding the cards and foreign banks are in an unfavorable situation. Hang in there, and then we will win."

This thinking was based on the judgment that first, even though Korea was driven into a dead-end, Rubin had no choice but to save Korea from default quickly upon recommendations from Secretary of State Madeleine Albright and Defense Secretary William Cohen, who had tended to their strategy for Asia. Second, during the consultation with Mr. Wilson and Mr. Brown on maturity extension, they said that banks in the US were looking for a safe place to invest since they had too much fund and the government guaranteed loan would become the best investment choice. There was even a report of *The Washington Post* that foreign banks had already agreed on debt rollover. Third, Citigroup Chairman Reed sent Mr. Long to promise his "commitment to Korea."

The foreign debt negotiation kicked off in New York on January 21, 1998 and an agreement was made on January 28 to transform the short-term foreign debt of US$24 billion maturing in 1998 into a long-term debt with maturity extended up to three years based on the government guarantee. The interest rate spread was set at the LIBOR (5.66%) plus 2.25% for loans due within one year; LIBOR plus 2.50 % for loans due in two years; and LIBOR plus 2.75% for loans due in three years. It was around 8.16% in terms of the interest rate of that time. The agreement clearly lifted Korea out of the currency crisis.

Vice Chairman of Citibank William Rhodes and Mark Walker, legal advisor for Korea, led the process. At that time, Citigroup had US$16.4 billion of assets in five crisis-struck Asian countries—US$4.9 billion in Korea, US$3.7 billion in Malaysia, US$3.1 billion in Thailand, US$2.6 billion in the Philippines, and US$2.1 billion in Indonesia.

Our winning position was further strengthened by the news report that Treasury Secretary Rubin called on international creditor banks to ease the conditions for extending the maturities of existing debts before the foreign debt negotiations between Korea and international creditor banks. Noting that economic reforms by the Korean government were taking effect, Mr. Rubin said that international creditor banks should give Korea some breathing room and let the country reach an agreement on comprehensive and long-term maturity readjustment. He also added that the banks should voluntarily plan to extend maturity of Korea's foreign debts and open a new channel through which Korean financial institutions can procure additional funds.

Chang Jong-Hyun, managing partner of Booz Allen Hamilton's Seoul office who accompanied our delegates as an advisor during the negotiation said it was regrettable for Korean representatives to accept the deal too quickly even when we could have agreed on more favorable terms. Mr. Chang said the interest rate was agreed at or below 3% of spread thanks to the German banks, who collectively acted like a savior. International financial experts said the winner of the New York negotiations was not the Korean government but international creditor banks, adding that international creditor banks had forgave 10% to 30% of the principal and suggested lower interest rates in the case of Mexico and Brazil, but they demanded the government guarantee and higher interest rate from Korea. Mr. Chang's words were backed up by media reports that the interest rate could have been decided at lower level if a bottom-up approach, which is based on bidding, was used rather than a top-down approach, which considers market interest rate. They also said that adopting "credit step-down" approach, which lowers interest rate when the sovereign credit rating goes up, would have been better.

According to some reports, there were excitements at the news of managing the government-guaranteed bulky capital of US$24 billion with the interest rate of 8% when the interest rate of US Treasury securities, which were safe and guaranteed an appropriate interest rate, was around 5%. Lending an umbrella on a sunny day and taking it away on a rainy day. That's how banks work.

When Korea's 10-year foreign exchange stabilization bond (FESB) worth US$4 billion was issued in New York in April, 1998 with Goldman Sachs and Salomon Smith Barney acting as lead managers, analysts said that its interest rate, decided at the US treasury bond rate (5.48% at that time) plus 3.55% (3.45% for five-year), was too high considering that there was no early repayment condition. The fact that the scale of the bond issuance increased from the originally intended US$3 billion to US$4 billion due to over demand—worth US$10 billion—showed the popularity of the Korean bonds. It was reported that the spread of the bond worth US$1 billion issued in early March by Mexico who had a lower credit rating than Korea was 2.88%. The interest rate of Korea's FESB dropped by 0.25 percentage point to the treasury bond rate plus 3.30% on the day after its issuance due to a sharp rise in FESBs price, proving that the interest rate at the time of issuance was too high.

A syndicated loan was not even tried due to the already promised FESB issuance. It was too unfair that early repayment was not even permitted for the 10-year government bonds given that the spread for 3-year loans was settled at 2.75% at the debt rollover negotiations in New York, additional financing looked possible through syndicated loans, and furthermore, Korea's credit rating was expected to rise. Some news report said that the employees of the US securities firms that were in charge of the bond issuance at that time were generously compensated. As Mr. Brown said, it seemed that we suffered because we had done things in reverse order.

While the US, holder of the smallest amount of short-term bonds, led the process, Japan, the largest creditor, stayed back, concentrating on the withdrawal of its money. Japan turned its back on all of our requests: the request on November 21, when we applied for the IMF bailout, for US$10 billion bridge loan until the IMF money was disbursed; the request for stemming the rapid withdrawal of money on December 2, the day before an agreement was reached on the IMF rescue package; and the plea for preventing further withdrawal of money through a desperate last-ditch letter on December 19, when moratorium risk was being raised after the bailout agreement. The country was a neighbor who seemed to be farther than the US across the Pacific.

I thought about how Citibank Chairman John Reed fulfilled the "commitment to Korea" that he promised as the bank did during the 1973 oil shock. Likewise, I appreciated the continuous stream of support extended from Citibank's Seoul branch general manager Robert Wilson, the bank's Asia Pacific Group head Stephen Long, and Vice Chairman William Rhodes. If it had not been for the help from Mr. Rhodes and Mr. Rubin in 2008, when I was the finance minister, we couldn't have entered into a currency swap with the US and would have suffered enormous pains. On October 30, 2008, when a US$30 billion Korea-US currency swap agreement was announced, a meeting of the Korea-US Business Councils was held in Hotel Shilla in Seoul. During my congratulatory remarks, I gave a round of applause with Korean participants to show our appreciation for Mr. Rhodes, who served as the chairman of the US side.

I send my heartfelt appreciation and respect to Mr. Reed, Mr. Rhodes, and Mr. Rubin. There were friends in need, though! I can never forget them, along with the 1997 Asian financial crisis and the 2008 global economic crisis that I faced as vice minister and as minister, respectively.

| Birth of a leftist government

Contributing to the tentative agreement on maturity extension of US$23.7 billion short-term foreign borrowings on December 23 and the passage of financial reform bills on December 29 at the National Assembly became my last service to the country. My remaining tasks after December 24 were reporting to the new administration's presidential transition committee and a hearing on the currency crisis and an inspection by the Board of Audit and Inspection of Korea. To prepare, I made a report on a full account of the currency crisis titled, "The 1997 Financial Crisis: Causes, Responses, and Outcomes" with the staff of the Foreign Exchange Market Division. The situation had changed and everything disappeared into the swamp of the IMF.

Politically charged criticism centered on the argument that the currency crisis was the "biggest national crisis in history." The rhetoric became harsher over time and criticism from the press became more acerbic. The first-ever transfer of power to the opposition in Korea brought about change of power in the Ministry of Finance, bringing a new atmosphere to the ministry. Finance Minister Lim became the one who had saved the country from the currency crisis while his predecessor Kang Kyung-Shik and those who had managed the crisis with him were all accused of causing the crisis. Those who didn't participate in managing the crisis joined the accusers. I stood on in the line of fire along with the staff that had grappled with the crisis, and I was the highest-ranking official that was remaining. We all worked hard together, but some of us weren't at the right time.

People in the Foreign Exchange Market Division almost never went home before midnight from August of the previous year. All their work up to that time had gone unrecognized. Who should pay the consequences became the only important matter without determining who was at fault. Not a single day passed without a barrage of reproach: the biggest national crisis, dereliction of duty, and false reports. Self-claimed patriots sprang up and they argued that warnings from everywhere on the currency crisis were ignored. All the tremendous efforts and hard work had gone unappreciated, criticisms poured down like a cloudburst, and interrogations began. When people meet disasters, they perform an exorcism. There were questions about dereliction of duty, false reports, and people who ruined the nation. But few asked who caused the fire, who fueled the flames, and who contained the blaze. Solitude and resentment surged up.

On January 3, 1998, I went to the presidential transition committee and briefed the new power brokers on "The 1997 Financial Crisis: Causes, Responses, and Outcomes" from 2 p.m. to 10 p.m. A hearing on the currency crisis with a long title of "Parliamentary Investigation on the cause of the currency crisis and the facts of the economic crisis" continued for 21 days from January 18 to February 13. I was summoned to the hearing. The hearing was overwhelmed with political diatribes in search of scapegoats rather than a serious analysis into the causes of the currency crisis and how it was being handled. It was a trial on the steps we had taken, capitalizing on the popular mood that denounced us using the expressions like "the biggest national crisis in history," "the President who ruined the nation," "false reports on foreign exchange reserves," and "dereliction of duty." The hearing turned out to be an inquisition, with questions overwhelming answers. The hearing ended up with becoming a bout of fury.

For one month from January 30 to February 28, the Board of Audit and Inspection of Korea began a witch-hunt referred to as a special inspection of the current state of management on foreign exchange and finance. It was a political inspection initiated upon the demand from the political circle to find a scapegoat. A lot of my subordinates received punishments. Minister Kang who strived with me to overcome the crisis was accused of dereliction of duty. My inauguration address reported in a newspaper and business logs of the staff of the

Foreign Exchange Market Division who wrote down my first order on exchange rates and foreign reserves absolved me from accusations of dereliction of duty. This incurred resentment rather than a sense of relief.

On Saturday, February 21, I had a farewell luncheon with the staff of the Foreign Exchange Market Division who helped me prepare the last report on the currency crisis. We were embittered, at a loss for words, not knowing how fate would roll toward us.

On the next day, Sunday, I went to my office and packed. I tied up a lot of materials and personal belongings in a bundle. After tidying up my office, I climbed up the hill behind the office building. Above the mountain across the government complex, winter clouds were drifting away. Twenty-eight years of my public career that began in 1970 were brought back in rapid succession. Those were times of passion and agony, tasting the bitterness of life and floundering around in deep anguish. Those were years of endlessly mounting challenges and rising to each dilemma. Those were days of reeling, stumbling, and being caught up in the vortex.

The IMF gave birth to the leftist government. On March 9, 1998, I left the ministry, wrapping up my 28-year public service. Leaving behind me farewell remarks that became a poem!

* * *

My public life that began in a rural tax office.
I remember times, works, and people for the last 28 years.
From value added tax to the IMF,

From financial liberalization to financial market opening,

It was a time of mounting challenges and rising to each dilemma, fighting against enormous waves.

I bumped, bled, and collapsed.

I drifted along from Seoul to New York.

I look back on the past one year.

I went through Hanbo and Kia default cases, financial reforms, and lastly the IMF bailout.

The reform of the central bank, which had been left in abeyance for more than 30 years, was achieved, and 20 financial reform bills were passed.

The largest-of-all-time deficit of US$23 billion was improved to US$ 8.2 billion.

However, it all disappeared into the swamp of the IMF.

Turning to the IMF was unavoidable.

Who caused the fire and who extinguished it,

A sober assessment is necessary.

Whether the IMF was a blessing or a curse,

Will be decided depending on how we respond from this moment forward.

The IMF policy program was based on what we had planned before.

It's shameful that we are forced to implement this by the foreign power.

But external shock can also become an agent for a new development.

Now, I am leaving.

I will cherish the years I worked with you as a great honor.

CHAPTER 3

LEGACY OF CRISIS

Repaying of Borrowed Income

Koreans refer to the 1997 crisis as the "IMF Crisis." More than a million Koreans lost their jobs and businesses as the IMF's intervention unfolded, so "IMF" became a word that the public resented. When the foreign money that we, without knowing the nature of capital, borrowed, succumbing to the temptation of the low interest rate, flowed out like the receding tide, we came to realize there was no friend in need. We experienced how risky the current account deficit was and how important the foreign exchange reserves were. The ruins in the wake of forced changes left many lessons behind. The crisis occurred at a moment when Asia was gaining confidence by eagerly implementing economic development. Before then, it didn't even have assets big enough to be hit by a financial crisis. We had never experienced such a crisis and we suffered dearly. The crisis clearly taught us that there was no free lunch.

The memories of Japan turning away from our requests three times—on the day of requesting the IMF bailout, on the day before the IMF bailout agreement, and on the day when concerns for moratorium were raised even after the agreement —were severe wounds, but at the same time great lessons. Crisis-hit periphery countries have limited options. There was no friend in need, and sound current account balance and foreign exchange reserves were conditions for survival. A proper management of exchange rates is the exertion of sovereignty.

| Eagerness and ignorance

During one year in 1997, US$37.5 billion foreign borrowings flowed out like the receding tide. Korea, which was an underdeveloped country and periphery nation, gained confidence for the first time in its history as it enjoyed rapid economic growth and improved living standards as a result of eagerly implementing economic development plans in the 1960s. Our eagerness for economic growth in the 1990s created internal bubbles and external imbalances. Excessive bubbles and imbalances are not sustainable.

The causes of the 1997 Asian financial crisis were speculative bubbles created by excessive inflows of short-term money from Japan, the US, and Europe to drive economic growth and an over-leveraged corporate financial structure. In 1997, more than US$207.3 billion foreign funds flowed into five Asian countries —Korea, Thailand, Indonesia, Malaysia, and the Philippines. The fruit of growth was not achieved through domestically accumulated money. It was through foreign borrowings. But like borrowed income, it must be repaid someday, and the income that does not exceed the borrowing rate is, in fact, a loss. The US$118.5 billion bailout packages provided by the IMF and advanced countries helped Thailand, Indonesia, and Korea to pay back their borrowed income, but they inflicted severe ordeals and wounds.

In retrospect, the 1997 currency crisis was a disaster caused by eagerness. Externally, the crisis left the brutality of forced transformations, and internally, it left negative growth and legions of jobless people. Personally, it left me political punishment, let alone rewards for hard work, ending my public life in remorse.

Externally, it left the cruelty of foreign funds and the inconvenient truth on the international financial order. When the IMF-arranged bailout fund of US$58.3 billion was agreed on December 3, 1997, foreign capital joined in a great flight, driving Korea into a near-moratorium. The bailout fund replaced dangerous speculative money with risk-free IMF money, bringing about moral hazard where pains were shifted to periphery nations. The IMF was beating the bush and speculative capital was catching the birds, making it unclear who was bailing out whom. A thought occurred to me that we could have shared the pains with foreign capital if we had rather declared a moratorium and then used the IMF money for new transactions.

I thought that a small open economy can achieve a balanced domestic development only when abrupt flows of short-terms funds are regulated. Comparisons of exchange rates and current account balances between 1996 and 1998—before and after the crisis—show that Korea, Thailand, and Indonesia all achieved current account surpluses that were high enough to sustain their foreign debts when exchange rates had been readjusted based on their fundamentals after the outflows of short-term foreign funds. I concluded that center and periphery nations should cooperate to create a mechanism that will prevent sudden inflows and outflows of short-term money.

On a personal note, I was the person who was sent to extinguish the fire during the 1997 crisis, but after I doused the flames, a political punishment awaited me. Those who caused the fire fell silent, and those who strived to put out the fire were subjected to witch-hunt-like exorcism due to the time lag in policies bearing fruit. Self-claimed wise men who claimed to have predicted the crisis joined in the witch-hunt.

The effort to rapidly bolster the won/dollar exchange rate to 920 won was met with criticism that foreign reserves were wasted to defend the exchange rate. I don't know if the BOK did that, but the Ministry of Finance did not waste even US$1 out of the foreign exchange reserves to defend the exchange rate. When short-term borrowings of banks began to be withdrawn after August 1997, the government was endeavoring to save banks from defaults almost every day. If foreign currency was in shortage at the business close of any day, banks took out overnight loans from the Hong Kong market, and if it was not possible, they went to Frankfurt, then to London, and lastly to the New York market. The effort to borrow money for the day at the global foreign exchange market ends at 2 a.m. The Foreign

Exchange Market Division of the Ministry of Finance checked the foreign exchange shortage of banks, took actions so that the BOK could lend money, and wrote a report on the day's situation, completing the day's work at 5 a.m. the next day. A situation like this happened almost every day since the mid-August.

I was criticized for my statement overseas: "There is no problem in the fundamentals of the Korean economy." In 1996, we had structural weakness of high cost and low efficiency and severe current account deficits. Amid the sudden reversal of funds by foreign financial institutions, I could not make any other statement. I believe no company on the verge of default would go to banks and say, "Our company doesn't have a future, but lend us some money even though you are not getting it back."

Some people argued that the government disregarded warnings of the crisis. In an attempt to manage the impending turmoil, government research institutes were prevented from making public statements that could cause alarm. Whenever stock prices or exchange rates fluctuated after April, 1997, the newspapers were faster than research institutes in reporting about financial turmoil. One of the BOK executives came forward, asserting that he warned about the crisis: "Putting emphasis on improving current account balance and stabilizing the foreign currency market, we should achieve stable management of macroeconomic policies, early expansion of foreign exchange reserves, and exchange rate management based on a supply-demand trend in the market while devising measures to enhance corporate management environment and prevent the diffusion of financial distress through the stabilization of wages and abolition of various regulations. If these measures do not produce real effects, it is necessary to seek emergency measures such as borrowing from international organizations like the IMF." What empty talk.

The situation had changed with the first-ever power transmission to the leftists since the establishment of the country, and change of power also occurred at public offices. Self-claimed patriots came forward and they were satisfied only after performing an exorcism through a kangaroo court. This human nature saddened me. Minister Kang Kyung-Shik, who strived to put out the fire suffered the humiliation of being brought into court, and many working-level officials received disciplinary punishments. Those who had been arrogant and misjudged the direction in the face of the crisis were not seen and remained silent. They have to make an apology, even in hiding, to people who suffered pains from the wounds of the currency crisis.

| Crisis wounds: Massive job losses and closures

The currency crisis was our most traumatic event since the 1950-53 Korean War. Massive unemployment and shutdowns were disastrous events that we faced for the first time in our history. As a small open economy, we should never forget the wounds from the crisis to survive in international competition and emerge as an advanced economy.

Financial institutions suffered the most damage in the 1997 currency crisis. The Korea First Bank and the Korea Exchange Bank were sold to New Bridge Capital and Lone Star of the US, respectively, at giveaway prices, and Seoul Bank disappeared after being merged with Hana Bank. Five regional banks were closed. Twenty-two merchant banks out of 30 that triggered the crisis were shut down and the rest of them vanished after mergers. More than 68,000 companies were closed and large buildings in Seoul were also sold away overseas.

A look into leading economic indicators reveals that the economic growth rate of 7.2% in 1996 crashed to 5.8% in the crisis-hit 1997 and to -5.7% in 1998, and the unemployment rate for the same period soared from 2.0% to 2.6%, and to 7.0%, respectively. The number of jobless people during the same period also skyrocketed from 430,000 to 560,000, and to 1.46 million, and per capita GDP collapsed from US$11,422 to US$10,371, and to US$6,863. Stock prices plummeted by 61% in 1997.

We could draw two important lessons from this comparison of economic indicators before and after the crisis. First, a recovery in economic growth rate to around 10% beginning from 1999 means that our economic fundamentals were sound except for current account balance. Second, as the won/dollar exchange rate jumped up to 1,415.2 won at the end of 1997 from 844.2 won in 1996, the current account balance turned around to a surplus of US$40 billion in 1998. This clearly shows that the exchange rate has a decisive effect on the current account balance, and that the current account balance is the basis for the management of a state.

Survival tools: Exchange rate and foreign reserves

Having gained confidence based on rapid economic growth since World War II and improved standards of living, developing countries in Asia pursued faster expansion and further enhanced life not through capital they accumulated on their own but through money accumulated overseas. This eagerness became the source of trouble. Through the Asian financial crisis both center and periphery nations realized the risk of choice. Periphery economies were not strong enough to satisfy the greed of foreign capital, and center economies were not flexible enough to absorb their money. Bubbles that used to be created only in center countries in the past became energy for bubbles in periphery nations in this era of global village where capital movement has become liberalized. An inconvenient truth that periphery countries pursued borrowed income, while center countries sought after profits through speculation was brought to light during the Asian crisis.

As the Asian financial crisis was being put under control, *Financial Times* reported on April 18, 1998, that one of the gains of the crisis was that Asian countries began to realize that the western-style market economy system, in particular, US-style capitalism was a superior model. According to the newspaper,

American-style capitalism promised a better life and higher growth, and that is why many leaders in the region were rapidly shifting their own economies to the US model.

In contrast, on July 24, 1997, when the Asian financial crisis was beginning, Malaysian Prime Minister Mahathir bin Mohamad stated that the country had been hearing that it should open its market, which meant a complete opening in trades and capital transactions. He deplored such demands by raising this question: For whom is the opening? Then, he implemented capital control and walked the path of isolation to manage the crisis.

The enormous pain, due to the 1997 crisis, was necessary to convince periphery economies to accept the western-style market economy and accompanying changes to their systems. Walking the path of isolation involved too much uncertainty. It was inevitable to pay the price of ignoring the nature of short-term foreign funds, and it was also inevitable to pay the price for reckless borrowing of excessive foreign money, trusting the IMF as the lender of last resort. Foreign exchange reserves equivalent to three months of current payment, which was recommended by the IMF, were based on trades in goods and services, not on international capital flows. We also disregarded a simple fact that market exchange rate is decided not by current account balance but by the supply and demand of key currencies.

Options of periphery countries that cannot issue key currencies are limited to domestic accumulation of capital or inducing foreign direct investment. Long-term foreign borrowings are not sustainable if they cannot create profits exceeding the interest rate, and short-term borrowings are dangerous without enough foreign exchange reserves. Foreign reserves can be accumulated only when the current account balance achieves surpluses. If achieving surplus is not possible, it is better to refrain from borrowing short-term money. I believe that would be less painful than receiving the IMF rescue package.

Unless the international financial order is changed to restrict excessive inflows and outflows of short-term funds, the ways that periphery nations can choose are limited to current account surpluses. There is no other way to achieve current account surplus than maintaining an adequate level of exchange rates, which is possible only when flows of short-term capital are regulated. An expansion of regional financial cooperation system was proposed as an alternative, but that too was merely a short-term measure.

With limited options available, periphery nations cannot but utilize exchange rates and foreign reserves for survival. Market intervention to maintain a proper level of exchange rates and accumulation of enough foreign exchange reserves through current account surplus are requisites for survival and also the exertion of sovereignty. The agreement reached on the principle of government intervention in the foreign exchange market at the 2010 G-20 Seoul Summit was a giant step for the global economic community.

When the US$37.5 billion, 60% of the short-term borrowings of financial institutions, flowed out like the receding tide during the 1997 currency crisis, our economy seemed to be on the verge of collapse. We made prodigious efforts, but they ended in vain and there was no friend to help us. There was no other way to avoid the crisis than to build strength on our own. I faced the 1997 currency crisis as Vice Minister of the Finance, and experienced enormous hardship in which banks, companies, and buildings were sold to advanced countries at giveaway prices amid a recession and massive unemployment.

After paying dearly during the 1997 crisis, I have learned five painful lessons. First, crises recur. Second, external balance should be our priority. Third, the exchange rate is sovereignty. Fourth, when it comes to foreign reserves, the more the better. Fifth, technology is the way to survive.

The economics that is equipped with the best technology or resources and can print reserve currencies is not the same with the economics which lacks technology and resources and has to suffer a crisis when in shortage of the US dollars. Center countries can print key currencies and arrange currency swaps to quell a crisis. They have no problems in their current account balance and foreign exchange reserves.

| Crisis repeats itself

Crises revisit a small open economy if it does not properly manage exchange rates and current account balance. Ways to manage crisis through exogenous variables do not exist anymore. If not prepared, a pitiless hardship is unavoidable. Besides, there is no friend who will lend us an umbrella when it rains.

Korea faced four crises while implementing five Five-year Economic Development Plans, which began in 1962, due to foreign capital inducement to supplement investments that exceeded domestic savings, and current account deficits arising from imports of capital goods that were scarce in the domestic market. With the financial market not opened yet, we resolved them by relying on exogenous variables such as reparation funds from Japan, special demands rising from the Vietnam War, and construction boom in the Middle East. We faced the 1997 currency crisis due to a sudden outflow of short-term foreign funds that had poured into the domestic market after the financial market opening in the 1990s, and suffered acute distress with banks, companies, and building sold to foreign institutions at scrap value amid recession and wholesale unemployment.

Now, with the Cold War order broken and China embracing a market economy, a special relationship among Korea, the US, and Japan has weakened. We cannot expect conditions like special demands from the Vietnam War or the Middle East construction boom. The crisis taught us a lesson that we have to strengthen international competitiveness only through steady efforts of our own, in particular, through capital adequacy at corporations, current account surpluses, financial innovation, and flexibility in labor market. And one more lesson: there is no friend who will lend us an umbrella when it rains!

| External balance should be prioritized

A small open economy that lacks technology and resources need to make more provisions and efforts to survive than countries with advanced technologies, resources, or key currencies. Our future lies in the broad foreign market rather than the small domestic market.

The 1997 financial crisis was Asia catching a cold from the sneeze of Japan's Lost Decade. The cold that began in Thailand moved northward to infect Korea. It is inevitable for us to put external balance, which is affected by exports and current account, above internal balance, which is influenced by inflation and unemployment, because a shortage in foreign reserves will drive us to a crisis.

The direct cause of the 1997 crisis was the carry trade where cheap short-term money from Japan, the US, and Europe was used for expensive long-term loans in Asia. For advanced economies, investing in higher yielding instruments in emerging financial markets with carry funds at low interest rate is like swimming while touching the ground, or throwing a stone at frogs in the pond for fun. Center countries may be enjoying the money game, but it is a matter of life and death to small open economies.

It is said, "If you write a good novel, you can live on it for all your life in the US, for ten years in Japan, and one year in Korea." As a small periphery nation, Korea produces less output with the same input compared to center economies. We are destined to work more and make more efforts than others to make a living. A way for Korea to become an advanced power can be found overseas. The Netherlands, despite being a small country, became a maritime power by making wealth abroad. Export is the way for us to become an advanced power. Our decision to broaden our economic territory through free trade agreements (FTA) was a really good choice.

The Korean won is not a key currency and we cannot issue as much as we wish. To prevent crises, we need to be more prepared in terms of exchange rates, current account balance, and foreign exchange reserves, and for this, we need to exert more efforts for exports. The economics of center countries with key currencies sometimes tells us to do the opposite, as they did during the 1997 crisis. They recommended that we maintain high interest rates and tight monetary policies to prevent outflows of foreign exchanges, and we did that in anguish. Upon facing the 2008 global economic crisis, the US Federal Reserve dropped more than US$3 trillion from a "helicopter" through quantitative easing under Ben Bernanke. Japan is also supplying the yen unlimitedly. Although not exactly known, the scales of quantitative easing of countries with key currencies until the year 2012 are estimated to reach US$3.6 trillion in the US, US$1.6 trillion in the EU, and US$2.1 trillion in Japan, totaling US$7.4 trillion.

Korea needs to always bear in mind the limitations as a small open economy since the won is not a reserve currency. Because we have no choice but to engage in financial transactions and trades with center economies, we must make more provisions and efforts to prevent crises. Moreover, Korea, which lacks resources, is different from periphery nations with abundant resources. This is the limitation that we should never forget when we deal with fiscal and financial policies.

| Exchange rate is a matter of sovereignty

The exchange rate equals to national sovereignty and the management of international balance of payments is the basics for the management of a state. As shown in the 1997 crisis, exchange rates had more correlations with capital flows than with basic economic indicators. There is no use in defending exchange rates with capital flows still unregulated. Unless speculation of short-term capital is restricted, there is no way to prevent crises. Proper intervention in the foreign exchange market to maintain exchange rates that can sustain price competitiveness is tantamount to protecting national sovereignty, and the establishment of institutional frameworks to prevent speculative foreign exchange transactions is a basic responsibility of the foreign exchange authorities. Leaving the exchange rates in the hands of the market and neglecting speculation is a breach of public trust.

As periphery nations cannot issue reserve currencies freely as center countries can, their economies cannot be said as sound if they have bad balance of payments even when all other economic indicators look positive. Interest rates were important variables in 1997, when corporate debt ratio was around 400% and lending rates were about 12%. However, interest rates are conventional bombs if exchange rates are atomic bombs under today's circumstances where the debt ratio is 100% or below, lending rates are around 6%, and dependence on exports exceeds 40% of GDP. Currency crises can emerge at any time, depending on changes in the international financial markets, and a poor management of foreign debts can lead to sovereign default.

The won appreciated 4.3% against the dollar from 808.1 won in 1993 to 774.7 won in 1995, causing current account balance to shift from a surplus of US$2 billion in 1993 to a deficit of US$9.7 billion in 1995, and then the deficit explosively rose to US$23.8 billion in 1996 right before the crisis. In 1996, Korea's current account deficit accounted for 4.2% of its GDP, which was far over the risky level of 3%.

In a market exchange rate system where exchange rates, measure of external transaction value, change every hour and every day, a proper management of exchange rates is an essential defense right of a small open economy for its own survival. The management of exchange rates is an exertion of sovereignty, which cannot be relinquished no matter who applies what kind of pressure. This is the most crucial lesson from the 1997 crisis, and the sovereignty should be cherished and never be relinquished.

| Foreign exchange reserves are life line

The only way that a small open economy can prevent the crisis on its own is to hold foreign exchange reserves large enough to manage exchange rates and foreign debts. Foreign reserves can be accumulated through current account surpluses, and current account surpluses can be achieved through exchange rates in the short-term and though technologies in the long-term. If a crisis cannot be averted through foreign reserves, there is no choice but to receive the IMF's emergency liquidity funds. That's why we took the painful steps in 1997. The foreign exchange crisis was called that way since it occurred due to a shortage in foreign exchanges.

Korea's foreign reserves amounted to US$29.1 billion in March, 1997 and it increased to US$33.6 billion in July due to the effort for overseas borrowing. The amount didn't meet the IMF-recommended US$36 billion, three-month worth of imports, and fell far short of US$50 billion, the target amount of reserves with short-term foreign debts taken into account. With this inadequate reserve holdings, Korea could not withstand the capital withdrawal of US$37.5 billion and in December its usable foreign reserves excluding foreign currencies deposited in domestic banks plummeted to US$7.2 billion. On November 21, we requested IMF liquidity support facilities and overcame the crisis through US$58.3 billion borrowed from foreign powers, including US$21 billion from the IMF.

By relying on foreign powers to resolve the crisis, we suffered great pains, experiencing bankruptcies of banks and companies and massive unemployment. We clearly learned that this kind of situation should never happen again. We concluded that the currency crisis could not be avoided even with foreign reserves of US$36 billion, which was recommended by the IMF to avert such crisis. As a small open economy, Korea should never forget that it cannot live without dollars. Foreign exchange reserves are a life line to us.

The only way for a small open economy to prevent a crisis is to hold foreign reserves and the more the better. This was the lesson from the foreign exchange crisis. A hefty stockpile of foreign reserves can be used to create sovereign wealth funds, allowing us to make active investments in foreign markets. We can buy back what we sold at giveaway prices and also participate in international M&As. We need to learn from Singapore's sovereign fund, Temasek.

| R&D supplies edge

Our underlying external competitiveness can be bolstered through technology. We can strengthen our competitiveness by improving price competitiveness in the short-term, which is determined by exchange rates and tariff rates; by enhancing product quality in the mid-term; and by developing new technologies in the long-term. The way to maintain external competitiveness in the market exchange rate system is to properly manage excessive flows of short-term capital, and ultimately, to develop technologies.

Managing capital flows can cause friction with countries that export capital, so the way for a small open economy to protect itself is to establish an independent technology development system. The technology development system consists of: expanding R&D investments; boosting technology financing to help set up a business with new technologies and support their business operations; and establishing a technology transaction system.

Technology is the only way we can survive the competition with low-wage China and high-tech Japan, and investments in technology development thus should be Korea's top priority. Right before the 1997 currency crisis, US consulting firm Booz Allen Hamilton likened Korea to a nut caught between China's low costs and Japan's technical excellence, saying, "the competitive nutcracker of Japan on one side and China on the other is putting enormous pressures to change on the economy." Without "making the irreversible changes," it warned, "plummeting fortunes eventually force change."

Before the 1997 crisis, Korea's deficit in technology balance of payments increased from US$900 million in 1993 to US$1.8 billion in 1995, and to US$2.2 billion in 1997. This increase in deficits despite our continued economic growth shows that imported technologies were more efficient than our own technologies. However, it also testifies to the fact that we didn't pay enough attention to technology development and our technological competitiveness was lagging behind.

Korea's R&D investments in 2005 were 2.79% of GDP, 24 trillion won, which was at a similar level with 2.51% of the US, 3.31% of Japan, and 2.49% of Germany (as of 2004), but the amount of investment was a mere 1/13 of the US, 1/6 of Japan, and 1/3 of Germany.

Technological development should be pursued not only in terms of investing in R&D to produce new technologies for long-term competitiveness, but also in terms of investing to enhance mastery of field technology for quality improvement to achieve mid-term competitiveness. To enhance the mastery of field technologies, we can learn from the early vocational trainings and the systems enabling working while learning of Germany and Switzerland which boast the world's best technological mastery. Bold investments in R&D and mastery of field technologies along with the establishment of systems for technology financing and technology transactions are the ways that can strengthen our national competitiveness and help us to become an advance economy.

10

Legacy of
Leftist Government

I spent ten years outside of government after putting all my heart and soul into the 1997 crisis as Vice Minister of Finance. Because I couldn't participate in the process of implementing the IMF policy program after the currency crisis, when assessing the result, I think the crisis was a half blessing in disguise.

Malaysia and Korea made exactly opposite choices during the 1997 crisis. Prime Minister Mahathir of Malaysia refused bailout funds of the IMF, arguing that the main culprit in the Asian crisis was hedge funds of advance economies. He criticized the international financial market as a jungle where rogue speculators were roaming along with no fear, and accused international financier George Soros of attacking the ringgit. He also asserted that foreign currency trading is abnormal and should be stopped. Malaysia overcame the crisis through capital control.

The Korean government negotiated a policy program for the IMF bailout funds on the premise that the crisis was our fault.

During a televised debate on December 7, 1997, presidential candidate Kim Dae-jung said, "If I am elected, I will renegotiate with the IMF," but in his letter to IMF Managing Director Camdessus dated on December 12, he changed his position by saying, "I fully support the IMF program." After the election, President-elect Kim Dae-jung invited George Soros on January 4, 1998 to dinner and asked for his "active support to make foreign investors come back to Korea."

Regarding layoffs, on December 24, President-elect Kim stated, "We will try to overcome this crisis by freezing wages, but if it doesn't work, we need to cut wages and if that fails, too, we have no choice but to endure layoffs," and during a meeting with the head of labor unions on December 26 he said, "There could be people who might lose their jobs in the process of restructuring. We are living in an era where attracting foreign investments is more important than selling products abroad." In a conversation with the public, which was live broadcast through TV on January 18, 1998, when Korea's foreign debt negotiation team left for New York, the new president declared, "We have just stepped into the tunnel of restructuring caused by the IMF bailout. The year 1998 will become the year of severe ordeal. Unemployment rates will become double-digit numbers. Layoffs are necessary to re-attract foreign investors who had already left Korea. Layoffs will also have a very important effect on extending the maturity of short-term foreign debts that reached US$92 billion. In a globalized economy, we cannot live without foreign investments. We have to change our perspectives on them. We have to welcome foreign investments."

Mr. Kim's position on layoffs was different from that of the IMF. Mr. Camdessus made his third trip to Korea in that year on January 12 to consult the Kim administration's implementation of the IMF program. He had a dinner at Hotel Shilla with the relevant government officials as well as key legislators. They included Senior Presidential Secretary for Economic Affairs; Minister and Vice Minister of Finance; the chairmen of the policy committees of three ruling and opposition parties, the heads of the Finance Committee and the Labor Committee of the National Assembly.

During the dinner, Mr. Camdessus emphasized the importance of financial and corporate restructuring. He used Japan as an example. It had been restructuring for eight years and still was not finished. Mr. Camdessus warned that if Korea dragged its heels too long, it could face another crisis and fall into huge trouble. He stated that expeditious and bold restructuring would guarantee a success. He also stressed the necessity of minimizing the scale of layoffs, pointing out that if massive unemployment occurs in the process of restructuring, those who lost jobs would become opposing forces and impede reforms, and that if the number of people who don't work and receive benefits increases, social costs would rise. On January 13, Mr. Camdessus visited the Federation of Korean Trade Unions to help its members better understand the IMF economic program and ask for their cooperation. But the Korean Confederation of Trade Unions refused to meet with him.

The ensuing restructuring in banks led to massive unemployment, which was not the intention of the IMF. The

IMF was regarded as the evil cause of joblessness and "IMF" was coupled with "crisis" to describe the anguish. However, I believe the root cause was wrongful policies. With the power transmitted to the leftist party for the first time in Korea's history, a sweeping power reshuffle tinged with strong political disposition resulted in the record layoffs.

| A half blessing in disguise

Some foreign news media described the 1997 currency crisis as a disguised blessing. This meant that the crisis was an opportunity for Korea to implement the tasks which the country had failed to do on its own to resolve its high-cost low-efficiency structure. The tasks included: reforming the financial and corporate management structures, enhancing flexibility in the labor market, and innovating technologies. It is necessary to examine the lights and shadows during the ten years of the leftist government to know how many of the problems that led to the 1997 crisis have been resolved.

At the end of 1999, the government affirmed, "We overcame the IMF crisis." Liquidity crisis could be resolved through currency depreciation and US$58 billion of the IMF funds. The 1997 crisis was a liquidity crisis caused by a shortage of foreign currency on the one hand, and a structural crisis caused by a high-cost and low-efficiency on the other. Substantial improvements were made in terms of currency overvaluation, current account deficits, and a shortfall in foreign exchange reserves, which were main factors of the liquidity crisis, but during the last three years of the leftist government, starting in 2005, they returned to the three-year trend that preceded the 1997 currency crisis. As for main causes of the structural crisis, improvement was made only in the over-leveraged corporate sector. The problems of underdeveloped technologies and militant labor unions still remained. Even the improvement in the highly leveraged corporate financial structure was a passive result achieved through sluggish investment. This led to another problem, a drop in growth potential. Investments in technologies were insufficient, there was no change in labor market flexibility, and more temporary workers were created.

While the bright side of the leftist administrations had restructuring in the financial industry and improvement in the over-leveraged corporate financial structure, a dark side of problems piled up as well. They included failure in achieving internal balance by being locked into low investments and failure in achieving external balance due to persistent current account deficits. While a reduction in corporate debt ratio, maintenance of fiscal soundness, and augmentation of foreign exchange reserves were successes on the static side, low economic growth, low investments, and current account deficits can be said as failures on the dynamic side. Crisis management capability based on the lessons from the previous crisis was a bonus. It enabled us to escape from the 2008 global economic crisis faster than other countries. When adding this bonus, I think the legacy of the leftist government's ten years was a half blessing in disguise.

▌Low investment

Korea's per capita GDP exceeded US$10,000 in 1995, and it did not become firmly entrenched at US$20,000 until 2010. Compared to advanced economies, who made the upward move in 9.8 years on average, Korea's 15-year rise was too long, though it was slowed by the 1997 currency crisis and the 2008 crisis.

From 2000 to 2007, Korea's average annual economic growth rate was 5.2%, while the average growth rate of investment was 4.5%. Among the OECD member states, there are few with a growth rate of investment (growth rate of fixed capital) lower than its economic growth rate. Being locked into low investment eroded the sustainability of the Korean economy, gradually reducing the share of Korea in the global market regardless of its growth. It also pushed down Korea's GDP ranking to thirteenth from tenth.

The low investment at that time can be ascribed to a weak business investment climate in Korea. We were beset with low exchange rates, high tax rates, excessive regulations, militant labor unions, excessive control on the concentration of economic power, expansion of anti-business sentiments, and lagging technological development. This deterioration in investment climate made the Korean economy fall into persistent low investment and caused a vicious cycle of low investment and low growth.

Return to current account deficit

In the three years prior to both the 1997 currency crisis and the 2008 global crisis, the current account balance declined sharply. The current account balance turned from a surplus of US$1 billion in 1993 to a deficit of US$23 billion in 1996, and it dropped from a surplus of US$28.1 billion in 2004 to a surplus of US$5.8 billion in 2007. It shifted to a deficit of US$5.7 billion in 2008 when the global crisis occurred. This shows a collapsing external balance may lead to a crisis.

If the current account balance continuously suffers deficits or suddenly deteriorates in a small open economy like Korea, the economy is not sustainable even if other economic indicators are positive. Even when the current account records surpluses, it could be the result of low investment or low exchange rates, evidence that the economy actually is steadily shrinking. The current account balance can serve as an overall health barometer of our economy.

The main culprit in the current account balance's sharp drop in the mid-2000s was overvaluation of the won. A comparison to the Japanese yen during the time period reveals the extent of the won's appreciation. Between 2001 and 2007, the yen appreciated against the dollar a mere 15.6% from 131.8 yen to 114.0 yen, but the won appreciated a whopping 41.4% against the dollar, from 1,326 won to 938 won. During the same period, Japan's current account balance greatly increased by US$122.7 billion, while the figure in Korea dropped by US$2.2 billion. If compared with the number in 2004, when Korea recorded a huge surplus, Korea's current account balance plummeted by US$22.3 billion in 2007.

| Inadequate R&D investment

The 1997 economic crisis can be explained as Korea being a nut in nutcracker with low-cost China on one side and high-tech Japan on the other side. Technology balance of payments, which indicates the level of Korea's technology, shows that a deficit of US$2.4 billion in 1999 increased to a deficit of US$2.9 billion in 2007. During the same period, the US and Japan saw their surpluses of US$26.5 billion and US$4.8 billion leap to US$33.6 billion and US$15 billion, respectively. The technological gap between Korea and other countries is ever-widening.

Korea's R&D investment before 2005 was less than 3% of GDP, a little above the OECD average. Its R&D investment in 2005 reached 24 trillion won, 2.79% of GDP. Although the percentage was similar level to 2.51% of the US, 3.31% of Japan, and 2.49% of Germany (as of 2004), the actual amount of the investment was only 1/13 of the US, 1/6 of Japan, and 1/3 of Germany. From 2012, Korea's R&D investment rose to 4.36%, surpassing Japan to record the highest level among the OECD countries. This was the result of implementing the world-class R&D support policies beginning in 2008. Development of technologies is the way to survive for the Korean economy and the key to strengthening our external competitiveness.

Labor market setback

The problem of militant labor unions, which was one of the reasons behind the withdrawal of foreign capital during the 1997 crisis, was not resolved even during the leftist government years, and labor costs, which were at the core of Korea's high-cost and low-efficiency structure, significantly rose compared to productivity. In particular, costs of labor-management disputes went up and the proportion of irregular workers sharply increased as conditions for layoffs became more stringent and more rigorous standards for irregular workers were introduced in 1998.

In February, 1998, before Kim Dae-jung was inaugurated, the Labor Standards Act was amended, based on a labor-management-government compromise. The change stiffened the acceptable conditions for layoffs by injecting "urgent managerial need." That made an agreement on employment adjustment between labor, management, and the government more difficult, making it almost impossible to carry out layoffs. The amendment put Korea in the footsteps of Japan's lifetime employment system, dealing a setback to labor market flexibility. In addition, stringent requirements for labor contract for two years or less and a provision that required conversion of irregular workers into regular workers after two years were applied. This created more short-term employment, constraining labor market flexibility further, and it became difficult for the socially vulnerable such as cleaners to work at one company more than two years.

After the amendment to labor acts in 1998, the number of labor-management disputes soared to 129 cases in 1998 from 85 cases in 1996, before the currency crisis, and sharply increased again to 462 cases in 2004. The number of work days lost also increased from 893 days in 1996 to 1,452 days in 1998, and 1,894 days in 2000. The number of irregular workers in 1996 was small, although the exact number is not known due to imperfect statistics, but it increased to 3.59 million, 37% of the entire work force, in 2004. After the 1997 economic crisis, the labor market flexibility weakened substantially.

| Strengthened financial base

During the 1997 economic crisis, Korea's debt ratio in the manufacturing sector was 396.2%, which was more than two times higher than those of the US and Japan and five times higher than that of Taiwan. We were barely paying the interest on loans with ordinary profits.

The IMF recommended us to lower the debt ratio to 200% or below. Upon this recommendation, companies made excruciating efforts to lower debt ratio, reducing the size of their businesses and disposing of their real properties. As a result, debt ratio in the manufacturing sector dropped to below 200% in 2001 and to below 100% in 2007, putting Korea at the top among OECD countries in terms of corporate financial soundness.

The foreign exchange crisis turned out to be a blessing in disguise in terms of corporate financial structure. However, this reduction in debt ratio, which was achieved mainly through disposal of assets and the scaling back of investment, caused another problem of eroding our economy's growth potential.

I I | Elections and Platforms

The 1997 currency crisis provided an opportunity for the leftist party to take power in Korea for the first time. I resigned from my Vice Minister of Finance post the following year and stayed outside the public sector for the next ten years. However, I eventually joined the election camp of a right-wing presidential candidate, who recaptured power from the leftists. Immediately after its inauguration, the new administration had to deal with the global financial crisis, which was increasingly affecting the country.

There is a saying, "The road to hell is paved with good intentions." In elections, many populist platforms are disguised as good-intentioned promises. To win elections, catchphrases and visions giving simple and clear images and platforms that can win votes are necessary. Good policies hardly ever collect votes or lose them. There is no place for the runner-up in elections. But to have a successful tenure, presidents should forget all their campaign platforms as soon as they are elected, political scientists say.

In a majoritarian democracy based on voting that is universal, equal, direct, and confidential, the majority is taxed less and assumes less responsibility. Under an election system where responsibilities and authorities are separated, decisions mostly involve good vs. bad rather than right vs. wrong, and are primarily based on individual interests rather than national interests. Candidates focus on popularity and the probability of garnering votes more than efficiency and legitimacy. What determines success in elections is how skillful a candidate can formulate populist platforms that appeal to emotions rather than reasoning.

The most important axiom for election strategies is the 10-20-30-40 principle. It stipulates that 10% of population consists of innovators, who are the leaders. Rational early adapters are next, constituting 20% of the total, followed by the common public, the 30% who are nonprofessionals. They are said to be largely emotional and receptive to populist platforms. The remaining 40% consists of the bottom public. Its members are influenced by the common public individuals due to frequent contact with them. The sheer number of common and bottom public individuals make them the pivotal voters in deciding an election. Innovators and early adapters are minor groups. They have developed views and amassed knowledge through a lifetime of learning, and are rarely swayed by election campaign promises. Moreover, they do not have a decisive impact on elections due to a lack of contact with the common public.

To devise platforms of presidential candidate Lee Myung-bak, his campaign staff members and I focused on what had gone wrong the past 10 years under two leftist administrations. The legacy of the administrations was financial restructuring, less corporate dependency on borrowing, sustained fiscal prudence, and increased foreign reserves. On the dynamics side, however, our economy had been held in check by low growth, low investments, and current account deficits. From 2000 to 2007, the economy grew 5.2% on average whereas investments rose just 4.5%. Per capita GDP, which had surpassed US$10,000 in 1995, stayed below US$20,000 until 2006.

Platforms were shaped around the idea of making Korea the "Top 7 Nation" in the world and the catchphrase "Working Economic President." The "Top 7 Nation" idea was encapsulated into a campaign slogan, "747," which recalled the Boeing 747 airliner. With the slogan attracting considerable attention as well as doubts, our team gained momentum for success. Lee Myung-bak won by 5 million votes.

| Election economics: Good policies are bad pledges

The first five-year economic development plan, which started in 1962, resulted in successful industrialization of the Korean economy and the 1987 Constitution stipulating direct presidential elections helped the country establish a democratic system. In 2007, the times called for shedding economic sluggishness, which had persisted since 1997, and further advancement of the economy.

The campaign platform of turning Korea into the Top 7 Nation meant achieving 7% annual growth and raising per capita income to US$40,000 within 10 years, thereby putting Korea on the list of the world's top seven economies.

The idea came from the Korean national football team's victory against Italy's to grab fourth place in the 2002 World Cup. Thus, it was an expression of our desire to again move past Italy. According to the IMF statistics, Italy had the 7th-largest economy in terms of GDP and Korea was 10th in 2005.

To give it a vivid metaphor, the abstract idea was embodied in the "747" slogan, the top Boeing airliner. The model number was not unfamiliar to most Koreans since they had traveled abroad. They considered the airplane to be the best aircraft.

The catchy but also controversial 747 slogan was recognized as a key pledge because it raised major issues for discussion before rival candidates did. Our campaign thus was successful. Our campaign book contained the term "Top 7 Nation," but not "747," which was used for public events only. We expected to increase Korea's per capita GDP to US$40,000, outdoing Italy to become one of the world's top seven by 2017. This goal called for realizing growth potential of 4% and achieving additional growth rate of 3%.

About 100 scholars and experts joined candidate Lee's platform committee to shape his campaign pledges. They formulated pledges with a set framework. The first step was defining national visions and government philosophies. Strategies to realize the visions, tactics to implement the strategies, and projects to execute the tactics followed. I acted as the coordinator and gatekeeper, making sure pledges did not conflict and reviewing financial support plans for specific agenda items.

Economic plans in election campaigns often are designed to spend now and pay later. In effect, debt is transferred to future generations of taxpayers to achieve victory today. Such plans pay little attention to issues regarding long-term national development or fiscal balance. One expert on fiscal matters I had known at the IMF said that "English disease" was caused by populism under which hard-working professors happened to feed drunkards. Social welfare should not exceed a minimum level of protection such as feeding the have-nots, treating the helpless, and sheltering the homeless so that a country can ensure sustainability as well as fiscal prudence, he argued. Welfare programs providing protection from the cradle to the grave adopted by advanced Western countries in the past have been increasingly abolished, but only after they have upset fiscal balance sheets and overall economic conditions. In most OECD countries, national debt ratio hovers at 100%. The harmful effects are also well illustrated by the economy of Argentina, which once matched that of the US. The economy, however, has lapsed back to the level of a developing country in the wake of Peronism.

Most of Lee camp's programs that likely would have lowered the chances of an election victory had to be repackaged with more enticing names even if they were reasonable, effective, and forward-looking for the country's future. For instance, withdrawal of the new capital city plan was rebranded as the science-business belt plan and the move to abolish high school standardization was reshaped as high school diversification. Some programs were kept out of the spotlight so they could be smoothly implemented after the inauguration. Eliminating excessive welfare support was put on hold for a post-elections push forward.

There is no place for a runner-up in elections. *Election economics* tells us that good policies could be bad pledges and populism to win more votes is a necessary evil in a majoritarian democracy.

| Vision of Top 7 Nation

The "Top 7 Nation" vision not only aimed for expansion but also to advance national defense, science and technology, culture, sports, etc. For this, we thought we needed to achieve 7% economic growth, and to accomplish that, meet several goals: 1. improving the business environment to attract more investments; 2. expanding investments into technology innovations to ensure sustained growth; 3. reinforcing social infrastructure to broaden the base of domestic demand; 4. increasing working age population to boost potential growth rate; and 5. establishing a peace regime on the Korean peninsula to lower the risk involved in investments; and so on.

After rising 7.1% during the Kim Young Sam administration, the Korean economy declined and flattened out under the two leftist governments, achieving 4.3% growth during the Kim Dae-jung administration and a 4.4% rise during the Roh

Moo-hyun administration. Stuck on a low-growth track, the country's potential growth rate hovered around 4.5%. In terms of size, the economy slid to the 13th place in the world from the 10th at its peak as Russia, India, and Brazil outperformed Korea. Under the circumstances, the 7% growth target was urgent and necessary for the country.

The content of the 747 slogan was taken as major promises, national visions, and goals of the Lee camp. Many questioned whether 7% growth was unachievable and said the Top 7 Nation goal was overly ambitious. The country's potential growth rate was calculated at about 4.5%. We felt the potential could be raised 1% through tax cuts, adjustment of foreign exchange rates to reflect the fundamentals of the real economy, and other measures to improve the business environment; 1% through further deregulation; and 1% by preventing illegal labor strikes. If those activities were achieved, the campaign goals of per capita GDP of US$40,000 and seventh largest GDP at US$2.5280 trillion in 10 years, were attainable, we concluded.

Visions may appear unattainable initially. I think visions represent hopes that can be realized but only with 120% effort as well as goals that should be pursued with all of the nation's resources. Having a 7th largest economy in the world larger than those of Italy, India, and Russia is an attainable goal if all of the 80 million people marshal their energy on a unified Korean peninsula.

To reach the 7% economic growth goal, we established strategies in five areas: improving the business environment; expanding investments into technology innovations; reinforcing social infrastructure; increasing economically active population; and establishing a peace regime on the Korean peninsula. Eight major pledges formulated in those areas were deregulation and lowering of tax rates; spending 5% of GDP into R&D; establishing Meister high schools and systems enabling working while learning; building the Grand Korea Waterway; building 500,000 new homes every year; providing public care services for infants and preschoolers; realizing the high school diversification project; and achieving the détente initiative with North Korea. In the past, campaign pledges were mainly based on the righteousness of strategies. However, the aforementioned pledges had practical tactics and were supported by project-specific action and budget plans.

First, we pledged to improve the business environment through deregulation and tax cuts. From 2000 to 2007, the Korean economy grew 5.2% on average, but investments upped only 4.5%. The current account balance had substantially deteriorated every year since 2004, reversing a positive trajectory after 1997. The trend in 2007 was strikingly similar to the situation before Korea's currency crisis ten years earlier. Against this backdrop, we attempted to lower the corporate tax rate below 20%, a level applied by our competitors. We also planned to ease regulations significantly by using sunset provisions and the negative list approach, meaning comprehensive permission except for those that are explicitly listed, to improve the business environment to the best in the world. In the meantime, the OECD urged member countries to refrain from competing to cut tax rates for the sake of fiscal prudence. The most important task was to adjust foreign exchange rates to reflect the fundamentals of the real economy. However, it was excluded from the list of pledges in consideration of external relations.

Second, we focused on increased investments into technology innovations for sustained growth. In 2005, Korea invested 2.79% of its GDP into R&D, the US, 2.51%, and Japan, 3.31%; but in terms of the value, Korea's R&D spending was only 9.3% of the US level and 23.8% of Japan's. Given the small size of the Korean economy, we planned to raise the share of R&D out of GDP to 5%, which would have been the world's highest level and nearly double that of our competitors.

For this, R&D investment in basic science and original technologies was earmarked to jump from 0.75% to 1.5% in the government sector and in applied science and technologies, from 2.04% to 3.5% in the private sector. To boost private sector R&D spending, we also formulated one of the most well-structured support plans. It called for lowering almost all corporate taxes according to the stage of activity, from preparation and investment to research. The plan included tax deduction if up to 5% of sales revenue was reserved for R&D activities, tax credit for 10% of R&D facilities investments; tax credit for 25% of spending for research.

Third, we planned to establish 50 Meister high schools as well as work-study systems. Meister high schools were modeled after vocational training in Germany and Switzerland which boasted highly-skilled workers. Their task would be development of technologies to enhance the country's long-term competitiveness and improvement of product quality to heighten mid-term competitiveness.

As for systems to allow students to work and learn side by side, we devised diverse plans. They included selection of students according to employment contracts with companies; completing half of school lessons with on-site training; total exemption of tuition fees; and tax credit for on-site training fees up to 20 million won. Meister high schools were a way of fostering highly-skilled field technicians and easing the financial burden on working families to educate their children as well as a means to increase the working age population in a practical manner. As of 2006, the average Korean began to work at the age of 25 while Germans did at 19. The OECD average was 23. In the meantime, the college enrollment rate was over 80% in Korea, higher than in any other member nation. The rate was about 35% in Germany, 45% in Japan, and 55% in the US with the OECD average reaching 60%.

Fourth, we pursued construction of the multifunctional Grand Korea Waterway. The plan to build Seoul-Busan, Geumgang, and Yeongsangang waterways and connect them into a multifunctional grand waterway running through the Korean peninsula was highly controversial during the presidential campaign. The name, "Grand Korea Waterway" reflected our intention to link them with Yeseonggang, Daedonggang, Cheongcheongang waterways in the northern side of the Korea peninsula following reunification. The idea was ambitious in its size and scale. The project plan envisaged 12 routes running 2,100 kilometers on the southern side of the peninsula and five routes of 1,000 kilometers on the northern side.

At that time, it was urgent to facilitate industries for domestic demand to lift the economy out of the low-growth trap. We thus needed a massive economic project similar to the New Deal infrastructure works of the US. The Grand Korea Waterway project was aimed not only at providing a convenient transportation method but also at laying the groundwork to further develop the service industry through development of periphery regions, thereby promoting balanced national development.

Fifth, we pledged to build 500,000 houses annually. We put more efforts on devising a plan to provide houses for working families than on making other pledges. Our Constitution stipulates rights to employment and education, but not housing, though these are three basic rights to ensure stable livelihoods. In a way, housing is more important than others since it is the basis of receiving education and working. One of the major duties of local governments of other advanced countries is to provide public transportation and affordable housing to working people. We thought real estate prices were excruciatingly high for them to buy a house and coupled with expensive private tutoring for children, were the main causes of labor-management conflicts and violent labor strikes over higher wages despite already decent pay levels. Thus, it was urgent to build houses for newlyweds to prevent young adults from marrying at an increasingly older age and having fewer babies. Considering these circumstances, we planned to shift the basic housing policy from curbing speculative demand to increasing supply and set forth specific proposals. They were to stabilize real estate prices by offering more than 500,000 new houses every year; to hold the government to be responsible to supply "national" houses of 80 square meter or smaller; and to build 120,000 units every year exclusively for the newlyweds.

Housing prices spiked in 2005 due to 120 trillion won paid by the Roh Moo-hyun administration to buy land to promote its various development projects for rural areas. The government had rolled out new measures every year to curb price hikes since then and finally introduced the Comprehensive Real Estate Tax. The tax violated the principles of universality, equality, sufficiency, and protection of tax sources. I considered it to be an act of political violence.

Regrettably, key items of the housing supply plan were modified or deleted while being implemented. I believe, however, the stabilization in real estate prices from 2008 was greatly attributable to the plan. Sharp falls in prices brought new problems. Nevertheless, a price-to-income ratio higher than that of other advanced nations is too high for our economy and makes it difficult for wage workers, especially newlyweds, to enjoy housing stability. Although heavy taxes and regulations on housing ownership should have been gradually abolished to ensure a slow, steady decline in housing prices, the efforts were regrettably insufficient.

Sixth, we attempted to strengthen public care services for infants and preschoolers. One of the most serious structural problems facing our economy is a shrinking working age population, which will ultimately erode growth potential. Five ways are generally used to increase a population: improve the fertility rate; promote early employment; extend the retirement age; increase the number of female workers; and accommodate more immigrants. Of these, improving the fertility rate is most impactful. Thus, we focused on resolving difficulties of working mothers to have more children while encouraging their participation in economic activities. According to a government report, Korea's fertility rate was the lowest in the world at 1.05 in 2005. If the rate continues, the country's working age population will peak at 37 million in 2016 and then begin to contract as Korea becomes the world's fastest aging population. The South Korean population, which currently exceeds 50 million, will be reduced in halve by 2100 and the whole Korean population will disappear by 2500, the report added.

The key to lifting the economy out of its low-growth trough was to increase the working age population. In the 1970s, the government provided tax credit for families with one or two children only and men were exempted from military reserve training if they got a vasectomy. Families with two children were jokingly dubbed the civilized; those with three, barbarians; and those with four, cannibals. Today, having more babies constitutes one of the most patriotic acts. The public childcare service plan was intended to assure prospective mothers of government support for stages from childbirth and post-natal care to child-rearing. According to the plan, support was to be provided on four stages from pregnancy and childbirth to child-rearing and school enrollment. Services included were medical fee subsidies for prenatal checks and delivery, childcare fee subsidy for all babies under the age of 5, and government-paid essential vaccinations for children from birth through 12 years old. The plan also included expansion of private and public childcare facilities, as a precursor to full and complete national childcare service managed by the government in the long-term.

The national childcare service plan was the first step toward the resolution of national tasks to reinforce the country's growth potential and ensure Koreans continue to thrive in their homeland. We thought the plan should be the top policy priority, even before free school lunches, regardless of the fiscal burden. Provision of public childcare to improve fertility rate and boost economic activities by women and establishment of Meister high schools to lower the entry age of employment were aimed at increasing the country's working age population. Other plans such as extension of retirement age, introduction of a wage peak system, and dual citizenships to encourage Korean expatriates to return to their home country were implemented after we took power.

Seventh, we set the high school diversification project. Behind it was a lesson from Japan, which abolished its 35-year-old high school standardization policy in 2003. The policy, which standardized classrooms regardless of student abilities, led to an overall decline in academic performance of high school students. That diminished opportunities for children from low-income families to enter top-tier universities.

Moreover, research linked Japan's chronic economic malaise since the 1990s to a decline in academic ability and lost ambition among youths. Our standardization policy was modeled after Japan's. Thus, we thought, if Japan withdrew the policy, we should do the same. However, given the strong opposition against abolishing the standardization system, we had to diversify high schools step by step to address the policy shortcomings, rather than total cancellation in one motion.

I believe students, parents, and teachers should take the initiative in educational matters, as is the case in other advanced nations. Some in Japan even argue that the Ministry of Education and Tokyo University should be shut down to normalize the country's education. The high school standardization policy is giving fewer and fewer opportunities to low-income families and lowering the intellectual level of our society. It should come to an end. The education policy came to Korea out of jealousy and will only drive our society toward co-destruction.

My own granddaughter's experience showed me how widespread private tutoring and advanced learning has almost paralyzed the country's official educational system. Accordingly, I concluded that education can be normalized only when middle and high schools are guaranteed autonomy in student selection and educational curriculum. Without it, parents cannot but have their children enroll in supplemental and private educations from primary through high school, while teachers must continue to struggle to find effective ways to instruct students with different academic ability, from dismal to excellent, within the same classrooms. What about the worries of high school students as they realize the result of their one-time university admission test may determine their future and even their whole life? Pre-college private education institutions and admissions tests for primary and secondary schools exist other countries. Will banning them guarantee equality and balanced opportunity? Why don't we use random assignment for university enrollment or for jobs the same it is done for assigning seats in primary, middle and high schools?

Eight, we set up the détente initiative with North Korea. The basic idea was to provide North Korea with aid for the economy, education, finance, infrastructure, and welfare if the North gives up nuclear programs and promotes an open-up policy that aims for a rise in per capita income to US$3,000 in ten years.

Specific programs included establishment of five free economic zones in the North and development of 100 companies with more than US$3 million in exports a year; establishment of North Korean versions of the Korea Development Institute and Korea Advanced Institute of Science and Technology as well as technology training centers in ten major cities to foster 300,000 economic and financial experts and technicians; form a US$40 billion economic cooperation fund with grants from the World Bank and the Asian Development Bank, the Inter-Korean Cooperation Fund, and foreign direct investments; laying the 400 kilometer-long New Seoul-Sinuiju Expressway, building waterways linking north Korean rivers, and reinforcing telecommunications networks and port; and food aid, support for medical staff and hospital equipment, housing, water, and sewage system improvement, and planting 100 million trees.

The initiative is aimed not only at laying the groundwork for national reunification but also at achieving 7% economic growth. The CEO at one of the largest British banks once said foreign banks had withdrawn their money during the 1997 currency crisis mainly due to their concerns over militant labor unions, lack of corporate transparency, and the unpredictable nature of North Korea. It is critically important for us to resolve the security issue in order to induce more investments, a precondition to accomplish the 7% growth target. It is also essential to establish a peace regime on the Korean peninsula to reunify the country and build a strong nation with its 80 million people. The initiative reflected the fact that the 10-year pursuit of the engagement policy by two former leftist administrations had unwittingly supported the North's nuclear development programs. Specific projects were proposed to express the sincerity in our desire to promote inter-Korean relations. However, the initiative bogged down due to the sinking of the South Korean corvette Cheonan and the artillery shelling of Yeonpyeong Island, both in 2010. In addition, the Six Party Talks entered a stalemate on the first-phase implementation plan toward denuclearization of North Korea, regrettably.

Among the pledges above, we selected three priority tasks to be pushed through in the first year in office: building the Grand Korea Waterway to revitalize the domestic economy in the short-term; creating the world's best business environment through deregulation and lowering tax rates in the mid-term; and boosting R&D investments to create new growth engines in the long-term.

Pledges: Toward advanced country and community of hope

In the run-up to the 17th presidential election, we produced a book containing pledges, titled "*Korea toward an Advanced Country and Community of Hope.*" Such books in the past were nothing but simple collections of pledges with no structure or order and lacked consistency in the contents. We referred to all of the campaign publications created both by ruling and opposition parties in Korea, the US and Japan to make ours more substantial and well-structured. We referred to nothing but the contents of Japan's since the country does not have presidential elections. The best reference was the book *Putting People First* by US President Bill Clinton. It expressed his pledges in a story telling manner so that voters can easily understand them and contained budget plans, too.

Our campaign book consisted of the needs of the time, national vision and administrative philosophies, President's economic philosophies and principles, pledges, action and budget plans, and five-year-after achievements. It was the first time action and budget plans, and five-year-after achievements had appeared in a campaign book. We held a magnificent ceremony to announce the pledges. Campaigners played a key role in election campaigns in the past. With significant progress made in the media environment, the election campaign moved mainly to the airwaves, not in the streets, through televised speeches and debates. Thus, pledges play a critical role in election campaigns.

We declared that the nation's time in history called for a power shift that could establish a new system for national development and develop the country into a world leader. The national vision was the "Top 7 Nation," and the administrative philosophies were a warm-hearted market economy, democratic activism, and creative openness based on empirical pragmatism. The principles for governance were autonomy and competition, consideration and tolerance, and the rule of law.

Candidate Lee's economics, popularly known as "MBnomics," called for a smart and open market economy supported by seven principles: 1. maximum guarantee of autonomy and competition; 2. protection of the less privileged and support a fresh restart by those who had failed; 3. economic matters prioritized over political issues; 4. supply expansion prioritized over demand control; 5. improved redistribution through job growth; 6. entrenchment of the rule of law across all sectors of the economy; and 7. pursuit of openness and global standards.

All the pledges were arranged into objectives, strategies, tactics and projects, which corresponded three goals, 10 strategies, 43 tasks, and 92 promises, respectively. Action and budget plans and five-year-after achievements were also included into the booklet.

The three goals were well-off people, inclusive society, and strong nation. The 10 strategies were: 1. economic recovery; 2. growing middle class; 3. co-prosperity; 4. basic welfare for brighter future; 5. public safety; 6. fight against exclusion and discrimination; 7. strength in soft power; 8. redesigning and reconstruction of national land; 9. effective diplomacy and peace on the Korean peninsula; and 10. pragmatism within the government.

These pledges were accompanied by action plans which contained yearly roadmaps from 2008 to 2012, budget plans, specific tasks for policy formulation and revision of laws and regulations. We estimated the cost for implementation of each pledge at 24 trillion won and set forth plans to save 10% from other government budgets and secure additional financial resources through mid- to long-term fiscal projects. Five-year-after achievements were illustrated with specific figures for each of the three goals, namely well-off people, inclusive society, and strong nation, as well as for individual projects mentioned above.

| Presidential transition committee

My three-year long journey to recapture power ended with Lee Myung-bak winning a landslide victory by a margin of more than 5 million votes on December 19, 2007. I joined the Presidential Transition Committee as a committee member and the secretary of the first economic subcommittee, which dealt with economic matters in preparation for the new president's inauguration.

I received reports from director generals of the Ministry of Finance, the National Tax Service, and the Customs Service on their impending issues and ways to put campaign pledges into practice.

I, along with many public officials dispatched from diverse

ministries, prepared a lot of reports for President-elect Lee. The most influential report was on implementation plans for the so-called MBnomics. The plans called for: reforms of business-related regulations; tax reductions to facilitate investments; better efficiency in budget spending; stronger competitiveness in financial and services industries; management of prices and the current account balance; expansion of investments into science and technology; and development of next-generation growth engine industries. Five-year action plans were established with 2012 as the target year for such goals as 7% economic growth, 12.0% investment growth, US$7.5 billion current account surplus, 580,000 new jobs, 3.6% consumer inflation.

We set a growth target of 6% for 2008. For this, we consulted with the Ministry of Finance and the BOK to facilitate immediate action when the new government took office in March. In addition, it was agreed to use the first regular session of the National Assembly in June to pass revised laws necessary to pursue the goal. Until then, we planned to do what was feasible in revising enforcement decrees or lower-level regulations during the first month after the inauguration.

Amid the preparation, the country's current account balance was shrinking and short-term debt was rapidly growing to reach US$158.6 billion as of the end of 2007. Given this, we were determined to take preemptive action if financial institutions experienced a crunch in foreign currency liquidity due to turmoil in global financial markets.

To execute the plans smoothly, President Lee would chair

monthly meetings to maintain the momentum behind the plans. The topics and host would be: economic facilitation, Ministry of Finance; trade and investment promotion, Ministry of Knowledge and Economy; and science and technology promotion, Ministry of Education and Science.

The Minister of Finance would host economic and financial review meetings, economic policy coordination meetings, and meetings on international economic affairs to review fiscal and financial policies, coordinate issues between government agencies, and continue to pursue more free trade agreements. To prepare to handle the instability swirling in international financial markets, we would hold closed-door meetings for economic and financial reviews on a weekly basis in the initial days of the new administration. The Senior Secretary to the President for Economic Affairs and representatives from the Ministry of Finance, the Financial Services Commission, and the BOK would attend the meeting.

Some who did not participate in the election campaign tried to insert tasks unrelated with campaign pledges into the new administration's projects. However, after assuming office, the new administration cancelled most of the additions. Unless members of the transition committee participate in the new cabinet, their efforts on the team lose much of their meaning and the activity and money poured into the committee's activities are useless.

The two-month long activities of the presidential transition committee were listed in a white paper, titled "Success and Sharing." I doubt the book influenced the actual operations of each government ministry since I was the only member of the transition committee placed in President Lee's first cabinet team. It is waste of resources for someone not expected to serve the government or the Office of the President to join the transition committee. The confusion and disorder caused by such practice outdo the merits.

The presidential inauguration committee must be formed in a similar fashion as the UK's shadow cabinet. First, the committee must consist of prospective members of the new cabinet. Second, the members should establish action plans on how to put the campaign pledges into practice in cooperation with relevant ministries. Third, they should obtain personnel records in order to appoint members of the Presidential office as well as the cabinet and devise personnel reform measures. Lastly, they should prepare for the inauguration ceremony and stay focused on organizational restructuring of the government.

CHAPTER 4

2008 GLOBAL ECONOMIC CRISIS

12

Unprecedented Global Crisis in 2008

An unprecedented global economic crisis erupted when global imbalances became unsustainable and the bubble in the financial derivatives market burst due to the bankruptcy of Lehman Brothers on September 15, 2008. The US subprime mortgage crisis in 2008 differed from crises which occurred primarily in the English-speaking world in the 18th century, the debt crisis in South America in the 1980s, and East Asia's currency crisis in the 1990s in that it reverberated around the world. Since New York's financial market was interconnected with global markets, the subprime mortgage crisis spread to the whole world, driving it into the Great Recession. Pains were more severe in advanced countries than in Asian countries because the former had lived without such an economic chaos since the Great Depression in 1929 while the latter suffered a crisis relatively recently in 1997.

Financial institutions continued credit expansion and greedy speculation in the 21st century as they did in the 18th century. In the past, speculation took place in real economy objectives such as textiles, railways, mines, stocks, real estates, and slaves. In the 21st century, speculation became a money game around financial derivatives, innovative securities created based on complex mathematics. Investing in financial derivatives was like playing in a casino in that the investment could not be sustained without repeated betting. The financial engineering that produced derivatives was like a casino that can maintain non-stop risk-taking. Complex mathematics behind the products fooled everyone in the financial market.

The US Federal Reserve Chairman Alan Greenspan offered the money needed for playing in the casino, through credit expansion and low interest rates, and Wall Street's genius created a great illusion that everyone can make money. Greenspan continued to step into the market whenever stocks fell to prevent everyone from losing money. The Great Moderation which began in the late 1980s collapsed in 2008 after his resignation. Behind it were the great twin deficits of the US—its troubled fiscal and trade accounts—and the consequent global imbalances, which had been supported by supply of cheap products to the world from China. Greenspan's Great Moderation which gave rise to the imbalances and the bubbles demonstrated that there is no free lunch in economic matters.

In an article in July 2005, *The Economist* warned, "The entry of China's army of cheap labour into the global economy has increased the worldwide return on capital. That, in turn, should imply a higher equilibrium level in real interest rates. But, instead, central banks are holding real rates at historically low levels. The result is a misallocation of capital, most obviously displayed at present in the shape of excessive mortgage borrowing and housing investment." Nuriel Rubini, a professor at New York University, also warned that yet-to-materialized housing bust could lead ... to "a systemic problem for the financial system."

| Imbalance and burst of bubble

Everything in the world moves toward an equilibrium. Water overflows after the cup is full and energy bursts when it became excessive. The imbalance between excess heat around the equator and energy shortage in the North Pole is resolved by typhoons carrying heat northward. This is the law of the nature. The imbalance between surplus in some countries and deficiency in others bursts by the law when it reaches a critical point.

There were fundamental differences between the 2008 global economic crisis and the 1997 Asian financial crisis. The cause of the 1997 crisis was mismatched maturities of liquidity while that of the 2008 crisis was an imbalance in the global economic structure, in particular in housing and fiscal sectors and international balance of payments. The former took place because of the bursting of bubbles created by eagerness for economic growth and lack of skill to steer it, and the resultant instability. The latter happened when bubbles created by greedy speculation and overconfidence burst.

At the root of the global financial crisis lay massive surpluses on one side of the global economy and ballooning deficits on the other side. Mounting surpluses enforce exports of capital and growing deficits require imports of capital or printing of reserve currency. Japan had run a surplus of more than US$100 billion every year since 1992, which amounted to US$136.2 billion or more than 3% of its GDP in 2003. Germany's current account surplus exceeded US$100 billion in 2004. After surpassing 5% of its GDP in 2005, Germany's surplus peaked at US$249.1 billion or 7.5% of the GDP in 2007. In China, current account surplus surpassed the US$100 billion mark in 2005. Then it doubled to US$200 billion in the next year and to US$412.4 billion in 2008. The share to the GDP jumped from 5% to 9.1% during the period. The US contrasted vividly. Since 1994, it had run a deficit more than US$100 billion every year. Its share to the GDP exceeded 3% in early-2000s, the known limit for sustainability, and 5% in 2004, and then peaked at 5.8% in 2006 with deficit reaching US$802.6 billion. The huge imbalance between Japan, Germany and China, and the US gave rise to a huge amount of excess capital.

Excess capital sparked investment into high-yielding financial derivatives. In 2007, worldwide market securities totaled US$61 trillion while financial derivatives amounted to US$596 trillion in value, almost 10 times larger than the market securities. In addition, worldwide export transactions reached US$17 trillion while foreign currency transactions, US$803 trillion, as much as 46 times larger than export transactions. Bubbles were estimated at more than US$1,000 trillion in the financial sector and to reach even higher if sovereign debt was included—the OECD countries' average sovereign debt ratio stood at 73.5% with that of Japan peaking at 162.4% in 2007. Excess capital cannot but arrive in the financial market if there are no appropriate enough investment targets in the real economy.

If low-paying excess capital ignited speculators' greed, housing loans with low interest rates added fuel. In the 2000s, the US' economic growth slowed to around 1% due to the burst of IT bubbles, the 9/11 terrorist attacks, the Afghanistan War, and the Iraq War. The Federal Reserve then began steadily lowering its benchmark interest rate from 6.5% to the ultra-low 1% in 2003 to spur the economy.

Excess capital, in search of higher returns, gravitated toward the home mortgage market, where even homebuyers with low credit ratings were getting loans. The loans became underlying assets of financial derivatives, which became underlying assets themselves of other derivatives, creating speculative bubbles in the process. Housing prices in the US soared 190% in the 10 years to 2006, and then plunged 34% over the next three years in the wake of the ending of low interest rate policy in 2004. The plunge lit the fuse on bubbles in the real estate market, setting the stage for the subprime mortgage crisis. Upon the fall of Lehman Brothers, one of the five major investment banks in the US on September 15, 2008, stock prices tumbled 6% during the following three trading days around the world and the London Interbank Offered Rate jumped to 4.29%. Citigroup, Merrill Lynch, and AIG, which were holding massive financial derivatives, practically went bankrupt. HSBC, the world's third largest bank, saw huge amount of its assets become irrecoverable and France's BNP Paribas suspended redemption of derivatives.

The financial crunch spread to Europe with housing prices tumbling in the UK, Spain, Italy, Ireland, and Hungary. All these countries had witnessed their housing prices double from 2000 to 2005. The bubble-and-burst cycle that started in a few center countries drove the whole world into an unprecedented panic.

The bursting of the bubbles in 2008 contracted the global economy by 0.6% in the following year with the economies of the OECD member countries shrinking 3.5%, and those of the US, Japan, and the EU, 3.2%. The contraction gave rise to a fiscal crisis in Portugal, Italy, Greece, and Spain in 2010, aggravating the situations even further. From the fourth quarter of 2008 to the first quarter of 2009, the world economy contracted by as much as it had done during the Great Depression from 1929 to 1931. On an annually adjusted basis, the US economy shrank 6% during the two quarters and Japan's economy, as much as 12.7% during a single quarter.

Japan saw its property market bubble burst in the 1980s and the ensuing Lost Decade and other Asian countries went into crisis with financial bubbles in 1997. Korea applied lessons it had taken from the experience of the 1997 crisis to its responses to the 2008 crisis. In 2008, it achieved a turn in its current account balance to surplus by adjusting its foreign exchange rates to reflect the fundamentals of the real economy. The government took fiscal and tax measures to supply about US$58 billion to the markets, representing as much as 7.1% of the country's GDP. These preemptive, decisive, and sufficient measures helped the economy grow 0.3% and raise its foreign reserves to over US$300 billion in 2009. In sum, Korea was able to weather the 2008 economic crisis thanks to lessons from the 1997 currency crisis.

Progress of crisis: Too connected to fail

When there are signs of a crisis, people withdraw their money from banks and banks curtail their loans. The resultant crunch prompts corporate bankruptcies, which then lead to bankruptcies of financial institutions, heralding the beginning of a full-scale crisis. Financial crunches and bankruptcies occur successively as crisis in center countries spreads to periphery countries. Bankruptcies cause severe recession and massive layoffs. Behind the establishment of the Bretton Woods system, the International Monetary Fund, and the International Bank for Reconstruction and Development at the end of World War II were reflections on past crises and need for international cooperation.

The financial connection between central and periphery countries strengthened thereafter. Mergers and acquisitions in New York's stock market created financial behemoths such as Citigroup, JPMorgan Chase, Goldman Sachs, Lehman Brothers, and AIG in the late-20th century. They launched a giant wave of market opening and globalization through the financial markets of emerging economies, expanding their networks worldwide. They created huge profits through reckless credit expansion and wild speculation and bankers and stock traders received generous bonus and stock options. These financial institutions were too big to fail and their networks around the world were too connected to fail.

The global economic crisis was difficult for center countries alone to cope with because of the complex connections of the global economic systems. The US injected US$9 trillion, 65% of its GDP, in bailout and economic stimulus programs and the EU, Japan, and China followed suits. Some predict, however, the crisis has never ended until today. The need for international cooperation to overcome the crisis gave birth to the Group of Twenty (G-20), which, along with the Bretton Woods system, has led the global financial order since its inception.

| Unprecedented responses: All means mobilized

The regular G-20 finance ministers' meeting, which kicked off in 1999, was elevated to a summit of state heads on November 15, 2008 due to the need for international cooperation to overcome the economic crisis. With the leaders of member states coming to an agreement on the need for cooperation, fiscal and financial programs accounting for about 6% of their GDP were implemented thereafter.

The G-20 states used every tool available from bailout and interest rate cuts to quantitative easing, tax cuts, and fiscal expansion as they had done to combat the Great Depression in the 1930s. They lowered interest rates to below 1%, supplied money as much as needed, cut taxes as much as possible, and increased spending as much as available. Reportedly, these measures were unprecedented in scale with the total value representing about 6% of their GDP. The US' tax cut amounted to US$317 billion, and increased fiscal spending, US$787.2 billion with the combined value taking up 5.6% of its GDP. Tax and fiscal spending programs reached 25 trillion yen or 5.7% of its GDP in Japan, 5.6% in Germany, 2.9% in France, and 1.6% in the UK. In the meantime, China announced a three-year plan for tax cut and infrastructure construction worth 5.5 trillion yuan or as much as 22% of its GDP. Emerging economies affected by the crisis also had to prepare similar measures. Professor Rubini estimated the combined value of bailouts, payment guarantees, economic stimulus, and other crisis measures adopted by the US government at US$9 trillion. Korea spent 72.8 trillion won in tax cuts and fiscal stimulus, taking up 7.1% of its GDP. Consequently, its economy grew 0.3% in 2009 when all other OECD member countries experienced negative growth.

The US measures were implemented in three aspects. First, on October 3, 2008, the Bush administration purchased bad assets from ailing banks, insurers, credit card companies, and even car makers or provided them with payment guarantees through the Troubled Asset Relief Program (TARP) worth US$700 billion. The beneficiaries were Citigroup, Bank of America, JPMorgan Chase, Goldman Sachs, Morgan Stanley, American International Group, American Express, General Motors, and Chrysler. Following up in 2009, the Obama administration formed a second relief program worth US$800 billion to buy more bad assets from financial institutions through bad banks. Second, the US federal government provided US$5 trillion in payment guarantees to the Federal National Mortgage Association, known as Fannie

Mae, and the Federal Home Loan Mortgage Corporation known as Freddie Mac, the country's two government-sponsored mortgage providers. Last, starting in November 2008, Federal Reserve Chairman Ben Bernanke employed what he termed a "helicopter drop" of money through three rounds of quantitative easing amounting to more than US$3 trillion, along with interest rate cuts to near zero.

Although bankers and stock traders in advanced countries who created bubbles received huge bonuses and stock options, no one held them accountable for their action. There was no strict judgment of legislators who loosened regulations for bubbles to form, or on supervisors who stood idly by. The Fed bought assets from financial institutions which needed money. In doing so, many zombie banks and firms were created, and the cost had to be paid by taxpayers. Moreover, taxpayers in even periphery countries had to foot the busted bubbles in center countries.

The unprecedented crisis required unprecedented solutions. Fiscal solutions inflated sovereign debt of the OECD member countries by almost 100%, causing another fiscal crisis in Europe in the end. Central banks' traditions disappeared and no one came forward to hold the responsibility for the widespread moral hazard. Meanwhile, oil prices nosedived to US$30 per barrel in 2009 after soaring from US$80 to US$145 in the summer of 2008. The fluctuations in oil prices vividly show the greed of speculative moves seeking profits out of crisis.

Unprecedented currency war: Open the safes

The quantitative easing that Fed Chairman Bernanke began in November 2008 prompted central banks in Japan and Europe to follow suit. This amounted to the currency war ever fought to protect jobs and exports.

The Fed opened its discount window to investment banks, securities firms, and other primary dealers other than commercial banks for the first time after the Great Depression in the 1930s and extended anything to anyone at a 2.5% rate without penalties. The Fed depended on a number of channels to supply money. They are Term Auction Facility (TAF), Primary Dealer Credit Facility (PDCF), Term Securities Lending Facility (TSLF), Commercial Paper Funding Facility (CPFF), Money Market Investor Funding Facility (MMIFF), and Asset-Backed Commercial Paper Money Market Mutual Fund Liquidity Fund (ABCPMMMFLF), whose name is too long to memorize.

In 2008, Japan launched quantitative easing without a limit as far as inflation remained below 2% and the European Central Bank bought national bonds from countries under a financial crunch, including Spain, Italy, and Greece. The UK bailed out its banks by purchasing bad assets, thereby supplying liquidity to the market.

The total value of quantitative easing carried throughout the world is not known exactly. An estimate in 2013 puts it at US$10 trillion, considering the combined total of US$7.4 trillion—US$3.6 trillion in the US, US$1.6 trillion in EU, US$2.1

trillion in Japan —plus those implemented in the rest of the G-20 countries. How enormous it is!

Fighting the crisis of 2008, the US Fed rewrote the history of central bank by turning from the lender of last resort to the lender of first, last, and only resort. The Bank of Japan and the European Central Bank came along side by side.

Quantitative easing could be inevitable from the standpoint of center countries, which had a reserve currency to protect their jobs and pull their economy out of recession. However, it is not different from a new form of currency war that wounds periphery countries. Capital with near-zero interest rates formed through the policy in the US and Japan flocks to periphery countries, strengthening currencies of periphery countries, making their exports more expensive and thus eroding their competitiveness. Quantitative easing kept currencies of center countries from appreciating, but it did the opposite to periphery states, which created confusion in the international financial markets. In this sense, it was like a double-edged sword that might ignite a currency war.

In the G-20 Summit in Washington on November 15, 2008, Korean President Lee Myung-bak proposed a "stand still", which urged all countries not to engage in a tariff or currency war as they had done in the 1930s during the Great Depression and countries with a reserve currency to strive to maintain the value of their currencies. Member countries agreed on the proposal. As countries remained under the World Trade Organization system, tariff- or non-tariff wars did not occur. A new form of currency war broke out though as countries sought their own national interests. Brazil imposed 6% tax on capital transactions to protect itself from volatile speculative short-term money from advanced countries and Korea enacted a 0.2% bank levy. A currency war is retaliatory in that central countries produce short-term carry money at low interest rates while periphery countries control them. I believe the world needs a new monetary order which countries with a reserve currency cannot print freely as they wish as is the case of the WTO system.

❘ Results of crisis management: Long road ahead

Despite all the efforts, the world economy is still weak. Some argue the unprecedented measures have only transferred private debts to governments. Others foresee a long road of more than 10 years to sustainable recovery. Even though Professor Roubini forecast a U-shaped recovery, some are more skeptical, giving an L-shaped trajectory, meaning that recovery to pre-crisis level is a long shot. With four decades of experiences in fiscal and financial policies and in fighting the 1997 Asian currency crisis and the 2008 global economic crisis, I am on the skeptical side.

In 2009 when the full brunt of the economic crisis swept across the world, the OECD countries saw their economies shrink 3.5% and unemployment jump to 8.2%. The global economy contracted 0.6% with trade shrinking 16%. The impact was most seriously felt in the US and Japan, which suffered negative growth of 2.8% and 5.5%, respectively, as well as in Europe, where unemployment soared to 10%. In 2012, the OECD economies grew only 1.6% and the eurozone economies shrank 0.6% after four years from the crisis. Given these, a recovery to around 3% pre-crisis growth will be difficult to realize. In the meantime, the Korean economy registered 0.3% growth in 2009 while other members of the OECD were still struggling with their shrinking economies, and in the following year, it grew 6.3%, the fastest recovery in the rich nations club.

The failure of advanced countries to achieve a sustainable recovery is attributable to the lasting structural imbalance of the world economy and too much emphasis on liquidity supply due to their excessive fiscal deficits. The sovereign debt ratio of the OECD countries reached a dangerous level of 102.5% in 2011. The ratio stood at 104.1% in the US, 106.4% in Europe, and 227.2% in Japan in 2013, which implies they have no more rooms for fiscal maneuver. Household savings have doubled to 6% from 3.0% in 2007 in the US. Unemployment in 2009 hovers at 8% not only in the US but in other OECD countries. The US' current account deficit accounts for more than 3% of its GDP, a point known to be dangerous. The prospect for the world economy to recover to pre-crisis levels is grim, but there are no signs of global leadership to manage the crisis at present.

Households spending above their means, corporations borrowing more than their capability to repay, financial institutions obsessed with speculative operations, supervisory authorities standing idly by, and legislators indulged in populism were all responsible for the fundamental imbalance of the global economic structure. Without extensive reflections of what happened and fundamental innovations in all countries and economic players, it would be difficult to avoid an L-shaped recession. Limitless printing of money has probably made the economic illness worse. If it was to be tackled through monetary supply, operating a high performance currency printer would have been more effective and cheaper than resorting to Ben Bernanke or Haruhiko Kuroda.

The IMF should take the initiative in implementing fundamental innovations since it functions as the world's central bank. However, the fund itself lacks the power balance and is heavily influenced by a few center countries of the past. This makes me worry about discussions filled with rhetoric, but no actions, thereby causing more pain to the people around the world. It would be extremely difficult to completely break the bubble-and-burst cycle unless the free printing of reserve currency is controlled.

13

Reflection of 2008 Economic Crisis

After being banished from the Garden of Eden, people faced the fate of toiling for food. Martin Wolf at *Financial Times* described Germans, Chinese, and Japanese as the ants and American, British, and Spanish as the grasshoppers in Aesop's fable to account for the economic crisis. Ants should spend more, grasshoppers, less; and ants should not lend grasshoppers money, he wrote.

The experiences of the Asian financial crisis and the global economic crisis led me into a belief that the fundamental cause of a crisis was "obesity from overeating." Habitual overeating driven by affluence leads to obesity, which has become a fact of our life. Obesity may cause high blood pressure and diabetes, and even death unless properly treated. Everyone knows a healthy diet and exercise are necessities, but putting them into practice is not easy. When I was young, we had to work hard in the fields to have food, which was scarce. We had no idea about diet or exercise to lose weight. What we needed then was not exercise, but rest after working hard. Amid the global economic crisis, what center countries needed to treat was "obesity" of their economy while periphery countries needed to address the fragileness of their economy. What would be the means to transform an obese economy into a healthier one?

Center countries that have a reserve currency may tolerate economic liberalism and speculation operated by invisible hands of the market; but periphery countries cannot but step into the markets to ward off speculative capital flows. Financial derivatives were regarded as innovative financial instruments in center countries. However, in periphery countries, the same financial products were treated like casinos.

| Obese economy:
Excessive consumption and investment

Consumption is a virtue according to John Maynard Keynes. Although it was a bit confusing since we were taught that frugality and saving were virtuous at school, I implemented economic policies for 40 years based on Keynes' assertion. I once told my granddaughter, who was nagging me for a toy, too much consumption was bad. She replied consumption was necessary to revive the economy. This episode made me wonder if students these days are taught that consumption is virtuous.

In 2008, the US' GDP amounted to US$14.7203 trillion; net disposable income, US$12.2926 trillion; final consumption expenditure, US$12.3741 trillion; net saving, US$81.5 billion below zero; and gross fixed capital formation, US$3.594 trillion; and net borrowing, US$772.1 billion. The US had heavy foreign debt and its consumption outstripped disposable income. European countries excluding Germany, and Japan, had similar situations with their consumption and investment dwarfing income and saving.

How sustainable will be an economy with about 80% of the income flowing into consumption, about 5% into saving, and about 20% into investment? The economies of advanced countries are obese in that their excessive consumption and investment are sustained by excessive savings in Germany and China. The obesity was caused by three factors: global imbalances of consumption and investment, freewheeling financial sectors disconnected from the real economy, and over leveraging. Housing bubbles and the Lost Decade of Japan, housing bubbles in the US and Europe, and the global economic crisis are symptoms of an obese economy.

As for global imbalances, Mr. Wolf described Germans, Chinese, and Japanese as the ants and American, British, and people in South European countries as the grasshoppers in Aesop's fable in 2010. The imbalance created bubbles in the financial markets and capital transactions, he said. How long will the grasshoppers live without working, and how long will the ants continue to work?

Freewheeling financial markets disconnected from the real economy created huge financial derivatives and foreign currency transactions, let shadow financing thrive, and formed great bubbles. In 2007, the world's market securities amounted to about US$60 trillion whereas financial derivatives totaled US$596 trillion, 10 times larger than the market securities. In the same year, trade of goods and services reached US$34 trillion while foreign exchange transactions totaled US$802 trillion, as much as 23 times larger than the trade volume. Greed and speculation led shadow finance and let the Ponzi scheme continue. CEOs in Wall Street reportedly received a salary that was as much as 250 times more than their employees' and enjoyed US$240,000 vacations. It is fair to term the situation "casino capitalism." I doubt if freewheeling financial markets not based on the real economy and the secondary market disconnected from the primary market will be sustainable.

Financial markets disconnected from the real economy encouraged people to buy goods and houses on "borrowed income," and financial derivatives based on that created massive "unearned income." In addition, governments spent "borrowed revenue" into populism–oriented policies. All of these gave rise to an exorbitantly large amount of debt which is almost impossible to be paid back. Excessive debt prompts lowering of interest rates to zero, which then make debtors not hesitate to take more debt. The sovereign debt ratio exceeded 100% in the OECD countries and 200% in Japan in particular. How long will borrowed income, unearned income, and borrowed revenue be sustainable?

The bubble economy created by households, financial institutions, and governments turned capitalism into "debtism." It was possible to sustain accumulation of debt with the production by the world's ever–growing population in the

1980s. The world's workforce, however, began shrinking without a rebound in the 2000s after doubling from 1.46 billion to 2.93 billion in the 1990s thanks to the entry of Chinese, Indians, and Russians into the global market. The ever shrinking workforce implied bubble implosions were inevitable because the speculative debtism no longer could be propped with production. As individuals from emerging and developing countries who were putting skin into the game disappeared, the game ended. This can be likened to serious obesity, causing high blood pressure and diabetes which have to be treated by doctors.

The global economic crisis was a part of the boom-and-bust cycle created by speculative investments into derivatives with over-leveraging from short-term funds from the point of advanced countries. It was a part of the dash-in and rush-out cycle created by reckless investments into emerging markets with over-borrowed carry funds from the point of emerging economies. The former sees the crisis was caused by uncertainty formed by greed and overconfidence over speculative profits whereas the latter points to instability created by over eagerness and lack of skill over economic growth. Excessive investment on derivatives through financial innovations was to blame from the view of rich countries while it was overexposure and contagion effects spreading via financial conduit was to blame from the view of emerging countries.

At the center of the crisis were bloated economies where consumption outstrips income and investment exceeds savings. Their obesity was tethered to global imbalances between income and consumption, savings and investments, fiscal revenue and fiscal expenditure, and exports and imports. Current account deficits of the US, the UK, and Southern Europe were offset by capital account surpluses of Germany, Japan, China, and others. The essence of the global economic crisis was the imbalance of current and capital accounts. The economics we need now is not that of uncontrolled greed, but of managed restraint.

| 'Diet' economy:
Work hard, save more, and invest more

History tells us that bubbles burst someday. Money game in which bubbles are formed and then burst needs new skin in the game to go on. The inputs were profits from colonies in the 18th century. After the liberalization of colonies at the end of World War II, the new skin was profits from emerging and developing countries earned through financial market opening and globalization. In the process, regulators deregulated their markets, supervisors looked on speculative moves with their arms folded, and central banks increased the skin.

Ahead of the crisis, *The Economist* in July 2005 sent warning signs about increasing skin that central banks were delivering.

「Cheaper goods from China have made it easier for central banks to achieve their inflation goals without needing to push real interest rates sharply higher. This has encouraged a borrowing binge. The resulting excess liquidity has flowed into the prices of assets, such as homes, rather than into traditional inflation.

Central bankers like to take all the credit for the defeat of inflation, but China has given them a big helping hand in recent years... For instance, the average prices of shoes and clothing in America have fallen by 10% over the past ten years —a drop of 35% in real terms... Today, we would again have had "good deflation" —but central banks have instead held interest rates low in order to meet their inflation targets.」

While fighting two economic crises, I received advice and suggestions from a lot of experts and finally realized a simple truth that humans can make a living on their own toil and sweat only. When Adam and Eve were banished from the Garden of Eden, God condemned them to painful toil and sweat for their food. Thus, the fundamental solution is to work hard, save more, and invest more. A good printer will be enough if more money ensures economic recovery, but the reality is much more complex.

Crisis will be prevented if commercial banks extend loans with money they receive from depositors, investment banks earn returns for their risk-taking, the primary market takes the initiative in stock markets, and supervisors control greedy speculative moves. We have to break from the recurrence of chaos and panic in times of crisis, which lead to oblivion in times of no-crisis. The Brady report of the US Presidential Task Force on Market Mechanisms created in the wake of Black Monday of 1987 made five recommendations. One of them was that one agency should coordinate a few critical regulatory issues. The country seems to have forgotten the recommendation. Meanwhile, many regulatory authorities were incorporated into one agency in the aftermath of the 1997 crisis in Korea. Center countries should have big thinking and lead radical reforms and periphery countries should collaborate with them to solve the current problems. Who will do that and how?

The inconvenient truth is that free printing of reserve currency lies beneath bubbles and imbalances, which are poisonous to both center and periphery countries. Emerging economies in Asia were hit by the 1997 currency crisis mainly due to carry trade which converted cheap short-term money to expensive long-term loan. In retrospect, arbitrage trade by financial institutions in advanced countries seeking profit in foreign exchange markets and swap funds they operated in emerging markets made things even worse. Practicing the carry trade strategy was an easy option for financial institutions in advanced economies like swimming while touching the ground, but it is very risky for us. A mischievous boy throws a stone at frogs for sport, but the frogs' lives are at stake. Likewise, bankers and traders in advanced countries simply enjoy the money game, it is a life or death matter for emerging countries, which have no choice but to depend on short-term funds from their advanced peers.

I was the one of the frogs when foreign banks aggressively pushed me to raise swap funds in the 1980s and when under pressure for financial market opening and globalization in the 1990s. I believe periphery countries need to introduce capital transaction tax to protect themselves from reckless attacks by speculative funds. To tackle the fundamental problem of the global economic crisis, sharp flows of speculative short-term funds, which do harm to not only emerging but also advanced countries, have to be regulated.

Inconvenient truth:
Troubles in financial system

Since the global economic crisis was caused by the imbalance of over-consumption in advanced countries and over-saving in emerging economies, the solution to this structural problem is hard work, increased saving, and increased investment by the former combined and increased spending by the latter.

Professor Roubini emphasized that we need "some big-picture thinking and some radical reform" to tackle the crisis in a fundamental manner. Prolonged peace and abundance lead to indolence, corruption, and then crisis. Even though it is very difficult to convert an obese economy built on speculation and bubbles into a healthier one based on moderation and hard working, we now need to think about how to do it. Obesity causes potentially fatal health problems like high blood pressure and diabetes. At the root of bubbles and crises was obesity, which may kill the global economy unless treated in time. The Great Depression of the US was an opportunity for the people to think anew about their economy and make necessary reforms. Many have changed since then in advanced countries.

In the past, the problem was not about production which was flexible, but about demand. Today, however, supply has become less flexible, but demand has increased in flexibility in many advanced countries. We need new reforms to deal with new problems.

From my experiences of dealing with fiscal and financial policies for four decades and fighting the 1997 and 2008 crises, I think it will be difficult for advanced countries to do big picture thinking and apply radical reforms or find fundamental ways out of the crisis. There are seven grounds for such pessimism. On the economic side, the issues are current account deficit, speculation related with the financial account, volatility of the asset account, and rigidity of the capital account. On the non-economic side, they are bureaucratism of regulators, political populism of legislators, and oligopolism of international financial systems.

The first ground is current account deficit incurred by activities of households, corporations, and financial institutions as well as trades and government's fiscal policies. Excessive consumption, investments, speculation, spending, and imports can only be resolved by self-control and productivity increase by households, corporations, financial institutions, and governments. This is not easy to resolve, just as it is not easy to lose weight.

Second, financial speculation works irrespective of the real economy while constantly disturbing it. I believe the financial industry essentially cannot move along completely disconnected from the real economy. Financial speculation is especially tricky to resolve because human greed for money lies beneath it.

The third issue is asset account-related volatility due to foreign exchange rate fluctuations. During the Asian and global economic crises, market exchange rates were more influenced by capital flows than by current account balances, and showed wider fluctuations. Japan's external assets denominated in the US dollar halved in value following the appreciation of the yen according to the Plaza Accord in 1985. Japan tightened its belt thereafter to restore its competitiveness, but slipped into the 1990s Lost Decade in the end. The Bretton Woods system built on the gold standard and fixed exchange rates collapsed in 1971. We now need to reexamine the correlation between foreign exchange rates, economic indices, and capital flows and to revisit the international financial order accordingly. We cannot expect rational transactions in commerce when the standards for transactions change constantly.

The fourth is the rigidity issue of the capital accounts of Germany, Japan, China, and other countries which hold huge savings and the US, the UK, and South European countries with excessive investments. The rigidity is deeply related with the instability of the international monetary order as well as social security networks and life habits. Thus, it needs a long time to be fixed. This is like physical fitness cannot be achieved through one or two days of exercise.

The fifth is bureaucratism. Under the system, regulators are complacent and do not pay much attention to a potential crisis. The system has been one of the most complicated dilemmas with a long history. Despite ceaseless efforts to make changes and innovations, it still remains to be resolved.

Sixth, political populism of legislators makes matters worse. In universal and equal democracy based on the principle of majority decision, political populism is a necessary evil. It is difficult to prevent populist legislations in such a political system allowing funds for election campaigns and legislations influence voters. Behind the subprime mortgage crisis in the US were the Financial Services Modernization Act of 1999 and the Commodity Futures Modernization Act of 2000, which allowed to merge commercial banks, investment banks, and insurance companies and deregulated financial derivatives. Both measures were the results of strong lobbying efforts by financial companies. This then raises a question: Is there any alternative to the majority democracy?

The last one is the unstable oligopolism of the international financial system where the US and Europe take the lead in making important decisions. Since the fall of the Bretton Woods system in 1971 by the US's declaration of no more conversion of dollars to gold, mercy and restraint of countries with a reserve currency have been the only safeguard of the international financial order where they can freely print dollar, yen, or euro.

Under the international financial system based on dollar, the currency itself is a commodity with indefinite demand. Therefore, the US is technically free from external liabilities and needs not worry about foreign reserves and exchange rates as far as its dollar printing machine keeps working on. For the US, it is paradoxical that the value of dollar appreciates when its economy is weak. The reason lies with the unstable international financial order, which can be fixed only by the US' leadership. The only way for periphery countries to avoid a crisis is to maintain current account surplus while keeping sufficient foreign reserves. In this sense, their governments' intervention into the foreign exchange market is a form of exercising sovereign rights and the only way to ward off a crisis.

The global imbalance of the real economy and the unstable financial structure are not sustainable. The imbalance in particular requires strenuous efforts and a long time to be fixed. The international financial order without the gold standard is like a market without a measuring standard. If the size of measuring unit in a rice market changes every day, people will lose their confidence in the market, and if the length of one mile differs daily, people will no longer respect the measurement. Trade imbalance is not definitely sustainable, and unstable market foreign exchange rates are theoretically impossible. The inconvenient truth of the international financial order requires big picture thinking and radical reforms to be resolved.

| Leadership and cooperation: Birth of G-20

In the wake of the 2008 global economic crisis, the G-20 emerged. As the share of Brazil, Russia, India, and China (BRICs) out of the world's GDP increased, that of the existing G-7 slid below 50%. This consequently exposed limits in terms of representation and crisis response capability. Against this backdrop, the stature of G-20 finance ministers' meeting was elevated to a summit status on November 15, 2008 to facilitate global cooperation to fight the economic crisis. On that day, the front page of the *Washington Post* described the summit as a "historic power shift." The meeting was indeed a harbinger of a shift in the world power, considering that the G-20 accounted for two-thirds of the world population, 85% of the global GDP, and 80% of the world trade.

In the G-20 Seoul Summit chaired by Korea on November 11, 2010, the country took the initiative in forging an agreement on new foreign exchange rate principles, which would bring significant changes to the international financial order. Agreed principles were to ensure exchange rate flexibility to reflect underlying economic fundamentals, to have advanced economies with a reserve currency remain vigilant against excessive volatility and disorderly movements in exchange rates, and to include carefully designed macro-prudential measures into emerging countries' foreign reserve and exchange rate policies.

I pay my respect to the IMF and the US for their agreement with the new principles by changing their initial position from opposing to government intervention into foreign exchange markets. The only response from periphery countries to center countries printing their reserve currency is to use the foreign exchange rate policy as one of their sovereign rights. Korea has striven to achieve that right. I believe, the agreement on the new principles is a Copernican change that will go down in the history of international finance. Meanwhile, it is another miracle for Korea to have risen from a rule taker in the past to a rule maker making a contribution to the international financial order.

The G-20 is still in its infancy. Leadership by center countries and cooperation by periphery countries are a must to resolve global imbalances and instability, and revamp the oligopolistic international financial system. This is my honest belief gained by the experiences of the 1997 Asian financial crisis, the 2008 global economic crisis, and the G-20 finance ministers' and summit meetings.

14 Economics of Restraint

It is said that history provides us the basis of wise judgment and math provides us wise solutions. The history of repeated booms and busts gives us the criteria to judge a crisis and mathematical economics shows useful solutions to it. We need to rethink trade imbalance, volatile exchange rates, oligopolism of international financial system based on the reflection of the global economic crisis to avoid another crisis. Many economists have formulated a number of solutions to the problems which surfaced during the crisis.

However, the world economy is still struggling despite unprecedented actions prescribed according to the solutions. Some predict it will take more than a decade for recovery to be on a sustainable track. The global financial crisis was mainly caused by the imbalance in current and capital accounts and unstable financial system. What we need now is not the economics of unbridled greed, but the economics of managed restraint. A new development requires a new spear, which then requires a new shield. This is the same with economics.

Finance based on greed and speculation incapacitated human toil and sweat. Finance is a decisive factor of the real economy. Economic principles which did not take finance into account were useless as was proven during the Asian financial crisis and the global economic crisis. Sharp flows of capital and speculation in the financial sector caused the two crises. *The Economist*, January 19, 2013, pointed to the problems of the standard macroeconomic models used by central bankers and other policymakers.

『The crisis showed that the standard macroeconomic models used by central bankers and other policymakers, which go by the catchy name of "dynamic stochastic general equilibrium" (DSGE) models, neither represent the financial system accurately nor allow for the booms and busts observed in the real world. A number of academics are trying to fix these failings. Their first task is to put banks into the models. Today's mainstream macro models contain a small number of "representative agents", such as a household, a non-financial business and the government, but no banks. They were omitted because macroeconomists thought of them as a simple "veil" between savers and borrowers, rather than profit-seeking firms that make loans opportunistically and may themselves affect the economy.』

Lessons from crisis: Restraint and reform

The 2008 global economic crisis told us inconvenient truths of the global village and left lessons to learn. The global imbalances and instability rooted in the oligopolism of international financial system aggravated problems associated with current account, financial account, capital account, and the international financial order. Now, enriched with lessons, what matters now is whether we have become more capable of making right decisions and implementing correct response plans.

First, to deal with current account deficits, households need to live in frugality and save more, corporations need to expand retained earnings and make investments more efficiently, and governments must respect the principle of basing expenditure upon revenue and maintain foreign exchange rates at an appropriate level. Specific methods for these may differ from country to country, according to their actual conditions. Economic slowdowns stemming from lackluster consumption will be eased when income starts to grow following investment growth. Nevertheless, workers and entrepreneurs who pay attention to short-term performance cannot wait and politicians succumb to demands of unsatisfied voters in the same manner as it is difficult to lose weight.

Second, greed associated with the financial account can be controlled through well-structured regulation and supervision. However, it is hard to ignore constant lobbying by financial firms since greed is instinctive and cannot be measured. What make matters worse are regulatory arbitrage and innovative financial instruments that bypass regulations and supervision.

Third, volatility of the financial account can be soothed through rational intervention into foreign exchange markets by governments. Principles on market intervention were agreed at the G-20 Seoul Summit, but specific action plans have yet to be hammered out. There have been no such things as market exchange rate in the past. If the yardstick for measuring speed changes all the time, there is no way of driving under the speed limit. The IMF and advanced countries have long put pressure on periphery countries with no tools but foreign reserves to refrain from stepping into the market. Still, market intervention is a matter of life and death for the periphery countries.

Fourth, rigidity of the capital account will be resolved through increased spending in countries with excessive savings, and increased savings in countries which consume heavily. The rigidity is associated with the instability of international monetary order, inadequate social safety nets, and poor lifestyles and thus hard to be tackled once and for all. Japan did spend its surplus built from the 1960s not for commodity import, but for export of dollars. This backfired in the form of the Plaza Accord in 1985, which cut the value of country's dollar-denominated assets in half, driving the country into the Lost Decade in the 1990s.

Fifth, although everyone agrees there are problems with bureaucratic system and political populism, it is hard to find plausible solutions. In a majoritarian democracy based on universal, equal, direct, and confidential voting, the majority pays less tax and assumes less responsibility. Under a system where responsibilities and authorities are separated, decisions are made more often between what is good and bad than between what is right and wrong, and more often based on individual interest than based on the national interest. Realistically, majoritarian democracy on which bureaucratism depends cannot bypass populism. Some bring forward techno-democracy as an alternative to majoritarian democracy. Overcoming bureaucratism and populism requires ceaseless efforts.

Last, center countries may be aware of the oligopolism of the international financial system even though they do not raise the issue by themselves. Reshuffling of international financial system will provide the basis to resolve global imbalances and to prevent creation of speculative bubbles. It is hard to break the bubble-and-burst cycle based on imbalance and instability unless free printing of reserve currencies is controlled. Center countries are technically free from foreign exchange rate fluctuations and external liabilities, but periphery countries cannot avoid the fallout from them without resorting to exchange rate and foreign reserve controls. This shows different positions between children throwing stones at frogs for fun and the frogs whose lives are at stake.

Keynes proposed Bancor, tied to 30 representative commodities, as a global super currency in 1944 when the Bretton Woods system was established. Former President of France, François Mitterrand argued for a new international monetary system in 1984, and former British Prime Minister Gordon Brown advocated extensive reforms of the Bretton Woods system in

2008. The time has come for us to discuss a new monetary standard tied to gold, silver, iron, oil, grains, and other commodities which are omnipresent all across the world.

To prevent another crisis from happening, the current international financial system should be reformed in a way of resolving global imbalances and instability. Things have changed too much for us to maintain the Bretton Woods system. The market exchange rate system lacks stability and will aggravate the imbalance if misused. Oligopolistic international financial system exposes limits in terms of representation. Under the current international financial order, center countries cannot but adhere to printing their reserve currency and periphery countries, accumulating the currency. It is hard to control the monster created by greed and speculative capital. We thus need big thinking and bold reforms by center countries. Hopefully, the IMF will take the initiative in creating a new international financial system in collaboration with the G-20.

| Dilemmas of economics: Keynes, Friedman, Hayek and Schumpeter

The relationship of spear and shield is a tricky dilemma. Striving to make a spear that can penetrate any shield and efforts to make a shield that can defend any spear are like Sisyphus rolling a rock uphill then watching it fall back. I was not able to tackle the spear and shield dilemma with diverse economic theories during the two economic crises.

Started as mercantilism in the 15th century, commercial capitalism evolved into industrial capitalism passing industrial revolution in the 18th century, and then into financial capitalism and security capitalism with a focus on financial markets in the 20th century. With the world becoming a digitally networked global village in the 21st century, digital capitalism and global capitalism emerged based on the single market of networked global village.

Economics provides solutions to specific issues of specific time. Therefore, economic theories once useful in the past become null and ineffective in other times as issues change with passing of time. The iron industry which had spearheaded capitalism in the US fell in the 1980s. Today, Samsung Electronics of Korea is a leader in mobile phones. With production and supply of goods facing their limit in advanced countries today, economic theories which were effective when supply was flexible tell nothing about today's problems. Without flexible supply, economic stimulus is highly likely to create bubbles. The theories that I had faced the most while dealing with economic and financial policies for the past four decades were those of John Maynard Keynes, Milton Friedman, Friedrich von Hayek, and Joseph Schumpeter. While trying to apply Keynes's principle of effective demand and Friedman's monetarism, I had to cope with restrictions from supply and liabilities, and when attempting to use Hayek's free market economy by the rule of law and Schumpeter's creative destruction, I faced with emotional resistance and political restrictions.

Above all, Keynes's effective demand principle does not

provide a solution to limited supply if the manufacturing sector lacks competitiveness nor tackle the limit of sovereign debt when government spending is excessive. Gregory Mankiw at Harvard University contended that the best fiscal tool to combat recession was tax cuts. This is based on the empirical study by Christina Romer, who chaired the US presidential Council of Economic Advisers, and David Romer. According to their analysis of post-World War II fiscal policies, a dollar of tax cuts raises GDP by about three dollars. Alberto Alesina and Silvia Ardagna at Harvard University looked at 91 stimulus programs implemented in 21 OECD member countries since 1970 and concluded that cuts in corporate and individual income taxes were successful, but increased government spending was not. These imply that, for a country with sizable debt, tax cuts will be more efficient than a rise in spending of equal value since fiscal prudence is as important as economic recovery.

Korea has continuously reduced tax rates since the 1980s. Nevertheless, the country's tax revenue has risen. Despite tax cuts during the 2008 crisis, the country's overall tax revenue, including corporate tax, has increased thanks to its economic recovery outpacing those of other countries. In addition, value-added tax accounts for around 30% of all of its domestic tax revenue although the rate is as low as 10%, far less those of others. Direct support for corporate production is obviously more effective when a country maintains flexibility in production. Supply was no problem in the US or the UK when Keynes suggested the principle of effective demand because their production capacity was large enough. However, things have much changed since then.

Friedman's monetarism is useful for a country with a reserve currency and flexible production capacity. Otherwise, monetary expansion will only create bubbles when the country does not have a reserve currency. Expansion of credit by a periphery country in crisis will lead to depreciation of its currency, encouraging sharp withdrawals and hoarding of foreign currency. Radical monetary expansion by a country with a reserve currency will probably spark a currency war, which will wreak havoc with periphery countries. Monetary expansion also spurs speculation, not investments when profits from speculation outdo interest rate yields.

Korea adopted a stringent monetary policy and raised interest rates as recommended by the IMF during the currency crisis of 1997. However, it did say nothing to the US, Japan, and many other center countries which executed quantitative easing and lowered interest rates during the 2008 economic crisis. The IMF applied different standards of monetary economics to different countries depending on whether the target has a reserve currency, which confuses me a lot. In 2008, Korea was capable of lowering interest rates and raising credit supply since its foreign reserves were large enough to absorb short-term debt. With its small, open economy, Korea was influenced more by foreign exchange situations than by economic fundamentals and had to place external balance ahead of internal balance. The difference between periphery countries putting a priority on external balance and center countries emphasizing internal balance is not due to the difference in applicable economic principles, but to the difference in power.

I wonder what will be there at the end of the road of quantitative easing through which the US has supplied as much as US$3 trillion with a zero interest rate. Although the value of the US dollar was supposed to decline in recession, the value paradoxically went up on growing dollar preference and dollar hoarding in increasingly uncertain markets in periphery countries. In a sense this justifies the US decision on quantitative easing. Nevertheless, I am still concerned that quantitative easing will aggravate matters even worse as stipulated by economic principles considering that expansion of low-cost credit without production growth caused the 2008 crisis. Once again, the subprime mortgage crisis was the result of great bubbles created by profits from financial derivatives dwarfing interest rate yields.

I believe that Hayek's free market economy by the rule of law is one of the most rational and logical economic theories. I would like to promote the theory in Korea where the rule of law has to be reestablished. However, given the majoritarian democratic system, the country would not be able to appropriately deal with unemployment, recession, and huge welfare demand with that theory. Human emotions are swayed by likes and dislikes, not by rights and wrongs and the majority of the public is influenced by emotions. You should at least pretend to weep at a funeral knowing that the deceased can never rise again. This shows an aspect of human emotions. The reality is sad; life is difficult; the public is impatient; and the ideals are too far away.

During the decade ruled by two leftist administrations, which successively took power in Korea after the 1997 crisis, the rule of law regressed, welfare increased too much, and anti-business sentiment swelled. Reforms promoted by the rightist government that ensued in 2008 stalled due to political populism.

Schumpeter's creative destruction provides fundamental solutions to economic crisis, I believe. For Schumpeter, not only technological progress but exploration of new markets, development of new products, and changes to product distribution were all innovations. Still, making a policy based on the theory in reality will require courage due to political pressure and resistance to layoffs. Voters' resistance is almost insurmountable in a majoritarian democracy. Faced with the subprime mortgage crisis, the US resorted to the "too-big-to-fail" myth, not creative destruction.

Korea failed to conduct creative destruction driven by innovations during the 1997 crisis. Politicians and labor unions further aggravated the rigidity of the country's labor market. Many labor agreements require consent by labor unions to make facilities investments for productivity growth or carry out layoffs for efficiency enhancement. This is one of the notorious conundrums in Korea.

The theories explained above have contributed to the establishment of economic policies. It is not easy for policymakers to understand the principles and devise policies based on them because they have to take into account their economy's unique conditions and environments. I would call theories by Keynes and Friedman, warm-hearted principles based on consumption and liquidity focused on economic stimulus, and those by Hayek and Schumpeter, cool-headed principles based on investments and productivity focused on organizational restructuring. Ideals are always far from the reality; and warm hearts conflict with cool heads. In reality, policymakers face the limits of supply and sovereign debt as well as emotional and political restrictions. Most of the actual policies were mix of extremes or conflicting choices depending on specific situations.

| Experiences of Korea:
Conflicting choices and policy mix

When the economies of other OECD members contracted 3.5% on average in 2009, the Korean economy grew 0.3%. Its economic recovery accelerated in the next year to the fastest within the rich nations' club. In 2009, Korea's trade tumbled 7.8% while that of the OECD contracted 10.9% on average and in 2010 the former made a turnaround to grow 15.5% while the latter rose 12.5%. As a result, Korea became the 7th-largest exporter in the world from the 12th. The country raised the share of R&D out of its GDP to 4.36% in 2012, jumping to the first place in the world from the fifth in 2008.

The fastest recovery was possible thanks to aggressive fiscal and financial programs, including fiscal stimulus of 37.9 trillion won (US$30.2 billion), massive tax cuts of 34.9 trillion won (US$27.8 billion), and the four rivers restoration project worth 22.3 trillion won (US$17.7 billion) along with exchange rate normalization and interest rate cuts. The combined volume of tax cuts and fiscal stimulus amounted to 72.8 trillion won (US$57.9 billion), representing 7.1% of the country's GDP in 2008. This was the largest percentage spent by a single OECD country and faster than any others implemented in the club.

Randall S. Jones, Head of the OECD's Japan/Korea Desk, expressed his view on Korea's fiscal and financial measures in 2008. He said weakening of the won boosted exports, contributing economic recovery; tax cuts and increased spending, larger than those in any other OECD countries, restored domestic demand; and monetary expansion lowered real interest rates below zero, thereby boosting investments. Subir Lall, Chief of Korea Division in IMF's Asia and Pacific Department, also praised Korea's countermeasures by commenting that the country set "a textbook example" on how to stimulate an economy in recession. Korea increased its global market share by raising production when the global economy was in crisis and the moves in foreign exchanges rates at that time helped the country lift its competitiveness, he said.

The fast, decisive measures did not hurt the country's financial status. According to the OECD data, its public debt ratio remained low at 35.5% in 2012 while the ratio reached 218.8% in Japan, 102.1% in the US with the overall figure for the OECD averaging 107.4%. Another factor behind the expansionary fiscal and monetary measures of the Korean government was the world's lowest level of debt-to-equity ratio of listed companies which was below 90%.

To cope with the 2008 economic crisis, we applied the lessons learned from the 1997 crisis rather than resorting to specific economic theories. We adopted various policies and made choices among tax cuts, increased fiscal spending, interest rate cuts, monetary expansion, selective destruction, and restructuring depending on the actual conditions of the country. The actions we took in the very first year the crisis broke out were preemptive, decisive, and sufficient. A small open economy must put external balance before anything else to ensure its own survival whatever criticism it faces. Personally, the war against US-anchored economics based on the country's capabilities of flexible supply and free printing of the dollar was tougher than the war against the crisis itself.

| Economics of managed restraint: Toil and sweat

Which one is a virtue between saving and consumption? In what ways investments are different from speculation? Which one is good for housing prices to go up or go down? Can the service sector be sustained without the manufacturing sector? Can the financial industry exist by itself? What meanings does the secondary market have when it operates independent of the primary market? Where should we draw the boundary between freedom and regulation? Why aren't there many economic theories regarding greed and wealth while there are many regarding labor and income? Isn't there any problem with severe exchange rate fluctuations whereas rice sellers use the same measuring cup? How can we drive under the speed limit if the measuring criteria for speed changes all the time? These are the questions I has been harboring for the four decades in the public sector while dealing with fiscal and financial policies.

Faced with such questions, I used to think about the hypothesis of a world of ten farmers and a story of hamburger sellers. According to the hypothesis, as more and more farmers opt to do other work such as agricultural technology development, fertilizer manufacturing, and management, productivity will rise as will overall wellbeing. However, production will begin to shrink after a certain point and then disappear completely if every farmer decides to do other work. This alludes to the limit of the service industry as well as the limit of bubble creation. What will be earned if two hamburger sellers sell a US$1 hamburger to each other? A professor who taught me in the US used this episode to explain the limit of the money game being played in Wall Street. These two assumptions give mathematical wisdoms to see things in a simplified fashion to help solve problems for policymakers. These were useful in distinguishing between finance and the real economy; services and manufacturing; and bubbles and real things as well as judging the sustainability of the economy. Nevertheless, I failed to find simple, clear solutions to the problems facing the country from the existing economic theories. Isn't there any other conclusion to the boundary between speculation and investment than it is investment if I do, but it is speculation if you do?

From the experiences of two economic crises, I concluded that a theory which encourages consumption growth and inflation without production growth is "bubble" economics and a principle which advocates consumption and investments without flexible production is *"obesity" economics*. I came up with a vision of *"diet" economics* which is supported by restraints and toil and does not allow speculation or bubbles. I also asked to myself if it was impossible to apply Keynes' warm-hearted economic theory and Hayek's cool-headed principle together or how we could utilize rational invisible hand, not greedy invisible hand. Bubbles are formed not by flows of labor and income, but by stocks of greed and wealth. People with stocks of wealth still have their chances of success by the law of probability even if they lose some. This is the reason why they can make gut decisions. Still, those who have labor and earned income only will go bust once they lost their bets. The secondary market and financial derivatives are futile grounds for greed, and thus need to be regulated strictly.

God had us sweat and labor to subsist. I envision economic theories of restraints and investments, not of greed and speculation, with warm hearts and cool heads, which remove fats and add muscles to the economy; regard frugality and saving as virtues; promote the manufacturing industry and the services industry together; have the real economy and the monetary economy run in parallel; and place the focus of the securities market on the primary market. Will it be possible to realize big theories by economists, big reforms by governments, big mercy by the haves, and big thinking in Wall Street and Lombard Street? The reality is not bright.

We need *"diet" economics* which discourages greed and

speculation; encourages restraints and investments; harmonizes warm hearts with cool heads; and engages the financial sector. As someone retiring from the field of fiscal and financial policies leaving behind the 40-year long experience, I envision a new economics based on managed restraint which incorporates Hayek's free market economy by the rule of law and Schumpeter's creative destruction by innovation and involves the financial sector as well. I see a silver lining through a cloud.

KOREA'S RESPONSES IN 2008

15   **Caught in Turmoil**

With Lee Myung-bak's landslide victory in the presidential election on December 19, 2007, my three-year effort to reclaim the government was realized and 10 years of vicissitudes washed away with heart-stirring gratitude. The new administration was launched on Monday, February 25, 2008, and I returned to the government complex in Gwacheon as the Minister of Finance. That weekend, I went to my office to prepare proposals for a reduction of the oil tax and an allocation from the reserve funds of budget. Both were to be submitted the following Monday at the administration's first State Council meeting. I climbed the hill behind my office building just as I did 10 years earlier. The pine trees had grown so much that they blocked the view of the mountain on the other side of the hill. I felt my 10 years away from public service was the most beautiful time of my life in a sense. I lived like the moon passing through the clouds and there was peace that ran like a river.

The uncertainty of the global economy in 2008 was so high that the IMF adjusted its global economic outlook every month. The BOK forecast a 4.7% economic growth for 2008, but the actual figure ended up being 2.3%. The subprime mortgage crisis that began in 2007 in the US led to the collapse of Bear Stearns, one of the five largest US investment banks, on March 16, 2008, just weeks after the new administration began, further stiffening the international financial markets. Having grappled with the 1997 Asian currency crisis as Vice Minister of Finance, I found myself in another crisis 10 years later as Minister of Finance. Few of my peers around the world had dealt with even one major financial conflagration. As in 1997, mistakes could not be allowed. My country's fate once again was at stake.

As noted earlier, the Korean economy already was stalled in a low-growth trough before the 2008 crisis, beset with low investment, low exchange rates, and underdeveloped technologies. The poor state of investment, exchange rates, and technologies, three main factors for external competitiveness, were driving Korea's current account into the swamp of deficits. The current account, which had deteriorated in the three years prior to 2008 just as it did in the three years before the 1997 upheaval, especially alarmed those of us who had experienced the harshness of the 1997 crisis.

Excessive balance of payments deficit underscored Korea's crises in 1965, 1971, 1975, 1982, and 1997. Exogenous variables spared Korea from much pain during each crisis, except in 1997 when we were not lucky enough to have such a variable and had to pay dearly to overcome the crisis by accepting the IMF bailout. To avoid paying such severe price in 2008, we had to depend not on the foreign power but solely on our own strength.

As the 2008 storm gathered pace, we had to determine the steps that were needed and the sequence. I thought of the lessons from the 1997 crisis. I recalled how Korea was forced to accept severe changes to secure the IMF bailout in 1997 after wasting years with talk and no action. And I remembered that we could not assume friends would assist us. This time, we had to pursue preemptive, decisive, and sufficient changes based on leadership full of deeds rather than words. We had to find measures for what was needed, rather than friends to help attain our needs.

The biggest lesson from the 1997 crisis was that a small open economy must manage its balance of payments to survive. Contrary to what we did in the 1997 crisis, we had to focus on first treating symptoms rather than dealing with structural problems. We had to begin with reining in foreign exchange rates and then address the current account balance, foreign debt, inflation, and then economic growth. When an economy slumps and its financial market is in distress, as it was during the subprime crisis, the situation does not become a matter of the strongest surviving. Instead, it is those who survive that become the strong. To survive, priority should be put on external balance, and it is inevitable to bear the costs occurring from the damage to the internal balance.

Already limping in three traps

The leftist government that began in 1998 weathered the Asian currency crisis thanks to the IMF bailout, but the three traps of low investment, low exchange rates, and underdeveloped technology became entrenched in the 2000s. Consequently, tepid economic expansion, current account deficits, and modest growth potential emerged even before the 2008 crisis erupted. Average annual economic growth was slowing down from 10.1% in the 1970s to 8.6% in the 1980s and to 6.7% in the 1990s, and it further dropped in the 2000s, recording 5.2% in 2007. On the static side, government debts and corporate debt ratio were relatively in good shape, and there was no severe problem in foreign debts and foreign reserves.

The investment growth rate was 1.3% (5.8% for facilities investment growth) during the five years of the Kim Dae-jung administration launched in 1998 and 3.2% (5.0% for facilities investment) during the succeeding five years of the Roh Moo-hyun administration. GDP rose 3.7% and 4.3%, respectively. As the growth in investment fell short of the GDP expansion, the potential growth rate slipped to the 4% range in 2008, highlighting the gradual shrinkage of our economy.

During the ten years under the two leftist presidents, average annual economic and investment growth (growth of gross fixed capital formation) was 4.0% and 2.3%, respectively. Normally, investment growth rate exceeds economic growth rate in an economy that grows in the long term. During the same period, average economic growth rate of the OECD member states was

2.8%, while their average investment growth rate was 3.2%. Korea was facing a critical situation in which its economy was losing its vitality and gradually shrinking in the long-term.

With regard to the low exchange rate, the won appreciated 11.3% from 1,043.8 won in 2004 to 938.2 won in 2007. The overvalued currency stabilized prices but wreaked havoc on the current account. It had a surplus of US$28.1 billion in 2004, but it plummeted to US$5.8 billion in 2007. After the figure turned around to a deficit of US$800 million in December 2007, the shortfall soared to US$5.2 billion in the first quarter of 2008. The three-year slide of the current account surplus from US$28.1 billion to US$5.8 billion resembled the runaway deficit from US$3.8 billion to US$23 billion in the three years preceding the 1997 upheaval.

As for development of new technology in the 2000s, progress stalled due to low investment in R&D, and this led to a rising deficit in the technology balance of payments. In 2007, the deficit hit US$2.93 billion and R&D investment accounted for 3.21% of GDP.

The IMF predicts in its 2014 report that Korea's potential growth rate will drop to 2.2% by 2020, less than half of what it was in the late 1990s, unless special reforms are implemented. Allowing for an expected decline in working age population from 2016 and the level of Korea's employment protection which is higher than the OECD average, the only variables that can increase our potential growth rate are development of human capital through stronger technology training and an increase in physical capital through higher R&D investment.

Japan is maintaining its R&D investment at around 3%, which is the highest among the OECD countries, and its surplus in technology balance of payments is increasing every year. If we cannot dramatically increase the level of R&D investment, which is far lower than that of Japan, it will be difficult to escape the economic nutcracker effect from Korea's neighbors.

On the static side, Korea's sovereign debt as of 2007 accounted for 30.7% of GDP, and debt ratio in the manufacturing industry was 97.8%, the lowest level among the OECD member countries. But even relatively good conditions in national budget and corporate financial structure did not brighten prospects since they were primarily ascribed to inadequate investment and insufficient technological development. There was no major problem with foreign debt because out of US$383.2 billion of gross external liabilities, short-term foreign debt amounted to US$158.3 billion, and we had US$262.2 billion of foreign reserves.

| Subprime crisis on horizon

When I was inaugurated as the Minister of Finance on February 29, 2008, the waves of the subprime crisis were rolling in and a global economic recession and international financial market crunch loomed large. We were gripped by fear after suffering from the severe wounds of the 1997 currency crisis.

The US Federal Reserve had dramatically lowered its benchmark rate from 6.5% to 1% in 2003 as the IT bubble collapsed and the economic growth rate of the US had deteriorated to around 1% in the 2000s. As homebuyers with low credit ratings could easily get low-interest rate mortgages, US housing prices soared by 190%. The prices plummeted by 34% after the low-interest rate policy ended in 2004, resulting in the subprime meltdown. The subprime crisis cast a huge pall over the international financial markets as Wall Street's largest investment banks such as Bear Stearns, Merrill Lynch, and Lehman Brothers teetered. Citigroup and global insurance titan AIG needed a US government bailout to survive.

The waves of the subprime crisis crossed the oceans, crashing housing prices in Europe and Asia and throwing the international financial market into disarray. The financial industry's boom and bust spilled into real economies worldwide, sending them into a tailspin and panic. From the fourth quarter of 2008 to the first quarter of 2009, the world economy contracted as much as it did during the Great Depression between 1929 and 1931. The global economy contracted by 0.6% in 2009. OECD member countries shrank by 3.5%, and among them, the advanced economies, including the US, Japan, and the EU, slipped by 3.2%. Furthermore, the meltdown set the stage for fiscal crises in Portugal, Italy, Greece, and Spain in 2010.

Along with the international financial market crunch, soaring crude oil and raw material prices caused considerable alarm in Korea. During the oil shocks in 1973 and 1979, the skyrocketing oil prices upended the trade balance of Korea, which imported 100% of its crude oil requirements, and drained its foreign exchange supply. We also had painful memories of our trade surplus turning red in 1989 due to high raw material prices. That ended our first streak of trade surpluses between 1986 and 1988 which could be achieved thanks to the "three lows"—low oil price, low interest rates, and the low value of the US dollar against the Japanese yen. Hence, a spike in oil and raw material prices aroused a great fear in Korea.

Managing crisis first

In early 2008, stabilizing inflation caused by spiking oil prices seemed more urgent than devising countermeasures against the effects of the US mortgage crisis, which had not fully materialized. On March 3, at the first meeting of the new administration's State Council, I introduced a reduction in the oil tax and lowered tariff rates of tariff-rate quota (TRQ) items. A week later, I presented a work plan for 2008 titled, "An Economy with the Capability to Achieve 7% Growth," to President Lee Myung-bak. It incorporated the key features of "MBnomics" created by the presidential transition committee and focused more on boosting economic capability rather than growth itself.

The main goals of the work plan were: 1. broaden the base of domestic demand, stabilize ordinary people's livelihoods, and stabilize the current account for economic recovery by lowering the oil tax and tariff rates on TRQ items, utilizing the budget surplus to implement support projects for ordinary people, building 500,000 houses every year, adjusting foreign exchange rates to reflect the fundamentals of the real economy, and keeping external liabilities at below 40% of GDP; 2. create the world's best business environment for sustainable growth by minimizing regulations and tax rates, fostering a leading Asian bank, and organizing regional consultative groups between labor, management, government, and the private sector; and 3. develop new growth engines for long-term growth by investing 5% of GDP in R&D, promoting the service industry through deregulation, actively pursuing FTAs, and implementing the détente initiative with North Korea.

The plan projected the economic growth rate to be around 6%, consumer prices to rise 3.3%, and the current account balance to record a deficit of about US$7 billion in 2008. Major policies were to be checked at meetings on economic facilitation, trade and investment promotion, and science and technology promotion, with the president leading the talks. Representatives of the private sector also were to attend. As Minister of Finance, I was in charge of adjusting and implementing action plans through economic policy coordination meetings, consultative meetings on macroeconomic policy, and ministers' meetings on international economic affairs.

The growth forecasts of the BOK and many research institutes were around 5%. The election promise of 7% growth was difficult to achieve under the circumstance, but the new administration could not admit it from the beginning. As signs of a crisis became more obvious, the goals of achieving 7% growth and making Korea one of the top seven economies had to be shelved. We had to forget about election promises and focus on strategies for crisis containment based on reality.

Based on the lessons from the 1997 currency crisis, we shifted into crisis management mode. We rearranged priorities and operational procedures, determined implementation methods, and revamped a market monitoring system.

Contrary to what we did in 1997, we made management of the current account and foreign debts our top priority. Accordingly, we began with exchange rate management. Fighting inflation and facilitating economic growth took a backseat for the time being. We decided to implement short-term symptomatic treatment to weather the crisis first, and long-term structural measures for growth later. We felt that even our worst-case scenario in 2008 would not be as damaging as 1997 thanks to our US$260 billion in foreign reserves, which were more than our short-term foreign debts, but we knew considerable pain would be likely. In formulating treatment of the looming crisis' symptoms, we realized if erred in our first move, a hard fight would be unavoidable, and if the sequence was flawed, we would lose the game that we had a chance of winning. We were in a situation where if we withstand the crisis and survive, we could become the strong.

In operational procedures, I changed the reporting system, putting myself in direct communication with director generals and relevant directors. Multiple chains of internal communication during a crisis can compromise needed speed and distort or confuse messages and orders. Vice ministers and assistant ministers, who normally were in the middle of reporting line, were briefed later.

Since the international financing was at the core of crisis

management, I gave Assistant Minister for International Finance complete authority over external financial cooperation, including currency swap and cooperation with G-20, and had Director General of the International Finance Bureau directly receive and implement my orders regarding foreign currency exchange rates and the current account balance. I planned to review and adjust major policies before implementing them with the Senior Presidential Secretary for Economic Affairs, the Chairman of Financial Services Commission (FSC), and the BOK Governor at closed consultative meetings on macroeconomic policy every Tuesday in the west annex of the Office of the President.

Uncertainty in the international financial markets naturally intensified in 2008 given the turmoil surrounding the US investment banks: Bear Stearns was merged with JP Morgan Chase on March 16; Merrill Lynch was forced to sell itself to Bank of America; and Lehman Brothers collapsed. Moreover, uncertainty was also growing in the Korean financial market as it began to hear rumors of a "September crisis" in May. On July 10, the regular economic policy coordination meeting chaired by myself and attended by relevant ministers was changed into "the crisis management meeting."

Regarding implementation methods, it was decided that, from beginning to end, I would decide on policies and the working level officials would be responsible for executing them. We planned to implement preemptive, decisive, and sufficient measures to the extent that the market would be surprised and find measures in need rather than friends in need. During the 1997 crisis, nobody could provide a solution with certainty and passive responses only aggravated the crisis. We needed to minimize sacrifice by taking preemptive countermeasures. I resolved not to bend to criticism or public sentiment and let the outcome speak for itself by dealing with the situation head-on.

In 1997, Korea introduced the early warning system established by the IMF to prevent crises, but the system turned out to be ineffective for crisis management. Therefore, we implemented a daily monitoring system that used "micro-targeting," which tracked every individual index of the financial and foreign exchange markets. The system monitored movements in exchange rates and identified foreign exchange trends on daily, weekly, monthly, quarterly, and yearly bases to take appropriate actions.

16 Strategies against Crisis: Get up and Go!

Korea experienced enormous frustration and received deep wounds during the 1997 Asian financial crisis. We should never repeat the mistakes we made during the crisis.

Regardless of the subprime meltdown, the Korean economy had already had the three problems of low investment, low exchange rates, and underdeveloped technologies and fallen into the swamp of low growth. Deteriorating current account balance for three years from 2005 was exactly same as in the three years starting from 1994, and without special countermeasures, Korea could easily go to a crisis irrespective of the subprime crisis.

As the effects of the financial crisis began to be felt around the world, the looming question was "Who's next?" The foreign media decided it soon would be Korea's turn and churned out articles that were too negative. *Financial Times* of the UK described Korea's economic situation in 2008 as "1997 rewind" after the country had been "asleep for 11 years" (August 13) and reported that Korea had been always Asia's "obvious trouble spot for financial contagion" (October 6). Keeping up the pessimistic tone on Korea, the newspaper published another article with the headline, "Sinking feeling" (October 14). The UK's *The Times* said that Korea was heading for "black September" and was pushed towards a "full-blown currency crisis" (September 1). *The Wall Street Journal* of the US described Korea as "Asia's Iceland" (October 10) and *The Economist* reported in 2009 that Korea was "as risky as Poland" which was ranked third after South Africa and Hungary (February 26).

Ride out with get-up-and-go

While the 1997 Asian crisis was the first crisis Korea encountered after its financial market opened up, the 2008 global economic crisis was the first of its kind after the world had been connected as a global village. We needed *"indomitable" economics* with a get-up-and-go spirit in order not to crumble as we did in 1997. On my first day as Minister of Finance, I sent staff members a message conveying that thought.

"History has been created by people who rise to the challenge with positive thinking. Mankind has achieved explosive developments through Agricultural and Industrial revolutions. We were stragglers during the Industrial Revolution and experienced the pain of losing our nation. Now, we are witnessing tremendous changes in this era of Digital Revolution. We are standing at a crossroads of being the center of the world history or being pushed to the periphery. Our future will change dramatically depending on the effort of the current generation.

Let's boost investment sentiment by easing regulation and reducing taxes in an expeditious manner, and make efforts for economic recovery by implementing supporting measures for small and medium-sized enterprises, small business owners, and self-employed microbusinesses. Let's continue with sustainable growth by creating the world's best business environment based on four principles: minimizing regulations, minimizing tax rates, introducing global financial standards, and governing labor relations within the rule of law. Let's foster new high-tech industries by expanding investment in science and technology to 5% of GDP and continuously develop new growth engines through innovations in the service sector such as tourism and medical industries.

For the past ten years, the Korean economy had run continuously to contraction. The economy grew 4.9%, but investment increased only 2.6%. The current account balance, which had posted a surplus of US$28 billion, almost fell by half every year and foreign debts soared to US$380 billion. We have 800,000 unemployed youths and 8 million temporary workers.

The world economy stepped into the path of a depression after a 10-year boom period. We missed out on those good ten years. We are in a worse internal and external condition than ever. The world economic growth has slowed down and international raw materials' prices are skyrocketing. Crude oil price has surpassed US$100 per barrel and the price of flour has increased by 100%.

As a leading government department, the Ministry of Finance will take the initiative in building a first class advanced nation and realizing an economy that has the capability of achieving 7% annual growth. Let's make it clear to the public what we can do and what we can't, and work expeditiously based on detailed action plans.

The fate of our next generation depends on us. We shouldn't be a failure in the world's history again. Let's open the second era of national prosperity. Let's make it happen again.⌟

| Crisis is opportunity

The global economy sank into low growth and polarization in the 21st century. The Great Depression of the 1930s heralded the "normal" era represented by the Bretton Woods system, expanded government roles, high growth and low prices, and strengthened welfare systems. The unprecedented 2008 global economic crisis appeared to recalibrate the economic order. Low growth and polarization in advanced center economies led to a historic power shift and created the G-20 system. The two phenomena became the new trend in this era and began to be called as the "new normal."

During the leftist government's ten years, the effort to overcome the new trend had been insufficient. Efforts alone cannot resolve weak growth and polarization, but at least it can abate the trend. If we exert efforts while advanced economies are caught in low growth and polarization, the effect would double and country rankings could change, allowing Korea to join the ranks of advanced economies. Investment-driven growth can create jobs, which is the best welfare system. Growth and distribution of wealth are not mutually exclusive. They should go hand in hand. Social welfare is not sustainable without growth. This is evidenced by the shift of the UK and Sweden, who have advanced welfare systems, into workfare scheme.

Implementing strategies to expand economic capability based on *"growth" economics* with a tenacious spirit is a critical obligation in this new era to go beyond the new normal. We have to make more investments to escape from low growth, and investment is affected by entrepreneurial spirits and investment capability. Meanwhile, to end polarization, we need to create jobs, and job creation depends on education and business environment. Therefore, magnifying economic capability can be achieved through promotion of entrepreneurial spirits and education, expansion of investment capabilities, and improvement of the business environment. *"Get-up-and-go" economics* will turn a crisis into an opportunity.

Promotion of entrepreneurial spirits and education requires deep reflections and national consensus, but this is being hampered by controversies swirling around economic democratization and downward standardization of education. Economic democratization, which is getting much attention in Korea, is at odds with entrepreneurial spirits. Moreover, today's uniform education system was rooted in a standardized system that churned out talented people, which was suitable for the mass production system that emerged after the Industrial Revolution in the 18th century. We need to devote a lot of energy in building an education system that cultivates creativity, which is essential in this digital era. We also should take notice of the fact that the standardization of high schools in Japan, which we benchmarked, already has been abandoned.

The world is in post-crisis survival mode, and we are living in the era where those who survive become the strong, not the other way around. Economic growth and job creation depend on companies, not government. Those who can rapidly improve their corporate investment capabilities and business environment will climb up the rankings of nations and escape from low growth and polarization faster than others. *Get-up-and-go economics* will help us to implement necessary measures expeditiously and expand our economic capability.

| Preemptive, decisive, and sufficient measures

Aside from the subprime crisis, the biggest economic threats to Korea in 2008 were the rise in oil prices and the current account balance turning into a deficit. We were in an unprecedentedly difficult situation. Obviously we had to deal with economic growth, prices, and the current account balance, but no one could confidently say in what order we should tackle the problems. We established comprehensive strategies to endure the crisis and turn the crisis into an opportunity.

Our strategies to respond to the 2008 global economic crisis were divided into three stages based on the lessons from the 1997 crisis: defense, transition, and offense. Symptomatic treatments and structural measures were fitted for each stage. Short-term emergency measures to endure the crisis were implemented first. Structural strategies to expand economic capability came later.

Managing the balance of payments is the fundamental task of running a state, especially for a small open economy. The balance of payments is affected by external competitiveness, which is determined by exchange rates in the short-term, product quality in the mid-term, and technology in the long-term. An exchange rate policy is a matter of survival, and a fiscal and financial policy in general is a matter of how to live. When internal and external balances conflict, the latter should be given priority. To maximize the effects of policies, we made sure that they were implemented preemptively, decisively, and sufficiently. The devastating effects of the subprime crisis had to be repelled before they could gain a foothold on our soil in order to minimize sacrifice. We realized that defense-only policies would end the fight in a draw at best. To truly win, we needed offensive steps that could seize opportunities. It was not that the strong survive but that survivors become the strong. This was a precious lesson that the 1997 currency crisis left behind.

Bearing in mind what we had learned in 1997, we established "Comprehensive Counterstrategies against the Global Economic Crisis." It built on *indomitable economics*. The counterstrategies included measures for surviving the crisis and for expanding economic capability to turn the crisis into an opportunity. They consisted of policy orientation, a national vision, strategic objectives, four key strategies, and 20 core tasks.

First, policy orientation was based on the recognition that survivors become the strong; the dollar is of the greatest importance; and country rankings can change during the crisis. In light of this, basic directions were decided as follows: 1. implementing strategies according to the three stages—defense, transition, and offense; and 2. preparing preemptive, decisive, and sufficient countermeasures.

Second, the national vision was to build a first class advanced nation, a vision that had been promised during the presidential election campaign. A vision means a goal that can be achieved when we use 120% of our ability.

Third, the strategic objectives were to withstand the crisis and expand growth capability, and the four key strategies were: 1. achieve current account surplus, 2. prevent an economic downturn, 3. expand economic capability, and 4. strengthen external capability.

Fourth, the 20 core tasks included the followings: 1. to weather the crisis, adjust foreign exchange rates to reflect the fundamentals of the real economy, raise a financial market stability fund, provide corporations with emergency funds, and release emergency fiscal funds; 2. to achieve sustainable growth, lower tax rates to the level of those of competing countries, employ expansionary fiscal policies, implement regulatory reform to expand investments, and initiate the Four Rivers Restoration project; 3. to ensure future growth, invest 5% of

GDP in R&D, foster highly-skilled field technicians, nurture new growth engines, and increase the working age population; 4. to expand social capital, establish the rule of law, create a system based on honesty, adopt global standards in broader areas, and establish new labor relations; 5. to strengthen external capability, support a G-20 system, continuously push ahead with FTAs, actively participate in international M&As, steadily promote an "Open Korea" policy; and so forth.

I told President Lee that I would frequently provide him updates on the counterstrategies and expressed my willingness to take on all the responsibility for implementing the measures. I asked him to grant me the authority to make decisions and implement policies when presidential secretaries and I had different opinions on major issues such as exchange rates, tax cuts, the comprehensive real estate tax, and the G-20 system. President Lee agreed. His support and special attention given to exchange rates were especially instrumental in giving us the backing that my staff needed. The staff at the Economic Policy Bureau greatly contributed to the establishment of the counterstrategies.

With the agreement on international cooperation reached at the G-20 Summit in Washington D.C., on November 15, 2008, our measures to overcome the crisis were crystallized into an unprecedented fiscal and financial package. The package, which included policies to be implemented from 2008 to 2010, scaled up to 72.8 trillion won, or 7.1% of GDP. It consisted of tax cuts worth 34.9 trillion won and expansion of spending by 37.9 trillion won. Other measures included 20.7 trillion won for Korean won liquidity, US$55 billion for foreign exchange liquidity, and a reduction in interest rates from 5.25% to 2.00%.

"Comprehensive Counterstrategies against Global Economic Crisis" was complemented later and some of the strategies were not implemented as planned, but I consistently tried to implement them as Minister of Finance and even while I was serving as the Senior Economic Advisor to the President and Chairman of the Presidential Council on National Competitiveness. As all other OECD member states recorded negative growth in 2009, Korea was escaping the crisis first, achieving positive growth at 0.3%. Our current account turned around to surplus territory starting in late 2008, and remained there. In 2010, Korea emerged as the seventh-largest exporter in the world. Once again, we realized the fact that proper management of exchange rates and current account balance is the basics for running a state.

17

Urgent Measures: Survivors Become the Strong

On January 16, 2008, we invited economists from Citibank, Deutsche Bank, and the Korea Capital Market Institute to have a meeting on the US's subprime crisis with President-elect Lee Myung-bak. No one sounded very sure, but the prospects for the world economy and international financial markets appeared to be bleak.

My first priority after becoming the Minister of Finance was exchange rates as it was when I became Vice Minister in 1997. On February 18, when my nomination as Minister of Finance was announced, the won/dollar exchange rate started to rise rapidly from the 930 won range. After I made it clear to the press on March 4 that foreign exchange market intervention was an undisputed sovereign right, the won depreciated around 10 every day and breached the 1,000 won mark on March 17. I thought that a rapid normalization of exchange rates should be our first move to manage the deteriorating conditions.

The effort to turn current account deficit into surplus was a rough road. The media, scholars, and politicians continuously criticized the high exchange rate policy and market intervention. They ascribed price hikes not to oil prices but to exchange rates. Economists who studied in the US claimed that exchange rates should be left in the hands of the market, and inflation, a favored item of political populism, strangled me. I was further hurt when even the ruling Grand National Party pressured me to resign, raising the specter of lost market confidence. Market confidence can be obtained not through words, but through actions and outcomes.

I went to an early church morning service and prayed, "O Lord, stop me if it's not the right way; if it's the right path, let me go on notwithstanding the stones being thrown at me." And I kept going forward and was stoned. I also suffered pains when the relentless criticism forced out Vice Minister Choi Joong Kyung on July 7. He had championed external balance and had been a good partner in the lonely fight. In addition to the relentless political sniping, I also had to cope with the effects of faulty remarks and stances of the BOK. The bank was repeating the mistakes it had made during the 1997 crisis while the US Federal Reserve was playing the role of not only the lender of last resort but also the lender of first and only resort. It was harder to fight against US-anchored economic theories and the BOK than to fight against the crisis.

I ended up resigning from my post after one year, having reached my primary objectives of exchange rate and current account balance despite the second-guessing and disagreements. This was how the fateful 2008 materialized.

First move: Normalizing exchange rates

Some of my predecessors said in the past that exchange rates should be decided by the market. But I feel that would mean abandoning one's responsibility. Buckling under international pressure for currency appreciation for fear of retaliatory actions is tantamount to relinquishing sovereignty. Managing exchange rates is part of exercising economic sovereignty and managing international balance is the cornerstone of running a nation.

When I was Director General of the International Finance Bureau and the IMF officials were pressing for a stronger won, I asked them, "Was it a market exchange rate when the yen/dollar exchange rate tumbled by half due to the 1985 Plaza Accord?" I explained, "I intervene in the market based on economic fundamentals, but I don't manipulate. Tell me which country lets the market decide exchange rates, if there is any." They were silent. Market exchange rates emerged when the Bretton Woods system collapsed in 1971, after the US had dropped the gold standard. If the length of one mile changes every day, how can any driver stay within the speed limit and reach his destination in the same time? If a measure of value changes every day, it is not a measure of value any more. The sovereign right to exchange rates is a matter of life and death to a small open economy.

Currency appreciation amid deteriorating current account balance is a major problem that foreign exchange authorities need to correct. We were hit by the currency crisis in 1997 due to a weakening current account balance, a result of currency overvaluation, during the preceding three years. The same situation occurred during the same time frame before the 2008 global economic crisis.

Proper management of exchange rates can be achieved: fundamentally, by stabilizing current account balance through enhanced external competitiveness; structurally, by preventing speculative currency trades; and temporarily, by conducting an adequate government intervention in the market.

The won appreciated in 2005 amid deteriorating current account balance because of the following reasons: internally, there was an excessive volume of foreign exchange forward transactions; and externally, transactions of speculative short-term funds and excessive non-deliverable forward (NDF) transactions in offshore markets impacted the won. Korea had no structural measure to control speculative transactions and no adequate means of market intervention to mitigate a tipping effect.

Domestically, in 2005, forward transactions based on real demand increased to hedge foreign exchange risk amid a boom in the shipbuilding industry, which typically has delivery dates several years ahead. Accordingly, banks achieved square positions by selling the forward they bought on the foreign exchange market, thereby boosting the won. Banks' speculative forward exchange transactions on offshore markets also accelerated the tipping effect of the foreign exchange market. There was neither adequate management of positions nor market intervention even under the pressure for currency overvaluation. Moreover, we had to contend with "knock-in, knock-out"

(KIKO) currency derivatives. If the won's value fell below the agreed upon "knock-in" price, companies would have suffered huge losses but banks would have reaped enormous profits. On the other hand, the contract would have been void if the won rose above the capped level. In short, banks enjoyed a one-sided fight that companies took the risks. This also created downward rigidity of the won value.

Externally, along with low-interest rate dollars and the yen-carry funds, speculative hedge funds that had bought stocks or bonds hedged positions in the forward market and hedged their risks on the Korean won NDF market. In this way, they were swimming while touching the ground, avoiding foreign exchange risks and further appreciating the won. No taxes on capital gains or transactions were imposed on the speculative short-term foreign funds. They flowed in and out of the country without restrictions, enjoying profits from interest rate differential or speculative trading. The fact that our stock index options market and the offshore market for trading the Korean won became the largest markets globally was inconceivable considering the scale of our economy. Korea was called an "Asian bonanza" or "Asia's automated teller machine." A foreign exchange market with no regulation and no taxes can be fatal to a small open economy.

As a result of neglecting excessive speculative trading in the foreign exchange market, the won appreciated 41.4% between 2001 and 2007, 25.8 percentage points higher than 15.6% appreciation of the Japanese yen. During this time frame, our current account balance decreased by US$2.2 billion, while it increased by US$122.7 billion in Japan. In particular, Korea's current account balance plummeted by US$22.3 billion between 2004 and 2007.

Since Korean exporters competed directly with Japanese peers in several key industries, the won/yen exchange rate calculated by their relative value against the dollar was a more important variable than the structural problem of the foreign exchange market. As in the 1997 currency crisis, our current account balance greatly worsened in the 2000s when the relative ratio of the won to the yen of 10 to 1 was broken. The biggest factor behind the 1997 currency crisis was the won/yen exchange rate falling below 8:1; the won was 844.2 won while the yen was 115.7 yen against the dollar in 1996.

A comparison between the relative ratio of the won to the yen and current account balance shows that current account balance moves in accordance with the changing ratio of the won to the yen. Since most of Korea's trade occurs in dollars and Korea competes against Japan in many products, the direct won/yen exchange rate is coupled with the won/yen exchange rate relative to the dollar regardless of the trade balance with Japan, and therefore, the movement of the current account corresponds to the changes in the relative won/yen exchange rate.

Correcting the won/yen exchange rate relative to the US dollar was imperative to structurally resolve the won's overvaluation while implementing other measures such as managing positions in futures trading, strengthening taxations on speculative income, and imposing transaction tax on capital flows. At that time, insecurity in the international financial market was palpable and the risk of overhauling structural problems was high. Under the circumstances, we decided to adjust exchange rates to reflect the fundamentals of the real economy by intervening in the market using foreign reserves and providing guidance, and then pursued institutional measures.

Past situations told us that deviations from the yen/won ration of 1 to 10 meant a rapid collapse in our external balance. Given that the yen/dollar exchange rate was around 110 yen, I thought the won/dollar exchange rate of at least 1,250 won was needed to quickly achieve a surplus in the current account.

The won/dollar exchange rate rose from the 930 won range to around 940 won on February 18, 2008, when my nomination as Minister of Finance was announced and it increased to the 950 won range on February 29, when I was inaugurated. At a luncheon meeting with reporters on March 4, I expressed my view as an upholder of sovereignty on exchange rates that foreign exchange market intervention was an undisputed sovereign duty. Subsequently, the exchange rate rose by around 10 every day, reaching the 960 won range in one week, and it jumped to the 1,000 won range on March 17.

However the exchange rate soon dropped because of unexpected remarks by BOK Governor Lee Seong-tae. On March 24, in his first meeting with President Lee Myung-bak, Governor Lee said the adequate level of the won/dollar exchange rate was between 950 won and 1,000 won, which was far lower than 1,250 won, which I estimated. The next day, at a forum for alumni of Hankuk University of Foreign Studies, he said the adequate exchange rate was between 970 won and 980 won.

This statement made the exchange rate drop to the 970 won range, a one-day plunge of 20.9 won. To borrow the expression from MIT professor Rudiger Dornbusch's comment during the 1997 currency crisis, the Bank of Korea, once again, acted as the currency czar.

Governor Lee's comment during the forum except the exchange rate was as follows: "Recent surges in exchange rates are a temporary phenomenon, and it might be proper to say that in the short-term, exchange rates have all tested their ceilings. The dollar will continue its weakness on a long-term basis since the US economy is not in a good shape. I think that the worst situation has passed. Since the Federal Reserve Board is determined to take every necessary action, the general opinion is that there would be no more severe incidents than this one."

Regarding the rise in prices due to soaring raw material prices at that time, he said, "People often say that the prices of oil or agricultural products are subject to supply shock and that the impact of the supply shock should be resolved through policy measures. However, as the recent surge in raw material prices was caused by an increase in demand from China and India, they will not plummet as they did during the past supply shocks. Therefore, policy measures will not resolve the situation."

I had to mend the situation urgently since Governor Lee's statement was directly contradicting the government's policy. In the evening on that day, in a forum hosted by the *Maeil Business Newspaper*, I said, "We were hit by the currency crisis in the past as the won appreciated amid deteriorating current account balance. Now, the current account is worsening again, but the won appreciated about 45% compared to the time when its value was the weakest. I experienced in person that we should put external balance before internal balance when the two collide with each other. This is not an opinion but a fact, and a fact should be only one. Considering the ongoing deficit in the current account, it is clear in which direction the exchange rate should move. It is always true that too much is as bad as too little. The competent authority in charge of exchange rate policies is the Ministry of Finance."

I added, "One economist said that Koreans whose income was half the amount of Japanese were travelling to Tokyo for shopping and this phenomenon would be recorded in the history of the economics. What is the meaning of the fact that playing golf in Kagoshima, Japan, cost cheaper than playing it in Jeju-do? Between 2002 and 2007, the won appreciated about 40%, while the Japanese yen and Chinese yuan appreciated about 15% and 13%, respectively. This is not right when the current account balance is still worsening." After my tough-talk, the won snapped back to the 990 won range in three days and in late April it reverted to the 1,000 won range.

Regarding interest rates, I stated, "The gap between the benchmark rates of Korea and the US was excessively widened up to 2.75 percentage points. The Minister of Finance not only deals with exchange rates but has veto power over the decisions made by the Monetary Policy Committee of BOK regarding monetary policies." As for prices, I rebutted, "Because the current increase in prices was mainly caused by a rise in cost, monetary policy alone has a limitation in containing inflation since it only manages aggregate demand." Regarding growth policies, I said, "From 1995 to last year, our economy annually grew 4.9% on average while our fixed investment grew only 2.6%. If a nation's investment growth is lower than its economic growth, it means that its economy is gradually going downhill. Without exceptional policies to reduce taxes and ease regulations, our economy will continue its downward trend. Some news reports said that President Lee agitated me by stating that he would put prices before growth, but he never agitated me and I wasn't agitated either."

I recalled the BOK that had taken a firm stand right before the 1997 crisis by saying, "890 is the Maginot Line. No more than that." The BOK, then as now, had been clinging to the impractical real effective exchange rate, and we were raising interest rates when every other country was lowering them. When corporate debt ratio falls below 100% and financial costs drop to around 1%, interest rates have bigger impact on the financial market than on the real economy, and the effect on flows of short-term foreign funds and exchange rates becomes more important. An idea of replacing the BOK governor was examined for effective crisis management, but it was dropped due to concerns that the issue of BOK's independence would be called into question again. I felt helpless. There was no other choice than to try to persuade him. All of the BOK's forecasts turned out to be wrong, with oil price plummeting to below US$100 per barrel in October and the won/dollar exchange rate rising to the 1,250 range in December.

The KIKO transactions ceased to exist as I recommended the Financial Supervisory Service to examine the situation and control further transactions. Firms that hedged their risks could recover their losses over time through profits from an increase in exchange rates, but companies that recklessly participated in the KIKO transactions suffered huge losses. These companies filed lawsuits against banks that had been active in selling the derivatives. The government's control on KIKO agreements was an inevitable action.

Exchange rates and foreign exchange situation of each bank were checked using the daily monitoring system on daily, weekly, and monthly bases and necessary actions were taken immediately based on the micro-targeting method. We were fighting a fierce battle every day. I made it sure that situations of conglomerates and those with immense real demand such as oil companies, Korea Gas Corporation, financial institutions, and public organizations were reported every day and I directly managed them. The exchange rate exceeded the 1,000 won range again in April after many complications with the BOK. The current account that had been recording deficit since December 2007 rapidly improved, shifting to a surplus of US$1.8 billion in June.

As oil price surpassed US$120 per barrel starting from June, exchange rates became a double-edged sword for current account balance and prices. Moreover, rumors on a "September crisis" acted as a drag on the economy. The rumors said if most of foreign investor-held US$8.4 billion treasury bonds maturing in September were withdrawn, exchange rates would skyrocket and bond prices would crash. The foreign news media's dire predictions of Korea's future fed the rumors, too. *Financial*

Times of the UK described Korea's situation as "1997 rewind" (August 13); *The Times* stated that Korea was heading for "black September" and was pushed towards a "full-blown currency crisis" (September 1); and *The Wall Street Journal* of the US depicted Korea as "Asia's Iceland" (October 10).

The situation was manageable since our foreign reserves exceeded US$240 billion and short-term foreign debts were about US$180 billion (US$365 billion of gross external liabilities, US$395.6 billion of external credits, and US$30.6 billion of net external credits as of September). The rumors about a "September crisis" and reports of the foreign media amplified insecurity in the financial market, compelling us to make an adequate level of market intervention to slow down the won's depreciation by lowering the exchange rate to below 1,100 won. Accordingly, the current account returned to negative territory in July and I was deeply frustrated. The reports of the foreign media turned out to be incorrect and the September crisis didn't materialize. We had suffered due to incorrect reports by US-based *Bloomberg* during the 1997 crisis, and again, the media of center economies enjoyed their freedom of throwing stones at us, periphery "frogs."

The price of Dubai oil, which Korea buys, began to slide after reaching its peak at US$140.70 in July, giving us a room for normalizing exchange rates. The exchange rate, which had been kept at below 1,100 won until August, rose to the 1,100 won range in September, and after the default of Lehman Brothers on September 15, the rate exceeded the 1,150 won range and surpassed 1,250 won, which I thought was an adequate level, in October. With the exchange rate steadily above 1,250 won, current account also turned around again to a surplus of US$4.8 billion in October, recording a surplus of US$7.5 billion in the fourth quarter. This helped us to limit the annual current account deficit to US$5.8 billion. The US$30 billion currency swap agreement signed with the US was highly instrumental in stabilizing market sentiment.

The rate exceeded 1,300 won in October and 1,400 won in November, and it peaked at 1,513.0 won on November 23. Following a fall in oil and raw material prices, it was closed at 1,259.2 won on December 30. We spent US$61.2 billion out of foreign exchange reserves, including US$13.9 billion to cover the current account deficit that had been accumulated until the third quarter of 2008 and about US$25 billion to supply foreign exchange directly to a grouping with immense real demand such as oil companies, Korea Gas Corporation, financial institutions, and public organizations, but we still had US$201.2 billion in reserves.

I considered a capital transaction tax to prevent volatility in exchange rates stemming from flows of excessive short-term foreign funds, but I left the issue for the future as a sharp rise in exchange rates made it more difficult to manage the crisis and raised concerns over inflationary pressure. In 2009, the won/dollar exchange rate was maintained at over 1,250 won in light of the adequate won/yen exchange rate of 10 to 1 and current account balance turned into a surplus of US$42.7 billion. The current account surplus remained intact through 2010, enabling us to surmount the global economic crisis and become the seventh largest exporter in the world.

Controversies surrounding the exchange rate put me under the pressure to resign. It became the most painful memory in my public career. Exchange rates are dictated by the supply and demand of foreign currencies. That is a simple economic common sense. Exchange rates are more closely correlated with capital flow than with economic indicators. Marginal quantity of foreign exchanges decides their rise and fall. If capital flow is not managed well, exchange rates cannot be managed properly, either. Intervention by means of foreign reserves is possible only afterwards and the cost is high. A central bank, as an institution in charge of price management, naturally prefers currency appreciation, but a government that takes charge of the economy as a whole naturally pays much attention to capital flow and prefers currency depreciation. In all nations, management of exchange rates falls within the scope of government authority. Looking at the daily check sheet I used during the fierce battle of every day, I am overwhelmingly touched by the passion and agony of that time. I am indebted to my staff for their dedicated efforts and struggles amid difficult situations.

❙ Second move: Lowering oil tax and tariff rates

When I took office as minister, oil price had already exceeded US$90 per barrel and domestic price of gasoline had risen to 1,900 won per liter. The consumer price index rose 3.6% in February, 2008 compared with the same month a year ago, and prices of major 152 living necessities increased 4.6%, putting inflation at dangerous trajectory. The highly elevated prices were due to spikes in oil and raw material prices. Normalization of the overvalued won became a double-edged sword due to rising oil prices, throwing us into a dilemma from the start. I was determined to not veer from my original judgment, which was based on the lesson from the 1997 currency crisis: the current account balance should not be sacrificed for the sake of prices.

Dubai oil price soared from US$56.99 at the beginning of 2007 to US$88.49 at the year's end. After rising to the US$90 range in early 2008, it surpassed US$100 in April and skyrocketed to US$140.70 on July 4. The rising cost terrified us since oil was the most important variable of current account balance; Korea imported 100% of its crude oil requirements and crude oil accounted for around 18% of its imports at the time. We were driven toward currency crises when skyrocketing oil prices sank our trade balance during the first and second oil shocks in 1973 and 1979. We also suffered pains when the trade surplus in 1986 which had been achieved for the first time in Korea's history reverted to deficit because of the soaring raw material prices. To make matters worse, the prices of wheat, corn, and soybeans also jumped around 50% in 2008.

To curb soaring prices, the State Council approved three emergency price stabilization measures. On March 3, it passed a revised bill on Presidential Decree of the Individual Consumption Tax Act to lower the oil tax by 10%, and on March 25, the council approved special measures to manage the prices of 52 daily necessities along with a revised bill on Presidential

Decree of the Customs Act, which would lower tariff rates on 82 TRQ items to 0% in most cases by the year's end. The special measures on 52 daily necessities were to crack down on hoarding basic necessities and strengthen curbs on exorbitant price increases. The 82 TRQ items eligible for tariff rate reduction included fishery and agricultural products, agricultural raw materials, nonferrous metals, and petroleum products. The reduction in tariff rates was estimated to have the effect of a 1.9 trillion won tax cut, lowering import prices by 0.27 percentage point and consumer prices by 0.1 percentage point.

Despite all the efforts mentioned above, prices continued to climb daily, and it became difficult to keep the annual inflation target at below 5%. Consumer inflation exceeded 5% in June and surged to 5.9% in July, when Dubai oil price rose to US$140.70 per barrel. A strategic compromise was inevitable to manage import prices: US$61.2 billion had to be used from the foreign reserves to prevent a sharp rise in exchange rates. Inflation was contained at 4.1% at the year's end as commodity prices plummeted following the collapse of Lehman Brothers on September 15 and Dubai oil dropped to below US$100 per barrel on October.

Due to speculative investment in raw materials and crude oil that took advantage of the subprime crisis, we were forced to choose between prices and current account balance. Although we had to suffer a lot, we pushed ahead with consistent policies. In the process, I became the target of considerable criticism, which became the seed for pressure on me to resign.

| Third move: Tax rebates of 240,000 won

Besides normalizing exchange rates and managing prices, fiscal policies for economic recovery awaited me. The government budget surplus, which consisted of excess tax revenue of 14.7 trillion won and unused budgets, reached 15.3 trillion won in 2007. With excess tax revenue of 5.2 trillion won expected in 2008, we had a total of 20.5 trillion won of excess revenue. We were too frugal in managing government finance in the run up to the crisis. To prevent a severe economic downturn, we urgently injected fiscal funds using diverse methods: extending the period for temporary investment tax credit, providing tax refunds to mitigate the effect of oil price hike, and drawing up a supplementary budget proposal.

On January 20, the presidential transition committee announced an extension of temporary investment tax credit. It came right after we heard a bleak outlook on the subprime crisis from the economists of Citibank, Deutsche Bank, and the Korea Capital Market Institute. The Presidential Decree of the Restriction of Special Taxation Act was passed at the first State Council meeting of the new administration on March 3 to provide tax credit for 7% of investment amount.

There were two obstacles in the National Finance Act in utilizing the budget surplus of 15.3 trillion won. First, according to the Act, the budget surplus had to be used first to subsidize local governments and education; 30% of the remaining amount had to go into public funds established during the 1997 currency crisis; and 30% of the remaining amount should be used to repay national debt. Second, a supplementary budget could be approved only when we were in a war, natural disaster, recession, or had massive unemployment. This was aimed at achieving fiscal soundness, but I thought that the provision was not effective for crisis management due to its lack of flexibility.

The ruling Grand National Party was too elated about its landslide victory in the April 2008 parliamentary election to think about the possibility of another financial crisis. Like the BOK, the parliamentarians were not speaking the same language as the Ministry of Finance. They opposed a supplementary budget for fiscal injection, saying the purpose was not in accordance with the National Finance Act.

I persuaded the Policy Committee of the Grand National Party that the nation needed a supplementary budget even if an amendment to the National Finance Act was required as a recession was looming. We agreed to draft a supplementary budget within the scope of the remaining budget surplus. Excluding 5.4 trillion won for the obligations to local governments and education system, and 5 trillion won for national debt, we were left with only 4.9 trillion won. We decided to add 5.2 trillion won of estimated excess tax revenue for 2008 for a mere 10.1 trillion won emergency fund, half of what I had initially expected.

Based on the hard-won consensus on financial injection plan, we announced "Comprehensive Measures to Overcome the High Oil Price" worth about 10 trillion won to stimulate the economy and support ordinary people's livelihoods on June 8, with an intention to execute them beginning from July 1. The 10 trillion won consisted of 5.23 trillion won of tax rebates, which was introduced through the amendment to tax laws, to alleviate the effects of the high oil price; and about 4.865 trillion won from the supplementary budget to subsidize oil businesses.

The comprehensive measures contained: 1) 3.14 trillion won for workers and the self-employed —240,000 won per person for workers whose annual salary was 30 million won or lower and the self-employed whose annual income was 20 million won or lower (workers with an annual salary above 30 million won and no more than 36 million won and the self-employed with an annual income above 20 billion won and no more than 24 million won received 180,000, 120,000, or 60,000 won, depending on their exact income bracket); 2) 1.76 trillion won for public transportation services, farmers and fishermen, and small truck owners; 3) 1.255 trillion won to cover electricity and gas suppliers' deficits caused by a rise in oil price; 4) 604 billion won for restructuring projects aimed at energy saving; and 5) 1.454 trillion won in subsidies for new and renewable energy businesses and development of overseas energy resources.

The tax rebates to ease the burden of high oil price were provided to 13.87 million people, 28.9% of total population, including 9.88 million workers (78.2% of a total of 12.63 million workers) and 3.99 million self-employed people (87.1% of a total of 4.58 million). The number of people who received 240,000 won was 12.92 million, 93.2% of the total number of beneficiaries, including 9.04 million workers and 3.88 million self-employed people.

The tax rebates, which were provided directly from tax

revenue, were unprecedented in other countries and the scale was huge. After oil prices stabilized, the Korean economy shrank substantially at the end of the year. The sales of the auto industry, which had strong forward and backward linkages with other industries, plummeted. Hence, we urgently reduced the individual consumption tax on automobiles by 30% for six months starting from December 19. That was equivalent to injecting 250 billion won into the economy. The whole world was seeking any available measure to counteract the global economic recession. In the US, a US$100 billion tax refund plan was implemented in 2008 to stimulate its flagging economy.

It was expected that the comprehensive measures to combat the effects of high oil price along with the reductions in oil tax and tariff rates would have the effect of injecting 10 trillion and 624.4 billion won into the economy, adding 0.4 percentage point to the growth rate in 2008. Moreover, tax reforms, including reductions in income and corporate tax rates, were expected to have a tax cut effect of 14 trillion and 235 billion won, making the economy grow 0.6 percentage point more in 2009. These measures greatly contributed to helping Korea record 2.3% and 0.3% of GDP growth in 2008 and 2009, respectively, while other OECD member countries recorded 0.2% and −3.5% on average during the same period. Without the emergency financial injection and tax cuts, Korea could not have avoided a negative growth.

Fourth move:
Cutting interest rate and injecting liquidity

Holding interest rates near zero, the US Federal Reserve Board began to drop more than US$3 trillion through three rounds of quantitative easing from 2008. The Fed also implemented unprecedented measures of providing financial support to investment banks and securities firms, apart from its assistance to commercial banks, by creating six types of new funds. There was even a fund with a name that was too long to memorize — Asset-Backed Commercial Paper Money Market Mutual Fund Liquidity Fund (ABCPMMMFLF). The Fed wrote a new chapter in central bank history, acting not only as the lender of last resort but the lender of first and only resort that provided funds to everyone as needed.

As the US housing market meltdown began to build, the Fed lowered its key interest rate from 5.25% to 4.25% in 2007 and to 2.25% in March 2008, when Bear Sterns teetered on default. After the demise of Lehman Brothers in September, the Fed lowered the rate again to near zero interest rate of 0.25% at the year's end, releasing unlimited amount of dollars. Other advanced economies were making a concerted effort by lowering their interest rates and releasing money.

However, the BOK maintained a hawkish stance even though the interest rate gap with the US had already widened to 3.00%. It was under pressure to lower interest rates amid the government's pre-emptive stimulus action, but the central bank raised the benchmark rate from 5.00% to 5.25% on August 7. It cited the high oil prices and foreign exchange rates.

On October 9, the BOK lowered its interest rate but only by 0.25% even though conditions were favorable for lowering it as oil price had plummeted to below US$100 per barrel. On October 26, during an emergency policy meeting chaired by President Lee and attended by BOK Governor Lee and myself, it was agreed that the BOK should lower its benchmark rate further the next day, at a special meeting of the bank's Monetary Policy Committee.

The next day, the bank slashed the rate by 0.75 percentage point and purchased bank bonds worth 10 trillion won, mitigating the financial market crunch. The rate cut was the BOK's largest single reduction ever and returned its benchmark interest rate to the level of 2006, 4.25%. On October 30, the Fed lowered its interest rate to 1.00% and Japan, the UK, the EU, and China joined the rate cutting. The BOK hurriedly lowered the rate to 3.00% at year's end, a demonstration of its isolation rather than independence. Its move was far less than preemptive, decisive, and sufficient in counteracting the global financial and economic upheaval triggered by the Lehman Brothers' collapse on September 15.

Along with the interest rate reduction, the Bond Market Stabilization Fund worth 10 trillion won was suggested by the Financial Services Commission (FSC) to ease the credit crunch in the bond market. However, the BOK refused to participate in the fund under the pretext of being the lender of last resort. The bank also made the same excuse and resisted joining in the effort to set up a 20 trillion won Bank Recapitalization Fund, which was to help banks shore up their capital base and provide financial support for corporate restructuring.

After a heated debate, the BOK was persuaded to provide 50% of each fund, injecting 5 trillion and 10 trillion won, respectively. Not long afterwards, the Federal Reserve, while lowering its interest rate to a near zero level, took on the role as the lender of first and only resort, providing more than US$3 trillion. The difference between the two central banks was startling. During the 1997 Asian currency crisis, the BOK opposed 1 trillion won in special loans to merchant banks under the same pretext of being the lender of last resort although it eventually gave in. Before long, we were hit by the crisis. To fundamentally resolve the problem of the BOK putting its role as the lender of last resort before crisis management, the Bank of Korea Act was revised in 2011 to require the bank to "pay attention to financial stability."

It was regrettable indeed that the conflicts with the BOK on exchange rates, interest rates, and funds shackled me with accusations that I was no longer trusted by the market and fueled calls for my resignation. I confronted the rebuking since I wanted to prove market confidence by actions and outcomes not by words. But this unswerving tenacity turned me into "Kang the Stubborn," leaving me a lot of wounds. The financial crisis was approaching and the conflicts were building up. The situation was so hard to deal with.

Fifth move: Korea-US currency swap

The core of crisis prevention is to achieve current account surplus and expand foreign reserves in order to secure enough foreign exchange liquidity. The foreign reserves can be expanded by purchasing foreign currency in the domestic market, borrowing foreign currency in global markets, and establishing currency swap lines between central banks.

Although the rumors on a crisis subsided, we spent US$20 billion of foreign reserves before September to ensure that our currency market would operate smoothly. We wanted to issue government-managed Foreign Exchange Stabilization Bond (FESB), although we were not in dire need of it. Our objective was to keep market sentiment stable and to help financial institutions borrow money overseas easily. Against this backdrop, I let Assistant Minister Shin Je-Yoon pursue the issuance of US$1 billion FESB. I thought that the US$1 billion FESB could be issued smoothly in New York on September 11, but due to plummeting stock prices of Lehman Brothers and rumors on Kim Jong-il's serious illness, we faced unexpected situation where the spread rose to over 200 basis points. Since the 200 basis points were too high compared to 85 basis points just one year earlier and we had enough foreign reserves to manage the crisis, I told the assistant minister to give up the issuance and come back. Following the default of Lehman Brothers on September 15, the LIBOR jumped 4.29 percentage points and the world stock markets lost more than 6% of their value in three trading days, further increasing uncertainty in the global financial markets.

Lehman Brothers' collapse upended the international financial markets. On September 18, the Fed boosted its currency swap lines with the European Central Bank, the Bank of England, the Swiss National Bank, the Bank of Canada, and the Bank of Japan to US$247 billion through a $180 billion expansion. We thought we could manage our foreign debts even in the worst case, considering that we had US$240 billion in foreign reserves and the short-term foreign debts were US$189.5 billion (gross external liabilities of US$365.1 billion, external credits of US$395.6 billion, and net external credits of US$30.6 billion as of the end of September). However, as additional overseas funding became difficult, I had ordered Assistant Minister Shin on September 19 to push ahead with currency swaps as a last resort to stabilize market sentiment. He had already been communicating through hotlines with the US, Japan, and China.

On Saturday, September 20, President Lee convened a meeting to examine the effects of the default of Lehman Brothers on the financial market. There were briefings and consultations on the repercussions of the default on the international financial markets and our countermeasures. FSC Chairman Jun Kwang-woo, Minister of Knowledge Economy Lee Yun-ho, Senior Presidential Secretary for Economic Affairs Bahk Byong-won, and BOK Governor Lee attended. I reported that the short-term foreign debt of US$189.5 billion was manageable with our US$240 billion foreign reserves and that a joint working-level task force would be formed between the Ministry of Finance, FSC, and BOK for an effective management of the foreign debt.

I also reported that as only 1.2% of US$61.5 billion of external assets held by domestic financial institutions, or US$720 million, were related to Lehman Brothers and the amount of investment by the Korea Investment Corporation in Merrill Lynch was only US$2 billion, the situation could be controlled even in the worst case of losing the entire amount and there would be no great turmoil in the local stock and money markets. The problem was that, due to credit crunch, the roll−over ratio of debt of domestic financial institutions, excluding foreign banks, fell below 20% and additional funding became difficult. After being briefed, President Lee recalled his experience as a CEO of Hyundai Engineering and Construction, saying that cash was most important during crises and that a crisis was an opportunity and companies could shift their rankings during crisis. Reproving us for having given up the issuance of FESB due to high spread, he ordered us to actively pursue currency swap arrangements.

At that time, the Federal Reserve was supplying dollars based on currency swap agreements with the European Central Bank, the Bank of England, the Swiss National Bank, the Bank of Canada, and the Bank of Japan. On September 30, it announced that it would supply US$620 billion by April the following year through additional currency swap arrangements with the central banks of Sweden, Norway, Denmark, and Australia. Assistant Minister Shin Je−Yoon consulted through the hotline with US Assistant Secretary of the Treasury Clay Lowery, but the US said that it did not want a currency swap line with Seoul because Korea's credit rating was below AAA and the US had to be fair to all emerging countries. However, the US established a swap line with Australia. I could not understand the US position, considering Korea had more stakes in the IMF and had larger economy compared to Australia.

When the US announced the Troubled Assets Relief Program (TARP) worth US$700 billion on October 3, we had a second meeting chaired by President Lee at the Office of the President to examine overall economic and financial situation. I reported a contingency plan that consisted of three stages depending on the level of tightness in the international financial markets. According to the plan, if we enter the worst stage where outflow of foreign capital becomes serious, we would impose safe guard measures under which money exchange would be controlled and foreign exchange concentration system would be implemented. I told President Lee that a currency swap with the US would not be easy to secure through regular working-level channels and that I would make personal efforts by participating in the IMF Annual Meeting to be held in Washington, D.C. from October 11. President Lee ordered me to promote financial cooperation among Asian countries, too, by holding a meeting of finance ministers of Korea, China, and Japan.

On October 11, an extraordinary G-20 finance ministers' meeting was held at the IMF building. Assistant Minister Shin who had arrived in Washington, D.C. before me reported that having consulted with Mr. Lowery, the currency swap was almost impossible. Mr. Lowery told me that I could meet Treasury Secretary Henry Paulson for only a moment at the meeting venue since he was too busy. At the venue I met Mr. Paulson and Mr. Bernanke, but I couldn't have a meaningful conversation. They both appeared distrait.

During the meeting, Mr. Paulson stated that "preemptive and decisive" TARP worth US$700 billion would end the crisis in December, and I told him that considering our experience in 1997, the US would need ten times stronger "preemptive, decisive, and sufficient measures." President George W. Bush also participated in the meeting unexpectedly.

After finishing my keynote speech at the IMF-World Bank Annual Meeting on October 13, I took a train to New York for a back-channel talk with former Treasury Secretary Mr. Rubin, which I had been preparing before my departure from Seoul. It was a final attempt at securing a currency swap arrangement with the US. The BOK had already consulted with the Federal Reserve only to receive the same answer as the US Treasury Department's refusal. Governor Lee returned to Seoul after stating in an interview that the currency swap was impossible.

At 10 a.m. the next day, I met Mr. Rubin and Vice Chairman of Citibank William Rhodes at the Helmsley Hotel, where I was staying. At that time Mr. Rubin was the advisor to Citibank. I asked Mr. Rubin for help after saying, "We can manage the crisis without the currency swap. But if we sell the US Treasury Bonds that we hold in order to manage the crisis, there will be reverse spillover effects that could undermine the monetary policy of the US. Establishing a currency swap line with Korea will be good even for the US. It is not right that we suffer from the crisis created by the US, and it is not understandable to see Australia establishing the currency swap, while Korea is excluded even when our economy's scale is larger and we have more stakes in the IMF compared to Australia." Mr. Rubin expressed his total agreement with my opinion. On that day, Mr. Rhodes were about to have a lunch meeting with Timothy Geithner, the head of the Federal Reserve Bank of New York, who had the actual authority on the currency swap. I had met Mr. Geithner who had been the assistant secretary during the 1997 currency crisis. Mr. Rubin asked Mr. Rhodes to delivor his full support for my opinion to Mr. Geithner. Mr. Rhodes told me that he would call me after the luncheon to let me know about Mr. Geithner's answer and we concluded our meeting. According to my experience in foreign relations and negotiations, one should never beg for help during negotiations. Persuading the counterpart based on the necessity of the deal and the benefits thereof is the key to success.

At 2:30 p.m., Mr. Rhodes contacted me on my cell phone. He said Mr. Geithner also had agreed with my opinion and a currency swap arrangement was totally possible. He said that it would take about 14 days to go through necessary procedures and asked me to keep it an absolute secret until the agreement was officially announced.

Looking down at the Central Park through the window, I felt a great relief as if all the heavy burden had been lifted, and thought about my longtime tie with Citibank and its "Commitment to Korea." I thanked God for the relationship that spanned 35 years: the jumbo loan of US$200 million during the 1973 oil shock; the supports from Mr. Rhodes and Chairman John Reed who took the lead in the process of the debt roll-over negotiations during the 1997 currency crisis; and the help from

Mr. Rhodes and Mr. Rubin on that day. They have been friends indeed in every need.

I returned to Seoul next day and informed President Lee about the Korea–US currency swap. Since I had to take every eventuality into consideration, I reported that the arrangement was 51% or more sure, not 100%, and that we needed to treat it with absolute confidentiality. In the evening of the 24th, when I was at a finance ministers meeting between Korea and China and the Asia–Europe Meeting (ASEM) Summit in Beijing, I received a call from Assistant Minister Shin that Citibank had notified him of the official confirmation on the swap arrangement. I informed President Lee, who was staying in the Regent Hotel, that a US$30 billion Korea–US currency swap agreement was official and the announcement would be made by the US on October 30. I had a celebration drink with President Lee, and we shouted bravo.

On the next day, Saturday, at the Beijing Capital International Airport, I told BOK Deputy Governor Lee Gwang–ju who accompanied me for the Korea–China finance ministers meeting about the swap arrangement so that he could report the matter to the governor and go to the US to proceed with necessary procedures in consultation with the Federal Reserve.

On October 30, a US$30 billion Korea–US currency swap arrangement was announced both in Korea and the US. The whole world changed, after it had ridiculed me. I felt betrayed by the public. We had been in a situation where exchange rates were far more important to manage the crisis than the currency swap and we could manage the crisis without the swap line with the US, albeit with some pain.

In the evening of the day when the swap agreement was announced, a meeting of the Korea – US Business Councils was held in Hotel Shilla in Seoul. During my congratulatory remarks, I expressed my gratitude to Mr. Rhodes, who served as chairman of the US side as follows:

『This morning, Korea and the US announced the set of the currency swap line. Again, Citibank has been a great help through various channels. Chairman Rhodes is the prime example of "A friend in need is a friend indeed." I would like to express my sincere appreciation to Chairman Rhodes for his continuous support and commitment for Korea. Please give a big hand to the Chairman.』

Here, I would like to inject some acknowledgements lest I should forget. First, I want to express my appreciation to Assistant Minister Shin Je – Yoon and financial attaché Yun Yeo–gwon in New York for their hard work and support. I also would like to extend my gratitude to Citibank Korea President Ha Yung–ku for his effort to arrange a meeting with Mr. Rubin. My appreciation also goes to BOK New York branch officials who worked hard in New York. I think the efforts there deserve high praise.

On the same day that I heard the news on the successful Korea – US currency swap arrangement, Chinese Finance Minister Xie Xuren and I agreed on a US$30 billion Korea–China currency swap line at Diaoyutai State Guesthouse in Beijing, and this served as leverage in helping us establish a US$30 billion currency swap line with Japan. China gladly agreed on the swap line, while Japan, at this time again, was somewhat reluctant, suggesting US$3 billion initially and then US$5 billion. So I told Director General of the International Finance Bureau Choi Jong-gu who went to Tokyo for the arrangement to drop the deal and come back. Japan reluctantly agreed on the US$30 billion swap line because of China, during a meeting of finance ministers of Korea, China, and Japan on November 15.

The dealing with Japan reminded me of its behavior during the 1997 currency crisis—how it was our largest creditor but focused on withdrawing capital and how my letter to the Japanese vice minister of finance pleading for him to stop the outflow was in vain. I was very confused about who they really were. In 2013, when Japan uttered an extreme view that even Samsung could fail if Japan cut off the source of funds, I told junior officials at the Ministry of Finance that if it held such position, Korea should end its currency swap pact with Japan. We did. Meanwhile, the swap line with China has been maintained. Japan has been a more distant neighbor than China, which was our enemy during the Korean War, and the US, across the Pacific Ocean.

| Last move:
Guaranteeing bank debt with US$100 billion

On the return flight from New York on October 15, 2008, carrying the good news on the currency swap with the US,

I thought about guaranteeing short-term debt of financial institutions as a third line of defense in our crisis prevention, after our US$240 billion foreign reserves and the US$30 billion Korea-US currency swap. In 1997, we were hit by the currency crisis before we could even try guaranteeing short-term debt.

Immediately upon arrival at the Incheon International Airport at dust on October 16, I called Director General Choi Jong-gu and told him that I was on my way to the office and that I wanted to be briefed on the status of short-term debts of financial institutions and measures to guarantee their external debt. According to his briefing, short-term foreign debts of financial institutions maturing within a year reached about US$29 billion. Working-level officials said that guaranteeing US$50 billion at most would be enough. I ordered them to prepare pre-emptive, decisive, and sufficient measures that would amaze the market by doubling the amount to US$100 billion. They doubted the passage of the proposal at the National Assembly, but I insisted on making it US$100 billion since I believed that it actually would cost the least. My reasoning was that if we guaranteed US$30 billion, all of it would be spent; if we guaranteed US$50 billion, some of them could be used; but if we guaranteed US$100 billion, it would be untouched.

The plan to guarantee US$100 billion in foreign debt was titled, "the Motion on a Sovereign Guarantee of Domestic Banks' Foreign Currency-denominated Borrowings from Nonresidents." Under the motion, the government guaranteed up to US$100 billion of the principal and interest of foreign currency-denominated overseas borrowings secured by 18 domestic banks between October 20, 2008 and June 30, 2009, for three years from the date of borrowing. KDB had the highest limit guaranteed, US$16.1 billion. Guarantee limits about US$10 billion were provided to each of the five largest commercial banks—Kookmin, Shinhan, Woori, Hana, and Korea Exchange—and government-run Industrial Bank of Korea and Export-Import Bank of Korea.

The motion was made public on October 23. The international financial markets were surprised at its unexpectedly spectacular scale. Some members of the National Assembly said the amount was too high, but we persuaded them that guaranteeing US$100 billion would actually save us money. On October 30, when the US$30 billion Korea-US currency swap agreement was announced, the National Assembly passed the motion for US$100 billion guarantee.

As expected, domestic banks, when their risk was removed thanks to the sufficient guarantee worth US$100 billion, could borrow money from foreign banks without providing guarantee, and we could secure enough foreign currency liquidity. I heard that the guarantee was provided several times for small amounts after I left the ministry.

Korea recorded positive growth while advanced OECD member countries recorded negative growth in 2009 and we emerged as the seventh-largest exporter in the world in 2010. We didn't go through any trouble in 2011, when southern European countries such as Portugal, Italy, Greece, and Spain were in fiscal crisis in the aftermath of the global crisis. We weathered the unprecedented 2008 global economic crisis without pain by shielding us from the crisis from outside of the country.

On the day the Korea-US currency swap agreement was announced and the US$100 billion debt guarantee was approved, I looked back what we had implemented. I had used all means available to endure the crisis: normalizing exchange rates, turning current account into surplus, reducing the oil tax and tariff rates, coming up with policies worth 10 trillion won to overcome the high oil price, establishing the US$30 billion Korea-US currency swap line, and guaranteeing up to US$100 billion as the final line of defense. I had not taken a day off, thinking I was performing my last tasks in public service. I timed my resignation for shortly after the National Assembly closed its session. Long ago, attending the National Assembly sessions when I was a junior-level official, I promised myself that if I become a cabinet minister, I would clearly deliver my opinions on what is right and what is wrong, and I kept my word. However, our politics and media were still not ready to accept my approach of tackling a problem head-on.

The year 2008 became the cause of great misery in my family. During my out-of-government years, I once said in a gathering that it would be good if only I could be a minister even if only for one day. After I became Finance Minister, my daughter, who fought all night alone with malicious comments on the internet that blamed me for high prices and high exchange rates, tearfully told me to quit since I had already have my wish fulfilled. It all started with abusive words of foreign music lovers and middle-aged women whose children were studying abroad. They blamed me for a sudden rise in the import price of music CDs and the amount of remittances to their children. My daughter's illness got worse because of the stress at that time, and she went to Heaven. My grieving heart never heals.

Oh! How can I forget the year 2008?
So many days of mounting challenges and responses
So much criticism and blame
Old boy, King Man-soo, and Kang the Stubborn
You would never know
The endless agonies of my soul
The painful wounds of a soul that lost its child.

18 Investment Environment: Maximizing Potential

In 2008, we also had to implement strategies to turn the crisis into an opportunity in tandem with establishing our lines of defense. The crisis was not only an opportunity to change our national ranking but also a chance to carry out offensive strategies and make a leap forward to become an advanced economy, overcoming many wounds from the 1997 crisis.

Even without the subprime crisis, Korea was in a critical situation in 2008. Ten years of leftist governance had left the economy in a swamp of underperformance. Investment growth was 2.3%, and potential growth rate had dropped to the 4% range. Normally, in a growing economy, investment growth surpasses economic growth.

To overcome the low growth and weak investment, we needed strategies to expand our economic capability, which boiled down to strengthening corporate investment environment and improving the management environment. The four key variables that determine corporate investment environment are: tax cuts to increase capital for investments, technological development to attract new investments, deregulation to increase investment opportunities, and a bigger workforce to run facilities. The primary variables that can boost management activities include expansionary fiscal policies, greater social overhead capital (SOC), a stable foreign exchange market, and development of the financial market. When we look back on the correlations between economic variables, low tax rates led to higher levels of investment and tax revenue, and high exchange rates led to high growth and low unemployment.

| Tax cuts: The best tool

Tax cuts are the first strategy to boost corporate investment environment. Lower taxes naturally allow companies to have more capital for investment. The risk of the leveraged financial structure was too high during the 1997 currency crisis. Making a sound investment with retained earnings is the first step toward enhancing economic capability. When retained earnings are combined with borrowed funding, an investment risk is lowered. Tax cuts aimed at increasing retained earnings not only serve as the first step toward expanding investment capabilities but also act as tax increase policies in the long term as they boost investment.

Any plan to cut taxes sparks intense debates since taxes act as the core variable in running the government and businesses. Controversies are inevitable because taxes, like death, are unavoidable. The rise and fall of a nation has often been decided on its ability to collect taxes. One thing is clear: both tax cuts and hikes are strategies to collect more taxes in the end.

Each dollar in tax cuts raises GDP by about US$3, according to Christina D. Romer, former chairwoman of the White House Council of Economic Advisers. Harvard professors Alberto Alesina and Silvia Ardagna compared 91 economic stimulus tools in 21 OECD member countries since 1970. To our surprise, they found that successful measures were related to cuts in business and income taxes and increases in government spending mostly failed. W. Kurt Houser put forward his proposition that no matter what the tax rates have been, tax revenues in the US after World War II have remained lower than 20% of GDP and that tax increases reduced both GDP and tax revenue. Recently, there are many other studies backing the argument that tax cuts are the best policy tools.

Statistics show that in Korea, too, lowering tax rates increased tax revenue in the long-term. I learned this firsthand since I played a part in lowering income tax rate from 70% to as low as 40% starting from 1974, when I began to work for the Ministry of Finance. The effectiveness of tax cuts can be also inferred through logical deduction besides statistical measures. Tax revenue becomes zero both when the tax rate is 100% and 0%. The highest amount of tax revenue that can be collected is when the tax rate is maintained at a level that is willingly accepted by taxpayers and encourages them to actively engage in their business activities.

It has been statistically proven that lowering tax rates,

especially in the cases of income, corporate, and inheritance taxes, boosts economic growth and increases income, resulting in more tax revenue. In Korea, the maximum rate of income tax was lowered from 70% to 35% between 1975 and 2012, but the tax revenue increased from 1.9% to 3.6% as a percentage of GDP. The highest rate of corporate tax was also lowered from 35% to 22% between 1981 and 2009, but the revenue rose from 1.20% to 3.61%. Inheritance tax showed a similar trend.

Confronted with the 2008 global financial crisis, I employed far-reaching tax cuts for the third time. I had implemented tax cuts when I was a working-level official. My approach was based on empirical facts, not theory. Tax cuts, apart from increasing tax revenue, are the best way to lift investment and consumption, which propel economic growth. Since Korea's tax-to-GDP ratio was 22.7% (2007), which was higher than 20.6% of the US (2005) and 17.3% of Japan (2005), we set the goal of reducing the figure to 20%. Our debt-to-GDP ratio was quite low at around 30%.

Tax cuts applied from 2008 to 2012 consisted of emergency measures to support those in the low-income bracket suffering from a rise in oil price; and structural measures to overcome low growth. The scale of tax cuts reached a total of 34.9 trillion won, about 3.4% of GDP: emergency tax relief, which included reduction of the oil tax and tariff rates, temporary investment tax credit, and tax rebates to mitigate the effects of the high oil price, was worth 9.8 trillion won; and structural tax cuts, which involved reductions in income, corporate, inheritance, and comprehensive real estate tax rates, were worth 25.1 trillion won. It was estimated that these tax cuts would increase 0.6% in GDP, 0.5% in consumption, 7% in investment, and 180,000 people in employment.

The structural tax cuts announced on September 1, 2008 involved extensive reforms of 17 tax laws, including Income Tax Act, Corporate Tax Act, Value–Added Tax Act, and Customs Act. They were focused on lowering tax rates to boost investments, promoting exceptional R&D investment that could bolster growth potential, and abolishing the comprehensive real estate tax, which conflicted with the principles of taxation.

First, the structural tax cuts were designed to lower the income tax rates from 8–35% to 6–33%, the maximum corporate tax rates from 25% to 20%, and the inheritance tax rates from 10–50% to 6–33%. At that time, the maximum income tax rates were an average of 35.5% in OECD member states, 35% in the US, and 40% in Japan. The maximum corporate tax rates were an average of 24.2% in OECD countries, 17.5% in Taiwan, and 16.5% in Hong Kong while the maximum inheritance tax rates were 45% in the US, 50% in Japan, and 30% in Germany.

Second, I devised an exceptionally generous system to support three stages of R&D. The system, which was unprecedented in other countries, aimed at having R&D investments account for 5% of GDP. It encouraged companies to earmark 3% of sales revenue for a tax–free reserve fund at the preparation stage, provided a 10% tax credit at the investment stage, and gave a tax credit for 25% (6% for large companies) of the R&D expenditure or 50% (40% for large companies) of the incremental portion of annual R&D expenses in research stage. The system was designed in a way that, if all these measures were utilized, companies could end up paying no taxes.

Third, since the comprehensive real estate tax, which had been introduced to control real estate speculation, conflicted with the principles of taxation and became a punitive system that created an excessive tax burden, I planned to gradually lower the tax rates and abolish the tax by integrating it into property tax. In 2008, at the first stage, I planned to greatly ease the tax burden by increasing the threshold for taxation from 600 million won to 900 million won, reducing tax rates from 1-3% to 0.5-1%, and providing a 10% to 30% tax deduction to a homeowner above the age of 60.

Reforms in income tax deductions, capital gains tax, and taxes on enterprises were also included. Earmarked taxes for traffic, education, and rural development were to be overhauled for integration into main taxes. Also, beneficiaries of earned income tax credit were to be expanded from those who earn 890,000 won annually to those who earn 1.2 million won.

The tax cuts were highly controversial. The opposition Democratic Party said they would benefit the rich and many university professors blamed that a tax cut was a mere ideology that increased the fortunes of the wealthy few without real economic effects and it was a big mistake to try to pump prime the economy through tax cuts by relying on supply-side economics of the Reagan administration era that had already lost its effect as an economic theory.

Against the political attack from the opposition party, I defended the tax cuts by pointing out that more than 70% of them would benefit the low and middle-income brackets and small and medium-sized companies, and that tax cuts were equal to tax revenue increase in the long-term. I said, "Personally, I have lived a life that had no reason to cut taxes for the rich. Which government in the world would want to take the big political burden of cutting taxes for the rich? Tax cut policies are for increasing tax revenue in the long-term." In the negotiation process with the opposition party, the tax package was revised to delay the 2% reduction in the maximum rates of income and corporate taxes until 2010. Lowering inheritance tax rates was shelved.

After partial modifications and adjustments, bills on 13 tax cuts worth 25.1 trillion won, excluding a bill on the abolition of earmarked taxes, were passed by the National Assembly on December 13 along with the 284.5 trillion won budget proposal for 2009. I can't forget the generous compromise made in the face of the crisis by key members of the opposition party. The tax laws would not have been passed without their help and there could have been major problems in crisis management.

Although the tax reforms were passed after many difficulties, the 2% reduction in income and corporate taxes, which was supposed to be implemented in 2010, was trashed. Moreover, no further discussions were made on lowering inheritance tax rates and integrating the comprehensive real estate tax into property tax. This was the result of political populism and the government's helplessness.

CRET change: Ending political violence

In 2008, income and corporate taxes took center stage in policy debates over tax cuts. But the Comprehensive Real Estate Tax (CRET) introduced by the opposition Democratic Party was the most disputed political issue.

Introduced in 2005 to curb speculative demand on real estate, the CRET was imposed and collected by the central government on top of property taxes, which were imposed by local governments. It had progressive rates of 1-3% for housing that exceeded more than 900 million won; and 1-4% for vacant land that exceeded 600 million won and land attached to buildings that exceeded 4 billion won in their combined assessed value. As speculation on real estate continued, CRET was toughened in 2006 by lowering the tax threshold for housing to 600 million won and changing the taxation basis from single person to single household. In 2007, there was considerable controversy over CRET because retired single house owners in an upscale district received tax bills of several million to several tens of millions of won. CRET was a punitive system that overburdened retirees to the point they had to get a loan or sell houses to pay their taxes.

CRET was unprecedented in the world history of taxation and it was a form of political violence disguised as a tax, targeting higher-income people who had overwhelmingly supported conservative candidates. First, the tax burden on retirees whose annual income was 40 million won or below was more than 45% of their income. This was nearly equivalent to confiscation, considering that even the principal would disappear if they paid the 45% rate for 20 years. Second, the system violated the principle of equity by excessively levying only 2% of all taxpayers and was not fair either since it excluded buildings. Third, the central government's intensive imposition of tax on certain district goes against the nature of property tax, which is characterized as payment by beneficiaries of local government services. Fourth, the progressive rates of 1–4% conflict with the principle of applying a flat rate of about 1% in the case of property tax, which is imposed for local government services. Fifth, tax imposed on holding property reached 3.7% of GDP, which was higher than 3.1% of the US and even higher than the OECD average of 2.0%. Finally, given that the speculation on real estate around 2005 was caused by a shortage in housing supply and an increase in mortgage loans, it was a policy mistake to impose severely heavy taxes on people who owned one house on a household basis and had nothing to do with speculation.

CRET was regarded as not only a byproduct of the leftist government's jealousy toward the rich on the excuse of curbing real estate speculation that occurred around 2005 but also simply administrative mistakes.

The Ministry of Finance made a great mistake saying, "We should raise holding taxes and lower trading taxes" when CRET was introduced in 2005. A property holding tax is regarded as payment for local government services, so it should be set as low as possible. The IMF recommended in 1975 that we should apply a flat rate for the holding tax. It said we could heavily tax real estate transactions to create sustainable sources of tax revenue because there should be income behind such transactions.

When I became the Minister, I resolved to re-establish justice in taxation by removing CRET. I called in working-level officials and ordered them to find any grounds that justified the argument for higher holding taxes and lower trading taxes. They reported that they could find no grounds and the argument was wrong. I ordered them to immediately prepare measures to abolish the tax. It was utterly absurd situation.

It is said that once a wrong policy is implemented, it takes 20 years to correct it. I thought that it would be very difficult to dismantle the tax in a short time, considering the way the leftist government had amended the tax code. Hence, I announced measures to make up for financial resources of local governments as well as a three-step plan to abolish the tax. The first step would freeze the ratio of the assessed price used to set the tax base for property tax in 2008. The second step would lower tax rates at a regular session of the National Assembly in 2008 from 1-3% to 0.5-1% and provide 10-30% tax deduction to a house owner above the age of 60. And the third step would abolish CRET by integrating it into property tax.

The reform measures for CRET were unveiled on September 23 separately from the comprehensive tax cuts announced on September 1 because further adjustments were needed due to strong objections from the Office of the President and the ruling Grand National Party. President Lee made a final decision on the three-step plan at a meeting attended by the President's chief of staff and relevant senior secretaries.

Who was to blame for CRET? The opposition party that introduced the tax was irresponsible; the ruling party who achieved a landslide victory in the general election was cowardly; and the presidential secretaries who tried to evade controversies were lackadaisical. None of them wanted to be at the forefront of ending the "political violence." My last comment at the Office of the President meeting was, "I will take full responsibility for implementing the measures." When the reform measures were announced, I was bombarded with political attacks that criticized the measures as tax cuts for the rich and CRET became the main reason of my resignation. I paid the price of removing the "large nail" of the leftist government.

A compromise was reached in the National Assembly. We adjusted the maximum rate to 2% and added a 20% tax credit for holding a house for more than five years and a 40% tax credit for holding it for more than ten years. This compromised tax cut measure for CRET and other tax reforms were passed on December 13 by the National Assembly. After I left my office, nobody mentioned aggregating the tax with property taxes again.

5% of GDP in R&D: Topping the world

The Economist (2011. 11. 12.) said, "To keep growing that impressively, though, Korea will need some new tactics ... When a country or a company is playing catch-up it can look at what others are doing and do it better. ... Hyundai has outcompeted Toyota in the market for reliable, efficient, cheap cars. Korea's shipyards have beaten everyone through economies of scale.

... Your economy comes to depend more on innovation and on learning from your own mistakes than on improving on the successes of others."

Our second strategy to expand corporate investment capability was the three-stage support plan to drive up investment in R&D to 5% of GDP. Economic capability can be strengthened by promoting new investment, and the key to new investment is development of new technology. We thus needed exceptionally bold assistance for development of new technology to emerge as a technology powerhouse. I painfully learned from the 1997 currency crisis that technology is the only way for a small open economy with insufficient resource and no reserve currency to survive in global competition. Technology also can be the way to mitigate a strong-won environment amid big inflows of foreign capital.

R&D was the only economic area where government support was allowed under the WTO system. Our hope in crafting the support plan was to foster new champions during the global financial crisis, providing them with preemptive and exceptional support for technological development and positioning them to help Korea join the ranks of advanced economies after the crisis ends.

Korea's technology balance of payments, which indicates the level of its technologies, worsened from a deficit of US$2 billion in 2001 to a deficit of US$2.9 billion in 2007. During the same period, the US and Japan recorded surpluses, with their figures surging from US$28.4 billion and US$5.7 billion to US$33.6 billion and US$15 billion, respectively. The technological gap is widening further. In 2007, Korea invested 3.21% of GDP in R&D, while the US invested 2.51% and Japan 3.31%. Korea's investment amount was a mere 10.8% and 27.8% of the amounts of the US and Japan, respectively.

To increase investment in R&D to 5% of GDP, the world's highest level, I set the goal of increasing investment amount in the government sector from 0.75% of GDP (5.8 trillion won) in 2005 to 1.5% of GDP (21 trillion won) in 2012. Basic science and original technology were earmarked for most of the spending. This was in addition to expanding the amount in the private sector from 2.04% of GDP (18 trillion won) in 2005 to 3.5% of GDP (49 trillion won) in 2012 to focus on applied science and manufacturing technologies.

To achieve 1.5% R&D investment in the government sector, I moved up R&D in the list of budgetary items to first from 11th — welfare was the first in the past — and required the amount to be increased at least 10% every year.

To achieve 3.5% R&D investment in the private sector, we created a system, for the first time in the world, which employed innovative methods to reduce corporate taxes in three stages. In the preparation stage, I included 3% of sales revenue earmarked for R&D reserve fund into expenses; in the investment stage, tax credit was provided for 10% of R&D facilities investments; and in the research stage, 25% (6% for large companies) of research spending or 50% (40% for large companies) of the incremental portion of annual R&D expenses compared to the average of the previous four years was deductible. Normally, this kind of policy is not implemented since it is equivalent to triple deduction according to taxation theories.

I included outsourced R&Ds and the areas where software development was critical such as design, advertisement, movie, and IT to the scope of R&D, and also included costs for human resource development to the research expenditure qualified for tax deduction. To facilitate industry–academia cooperation, I made R&D contributions to universities 100% deductible, provided a tax credit for 10 % of the amount invested in R&D facilities of universities. To attract top–level foreign human resources, a 15% of flat rate was applied to income tax rate for foreigners engaged in R&D activities.

If all of these exceptionally bold measures to support R&D were utilized, companies would nearly be free of taxes. The exempted amount could be fully offset through economic growth and increases in profits. By allowing companies to directly utilize their financial resources rather than collecting more taxes and use them as the government's R&D budget, the effectiveness of funds could be enhanced and the time lag between R&D and product development could be shortened. The three–stage plan to facilitate R&D investment, the core of the 2008 tax cuts, was the only agenda that attracted no controversy at the National Assembly.

After establishing this strong tax incentive system for R&D investment, we introduced Intellectual Property Right (IPR) transaction system and "techno–banking" service, thereby completing the foundation for technological development. In 2010, when I became the senior economic advisor to the President and Chairman of the Presidential Council on

National Competitiveness (PCNC), we established, through government-private joint investment, Intellectual Discovery Co. Ltd. which managed and invested in patent rights or IPRs created by newly developed technologies. In 2011, as the Chairman of the KDB Financial Group, I created an environment for boosting R&D activities by launching a techno-banking service through which the KDB invested in patents or intellectual properties and also provided loans.

| Quality improvement: Work-study regime

Effective strategies for technological development are inextricably linked with those for quality improvement. Competitiveness of a new technology is decided by product quality, which depends on workforce skill sets. The proficiency of workers can be achieved through skills and experience built up over a long time by entering into workforce at an early age. To enhance the mastery of on-site technologies and make Korea become a powerhouse of quality products, we can learn from the early vocational trainings and the systems enabling working while learning of Germany and Switzerland which boast the world's best technological mastery.

As of 2006, the average job entry age in Korea was 25 while the OECD average was 23 and it was 19 for Germans. In the meantime, the college enrollment rate was once over 80% in Korea while the figures were about 35% in Germany whose manufacturing industry has the highest global competitiveness, about 45% in Japan, and about 55% in the US, with the OECD average reaching about 60%. A low level of employment rate in Korea compared to its high college enrollment rate of about 80% is evidence that our education is being severely wasted.

To prevent the wastefulness of education and improve R&D outcomes, Korea needed a strategy aimed at becoming a powerhouse of quality products by enhancing hands-on experience. Central to the strategy was the establishment of Meister high schools, one of the core election promises of President Lee. Based on the vocational training system of Germany, the high schools were aimed at easing ordinary people's burden of educational expenses, serving as an incubator for highly-skilled technicians and launching pad to increase the working age population.

Twenty-one Meister high schools were opened in 2010 with a total of 42 schools operating as of 2014. Most of our plan was implemented as pledged during the election campaign: selection of students through employment contracts with companies; on-site training for 50% of school curriculum; total exemption from tuition fees and boarding expenses; and tax credit for on-site training fees up to 20 million won. In particular, on January 19, 2011, as the chairman of the PCNC, I led the process of creating a work-study system in cooperation with relevant ministries, including the Ministry of Education and Science, the Ministry of Finance, and the Ministry of National Defense. The system allowed students to pursue academic path further after graduating from Meister high school through various channels, including corporate university, partner university, evening college, open university, and contract-based customized courses, so that the graduates of the Meister high schools could grow into the world's greatest Meister.

To solidify the work-study system in our society, we revised tax laws in 2011 to include on-site training fees into human resource development costs eligible for a 25% tax credit (6% for large companies), and devised an exceptional support in which 100% of income tax is exempted for three years if a graduate finds employment. I think tax credits for on-site training fees and the exemption of income tax upon employment are the most productive R&D investments.

These benefits were also expanded to students at specialized high schools, innovating vocational education and lowering the average job entry age, thereby contributing to improving field mastery. Meister high school serves not only as an innovative vocational training system but also the best welfare system for ordinary citizens since graduating from the school will guarantee both employment and future. The program has been revised in the process of execution, but it has been a success, with Meister high schools attracting a lot of talented students and more than 90% of graduates being hired.

After I became the chairman of the KDB Financial Group in March 2011, I employed, for the first time in the financial industry, the graduates of specialized high schools as full-time workers. I also established the KDB Financial University, the first corporate university in the domestic financial sector, and was inaugurated as its president. Meister high school, the work-study system, employment of high school graduates as regular workers, and the KDB Financial University became the most beautiful memories in my public career, and thanks to these achievements I received *Mugunghwa* Medal, the highest Order of Civil Merit, at the end of my 43-year long public career in 2013.

| Regulatory innovation:
   Regulation Equity System

The third strategy to improve corporate investment capability was to ease regulation in order to expand corporate investment opportunities. Regulations on new investment impede companies with financial resources and new technologies from making investments. Although easing regulations was one of the core strategies for expanding economic capability, the Ministry of Finance was fully occupied with crisis management in 2008, and matters on deregulation were handled mainly by the Presidential Council on National Competitiveness (PCNC).

The PCNC was launched as a presidential advisory body with the start of the Lee Myung-bak administration in 2008. The council consisted of 30 people, including the Chairman, who concurrently held the position of the Senior Economic Advisor to the President, the Minister of Finance, the Senior Presidential Secretary for Economic Affairs, the Chairman of the Policy Committee of the ruling Grand National Party, and the heads of five leading economic organizations in Korea. At a monthly meeting, the council provided advisory opinions to President

Lee with regard to policies on deregulation and national competitiveness.

On February 10, 2009, after leaving the post of Minister of Finance, I took the position of Senior Economic Advisor to the President and PCNC chairman and began to deal with matters related to easing regulation and strengthening competitiveness.

I implemented many policies to strengthen national competitiveness in diverse areas. But most importantly except the work-study system, I put the highest priority on the introduction of the Regulation Equity System in relation to deregulation.

Deregulation has always been an issue. Numerous attempts by past administrations to relax regulations have been insufficient. Against this backdrop, I designed a fundamental regulatory relief system, taking into account the nature and reality of regulations.

Regulatory statutes and legislations intrinsically ban an act or control behavior based on average tolerance level. Therefore, in any individual case, a regulation may be excessive or insufficient; situations can change from the time of legislation or new circumstances may arise. For example, there was a case where a factory had to create more parking lots, even though its workforce was shrinking, as its floor space increased due to an extension of its building for automation. The factory obviously was overregulated, but providing a relief for an individual case is illegal from the executive office's standpoint. If a regulation is abolished, we cannot regulate matters that need to be really regulated. Although there is a system for reviewing constitutionality, legal methods take a lot of procedures and time.

Since the Regulation Equity System inherently created a new legal definition that would suspend the effect of a regulation, I asked the Korean Public Law Association to study the matter and it found similar regulatory exemption systems in the US, the UK, and Germany. Based on this, I concluded that the Regulation Equity System was compatible with our constitutional framework.

The system, which was devised through long-time researches and consultation with relevant government authorities, was designed to allow an independent regulation equity commission to grant an exemption to an individual case when a regulation was generally valid but caused "obvious and severe damage" in a specific case, as long as such exemption was in accordance with the intent of legislation and did not undermine the public's interest. Government offices would then take administrative steps accordingly if they found no "justifiable grounds" to oppose the decision.

The system could have been an innovative mechanism that could fundamentally deal with regulations that hinder corporate investments. We prepared an "Act for Damage Relief of Administrative Regulation and Guarantee of Equity in Regulation" in cooperation with the Ministry of Government Legislation and submitted it to the National Assembly in November, 2010. The bill stipulated that the Anti-Corruption and Civil Rights Commission would oversee regulation equity and the establishment of a new independent commission would be discussed later, if future workloads deem a need.

The bill went nowhere. It died when the National Assembly's term expired more than a year after the proposal was presented.

Future administrations will continuously raise the issue of deregulation, and amid such circumstances new regulations will be created whenever problems occur, and regulations that undermine equity in specific cases will increase accordingly. It's lamentable to think that how long we have to wait until companies who turn to government offices for unfair regulations that hinder their investments don't have to hear the same old excuse, "We are sorry to hear that, but we can't help it under the existing regulations."

Expansion of labor supply: Early employment and overseas Koreans

The fourth strategy to increase corporate investment capability is to expand the supply of labor. The rapid ageing of our society and the low birth rate have become the biggest threat to our economy. If labor is in shortage, investment is impossible even when all other conditions such as financial resources, technologies, and investment opportunities are met. Some research found that the biggest problem in small and medium-sized companies' investment environment is a lack of labor forces.

There was a government report that the working age population in Korea would begin to decline after reaching its peak at 37 million in 2016, and Korea's population, which surpassed 50 million as of now, would reduce by half in 2100 and the Korean race will disappear on the Korean Peninsula by 2500.

The government is exerting great effort to boost birth rate and utilize more female workforce aiming to expand the supply of labor, and the retirement age has been extended. Not much attention has been given to lowering average job entry age and accepting more immigrants. The late Nobel prize-winning professor Gary Becker at the University of Chicago once recommended accepting immigrants to deal with population ageing and low birth rates, but no effort has been made with regard to this except in marriage-based immigration.

To promote early employment, I made the establishment of Meister high schools into the election promise during the presidential election campaign, and after taking the post of the Chairman of the PCNC, I strengthened this effort further by creating the work-study system in 2011, which allowed students to pursue academic path further through various channels. In the same year, I also included on-site training fees into human resource development costs eligible for a 25% tax credit (6% for conglomerates), and came up with an exceptional support system in which 100% of income tax is exempted for three years if a graduate finds employment.

When I became the Chairman of the KDB Financial Group in March, 2011, I hired the graduates of specialized high schools as regular workers for the first time in the financial industry and also established the KDB Financial University, the first corporate university in the domestic financial sector. I actively pushed ahead with employment of high school graduates as full-time workers and plans on corporate university because they served as strategies for expanding labor forces.

The number of ethnic Koreans overseas is 7 million, and an unofficial figure is even higher than that. Immigration is a sensitive issue to Korea which is not a multiracial country. In Europe, severe social problems arose as the number of immigrants with different religious backgrounds exceeded 10% of the population. Taking Europe's experience into consideration, accepting the immigration of overseas Koreans or guaranteeing them free entry and departure from Korea can be a good solution to labor shortage.

While serving at the PCNC, I proposed a bill on the Nationality Act, as one of measures to expand population, to grant Korean citizenship to overseas Koreans and, if dual nationality was not allowed in their countries, to allow them to freely enter and leave Korea. The Ministry of Justice's concerns over possible abuse of the system to evade the nation's mandatory military service requirement prompted adjustments. The system would be limited to overseas Koreans with outstanding talent, those who made an important contribution to Korea, and those at least 65 years of age who intended to permanently return to Korea and reinstate their nationality. The bill was submitted to the National Assembly and was passed in April, 2010. The issue of guaranteeing free entry and departure to Koreans living overseas was resolved through flexible visa issuance based on the Immigration Control Act.

Failing to grant dual citizenship to all overseas Koreans was regrettable indeed. Ethnic Koreans in Uzbekistan or Kazakhstan are descendants of those who fought for Korea's independence or people who left Korea for their survival because of the failure of our government. Having lived in the land that should have been shared with them, we are not doing justice to our history when we restrict their reinstatement of nationality or examine their entry into this country.

While serving as the chairman of the KDB Financial Group, I implemented a Korean language program for college students of Korean heritage from Uzbekistan, where the KDB had made forays. The students were invited during their school breaks, to have an opportunity to work in Korea and learn about their grandparents' nation. I told them that they were historically entitled to the right to work in Korea, and that we needed them now. On the last day of the program, we all joined in singing *Arirang*—the most famous Korean folk song—standing around a campfire, which soon created a sea of tears. This made local newspaper headlines and received fervent responses. Looking away from their tears is being oblivious of the past and obstructs national prosperity. We are in dire need of ethnic Koreans living abroad right now. They may evaluate us, but we should not evaluate them. That is not doing justice to our history. The shift from single nationality to dual citizenship system was meaningful. Still, the Nationality Act must be revised at an earliest possible date to guarantee all ethnic Koreans dual citizenship and free entry and departure.

19

Management Environment: Best in the World

Robust investing and a solid management environment are mutually interdependent and essential to improve a country's economic capabilities. Even if tax cuts, technology developments, deregulation, increased labor supply, and other conditions needed to increase corporate investment capability are met, the efficiency of investments will degrade if the management environment is not improved. Conversely, the management environment cannot progress without rising investments.

To have a good management environment, a strong domestic demand base supported by aggressive fiscal policies and expanded infrastructure is critical. Other determinants are stability based on advanced financial markets and increased social capital and external capabilities.

Korea's national debt ratio is one of the lowest among the OECD nations. Therefore, to take advantage of the global economic crisis and move up to the next stage, the country needs to implement aggressive fiscal policies and reinforce infrastructure for the service sector, thereby strengthening its domestic demand base. From a business perspective, a jittery foreign exchange market puts enormous pressure on the Korean economy's trade potential and corporate profit margins. Nurturing of world-class mega banks capable of providing large-scale project financing is also important. The need became apparent when the country joined the international bidding for nuclear power plant contracts in the United Arab Emirates and Turkey. Accumulation of social capital is also essential for Korea, where the rule of law still has to be entrenched in the labor market. Increasing its economic presence to wider regions through free trade agreements is an effective way of strengthening external capabilities.

| Fiscal expansion: Offense brings victory

The year 2008 was extraordinary in that the government prepared two additional budgets in addition to the regular budget in response to the global financial crisis. The main budget for 2009 was 274 trillion won and focused on strengthening demand base. The 10 trillion won revised budget was added due to global crisis. The 10 trillion won supplementary budget plus tax refunds eased the impact of high oil prices in hopes of stimulating the economy. The extra budgets tripled the workload of the budget office officials and one senior official even fainted from the heavy volume.

The so-called Great Recession in the world economy that

came in the wake of the global financial crisis naturally rattled Korea's business environment. The economic freefall in the US and Europe cast a shadow over the prospects of Korea's trade-led economy. The situation demanded aggressive fiscal policy action that would shore up domestic demand and keep the business environment intact. Moreover, with the nation in better financial health than advanced nations, we had the means to take advantage of the crisis. We could position the economy for a leap over other countries before they could fully recover.

The collapse of Lehman Brothers on September 15, 2008 came just two weeks before the scheduled release of the Korean government's 2009 budget. With the destructive force of the US subprime crisis fully unleashed, the global economic outlook immediately darkened. We had to scramble to make adjustments.

A 274 trillion won budget was unveiled on September 30, 2008. As damage from the crisis scaled up, Korea's growth forecast for 2009 was revised down by 1 percent point to around 4% and I revised the budget before the National Assembly took it up on November 3. The revised 284 trillion won budget aimed at minimizing the fallout from the crisis on our economy and cooperating with the global community to overcome the crisis. It included a 10 trillion won increase in expenditure and a 1.7 trillion won reduction in revenue. That produced an 18 trillion won shortfall in revenue, which was covered by issuing government bonds. Consequently, the fiscal deficit rose to 2.1% and national debt increased to 34.3% of GDP.

I explained to the Special Committee on Budget of the National

Assembly on November 19 that the budget was designed to be a preemptive, decisive, and sufficient enough to effectively deal with the unprecedented global economic crisis. I said that the top priorities were placed on increasing growth potential, creating jobs, and stabilizing the people's livelihoods. To these ends, I adjusted the priorities of each item. Investments in R&D, industries and energy, and SOC were moved to the top, which was followed by welfare, education, and the environment.

The previous leftist administrations had put welfare before anything else. I made R&D investment the No. 1 item. I planned to raise it by 11.4%, faster than the overall 8.3% growth of expenditures, and on an annual average of 10% until it took up 5% of the GDP. Industrial and energy investment and SOC investment were planned to rise 10.2% and 20.2%, respectively. The salaries and the number of public officials were frozen. After being adjusted during the deliberation, the 284.5 trillion won budget which consisted of 217.5 trillion won in government accounts and 80.4 trillion won in funds was passed unilaterally by the ruling party on December 13.

The budget represented an increase of 27.3 trillion won or 10.6% of GDP from a year earlier, which rose further to 37.9 trillion won or 3.7% of GDP if 10.6 trillion won in tax rebates to ease the impact of high oil prices and the supplementary budget were included. Given tax cuts of 34.9 trillion won, including 1.9 trillion won in lowered tariff rates on TRQ item, the total fiscal injection by the Korean government at that time amounted 72.8 trillion won or 7.1% of its GDP. This was larger and faster than those by any other OECD economy.

The Finance Ministry presented a report of their work plans for 2009 to the President in the Office of the President on December 16, 2008 with representatives from all ministries present. The report, titled "2009 Economic Policy Directions for Growth into an Advanced Nation" was submitted earlier than usual —such reports had been usually submitted in the year's beginning. Following the first cut to 4% when preparing the revised budget in November, the growth forecast was lowered again to around 3%. We expected the current surplus to reach US$10 billion; the number of the newly-employed around 100,000; and consumer inflation, around 3%. Growth outlook was 2.2% for the world economy and −0.3% for advanced economies.

Other preemptive efforts to weather a slowdown included signing contracts for government-financed projects in December and deciding to spend 60% of the annual budget within the first half of the year. A number of special measures were taken in line with this. We formed project funds quickly through issuance of government bonds irrespective of tax collection schedule, shortened the lead time for concluding construction contracts from the usual 90 days to 45 days by using fast-track bidding process, and allowed individual ministries to place an order for their projects to expedite spending. Previously, project orders had to wait to be bundled by the Public Procurement Service.

The Finance Ministry presented a report on shifting of its fiscal policy to a balanced one from expansion at a fiscal strategy meeting on May 9, 2009 when the global economic crisis calmed down. As the Special Economic Advisor to the President, I contended that Korea needed to go on offense, not a defense, considering advanced nations had nosedived into a low-growth trough and were weighed down with national debt ratio of about 100%.

I strongly argued that it would be a mistake for Korea to strive for fiscal balance when its national debt ratio was a manageable 33.4%; there was no compelling need to join the debt-strapped advanced nations' push for fiscal austerity. I likened the situation to a soccer game in which a defensive play could produce a tie at best, but an offensive play could secure victory. I said that Korea should push through an expansion until the debt ratio reached 50% so as to become a new economic power after the end of the crisis. Increased national debt could be dealt with increased taxes and fiscal tightening after the end of the historic survival game being waged at the moment, I added. After extensive haggling over the policy direction, President Lee chose "expansionary balance." Even though "expansionary balance" was decided, the Korean government ran a 1.5% fiscal surplus and the country's sovereign debt stood at 34.0% in 2011. The next year it posted a 4.6 trillion won budget surplus.

The defensive fiscal policy along with the abolition of additional 2% cuts in income and corporate tax rates from 2011 turned out to be missteps. To me, the action was like a lightly-indebted, promising company rejecting additional financing from banks and beginning to repay debt because its rivals were doing so. It meant bypassing opportunities to beat competitors. I used the analogy several times to try to persuade relevant officials to shift the fiscal policy, but to no avail. The dominant principle for managing the Korean economy at that time was fiscal conservatism.

The Korean economy grew 0.3% in 2009 thanks to aggressive fiscal and financial stimulation. In the meantime, the world economy contracted 0.4% and in particular advanced economies shrank 3.2% in the same year. For three years from 2010, the world economy expanded by 5.2%, 3.9%, and 3.2% and advanced economies 3.0%, 1.7%, and 1.5%. During the same period, the Korean economy grew 6.5%, 3.7%, and 2.3%. These figures showed that we missed a great opportunity to become an economic powerhouse due to fiscal conservatism.

| SOC investment: Four rivers development

The second task to improve business environments was the multifunctional Grand Korea Waterway project. The construction project was designed not only to develop inland water transportation method but to achieve water management, water resources conservation, and inland development and to boost the economy and reinforce the infrastructure for service sector opportunities. The plan was first known as the Grand Korea Canal project although canals represented only a small portion of waterways to be affected. The project had to be renamed the Four Major Rivers Restoration project at the execution stage.

Ships traveled up and down the Hangang and Nakdonggang rivers until the 19th century but passage became impossible in the 20th Century. Too much soil accumulated on the river beds due to reckless logging in forests. Rivers became more and more polluted and summer floods increasingly cost lives and serious property damage. Thus, the necessity of water management increased. A canal on the Hangang river was considered as early as 1978.

Initially designed as a means to improve the country's inland distribution system, the project grew in size as other functions were added such as boosting of domestic demand and managing of water resources to prepare for water shortages. In other words, the project became the Korean version of the US New Deal infrastructure projects during the Great Depression years. It envisioned not only inland water transportation but also better water management as seen in Europe and new growth engines in the service sector.

I became involved in the Grand Korea Waterway project in 2005 by hosting the research into the ways to improve the distribution system, including the Seoul–Busan waterway which covered the Seoul metropolitan area as the President of the Seoul Development Institute. The Grand Korea Waterway project was adopted as an official campaign pledge of the then presidential candidate Lee Myung–bak in 2007 based on the results of the study. President Lee had first presented the proposal on the Seoul–Busan waterway in 1995 as a lawmaker. According to the proposal, 90% of the waterways used in the past would be employed. The less than 10% consisted of a canal that would be built through the Sobaek Mountains.

The project plan envisaged as many as 17 routes running 3,100 kilometers in total: Seoul–Busan, Geumgang, and Yeongsangang waterways with 12 routes of 2,100 kilometers on the southern side of the Korean peninsula and Yeseonggang, Daedonggang, and Cheongcheongang waterways with five routes of 1,000 kilometers on the northern side. The initial stage was construction of the Seoul–Busan waterway. The estimated cost was 15 trillion won with construction lasting four years. Build–operate–transfer contracts were considered to avoid additional financial burden on the public purse. Sale of sand and gravel dredged from the rivers, projected at around 8 trillion won, was expected to subsidize half of the project.

We expected the Seoul–Busan waterway to take up 20% of the freight transported on the Seoul–Busan Expressway at a cost only a third that spent for moving on the road. In addition, as a 2,500–ton ship would emit less pollution than 2,500 1–ton cargo trucks would do, we expected the waterway to serve as the second Seoul–Busan expressway boasting higher cost–efficiency and environment–friendliness. Redesigning and reconstruction of national land was another outcome we desired. We hoped inland cities to be transformed into port cities with thriving industries and the water sports industry, and especially the yacht industry to grow, creating 700,000 new jobs. All in all, the waterway project was designed to have more effects on reconstruction of national land and development of relevant industries, than on transportation.

The waterways plan was highly controversial. It stirred heated debate during the presidential election campaign itself. Environmental, religious, and civic groups were among the naysayers. After the election, the plan was repackaged as a water control project involving the four major rivers of the country, namely the Hangang, the Nakdonggang, the Geumgang, and the Yeongsangang. But opposing interest groups were unmoved and maintained strong resistance.

The Four Major Rivers Restoration project was kicked off on December 29, 2008 in the Nakdonggang area and lasted until April 22, 2012. During the period, 22.3 trillion won was spent to dredge the four rivers, build eco-friendly dams to raise water volume of reservoirs, restore nearby ecosystems, and lay the groundwork for the tourism and leisure industry. Up to now, the areas have been used only for recreational bicycling. However, if tourism and leisure infrastructure is constructed in the future, the areas will help boost private consumption and create jobs. People living nearby the rivers no longer have to constantly worry about floods.

Local governments and people in the affected areas welcomed the project. However, protests by religious, environmental, and civic groups, who warned of destruction of ecosystem, water quality degradation, and pollution continued throughout the project period. As someone involved from the beginning of the project, I would like to say that there were no other plausible options to bulk up the service sector infrastructure to create jobs. In addition, experts who examined the environmental aspects of the project asserted that the project would not damage the ecosystem or water quality and not pollute the environment. I believe time will tell the truth.

Forex controls: Stopping 'hot' money

To improve management environments, it is also important to control cross-border flows of short-term funds, thereby stabilizing foreign exchange rates and the markets.

In a small open economy, the correlation between foreign exchange rates and growth is high. This implies that the Korean economy is highly susceptible to short-term foreign funds, which have a high influence on foreign exchange rates. We learned from the 1997 currency crisis that short-term foreign funds act as a double-edged sword. They appreciate the won in normal times but are vulnerable to sudden outflows. Thus, it is difficult to control the supply and demand of foreign currencies during a crisis.

Korea's current account balance and economic growth rates moved in the same direction for ten years from 2001 while cross-border capital flowed in the opposite direction. This shows a negative correlation between foreign capital inflows and economic growth. Therefore, economic policies must focus on control of foreign exchange rates and short-term foreign funds. It was assumed that the net inflow of US$34.3 into Korea in 2004 shored up the won by 14.7%, undermining its economic growth and the net inflow of US$76.3 billion during three years from 2009 appreciated the currency by 9.0%, dragging down the economy into a low-growth trough in 2011.

Korea is a net creditor and has maintained a current account surplus since 2009. The time has come to shift the focus of its foreign currency management from capital import to capital export as the negative impact of cross-border short-term money on economies like Korea's is significant. The debt-to-equity ratio of the country's manufacturing sector plunged to 100% from around 400% during the 1997 currency crisis. Given that interest rates influence only 1.5% of the financial cost but foreign exchange rates completely affect sales revenue, interest rates are not as important a factor in business operations.

Economic forecasts by major international institutions such as the IMF and the OECD and central banks of advance nations have been wrong since the 2008 economic crisis. Data suggests that the predictions were drawn from the standard macroeconomic models or the dynamic stochastic general equilibrium models, which contain households, non-financial businesses, and governments, but not banks. Banks were a simple "veil" in the real economy although speculative transactions by banks were at the center of the crisis. As such, we need to develop a new leading indicator that mainly tracks flows of capital. Cross-border capital significantly disturbs the real economy. Speculative financial transactions were the primary cause of the 1997 crisis and put a tremendous burden on us during the 2008 economic crisis.

In 2008, I envisioned the capital transaction tax in a bid to prevent excessive volatility in foreign exchange rates caused by volatility of short-term foreign funds. The idea had to be shelved, however, as spiking exchange rates made it more difficult to manage the crisis and raised concerns over inflationary pressure.

Structural means to stop excessive flows of short-term money include control of positions on currency forwards, higher taxation on investment gains, taxation on capital transactions, and regulation of offshore currency markets. It is easy for speculative hedge funds and carry-trade money to make a profit by buying stocks and bonds, and then hedging in the forward market. Currency hedging in the offshore currency forward market in particular is a popular tactic. There was no income tax or capital transaction tax on gains earned by short-term foreign capital using interest rate or currency speculation. Korea's equity index option market and offshore currency market were once the largest in the world, which was absurd given the size of its economy. Cross-border speculators raked in profits, freely moving between the country's spot and forward markets and the offshore market without taxes and restrictions on depositing and withdrawing, a potentially fatal problem in a small, open economy. Not surprisingly, Korea became known as Asia's ATM and bonanza.

Backed by three layers of protection against a currency crisis—current account surplus, US$90 billion the US-China-Japan currency swap arrangement, and US$100 billion external payment guarantee—we were also able to issue US$3 billion FESB on April 30, 2009. At that time, we had to control inflows of speculative capital. However, the finance ministry granted tax exemption to foreigners on their interest income from government bonds and stabilization fund bonds on May 21.

Additional gains foreign speculators secured through the exemption of 14% income tax and 20% corporate tax were estimated at 30% at the most, considering the around 4% profit they were realizing in the form of interest rate differential and currency speculation. Granting of tax exemptions was a serious misstep taken at a time when the country had to introduce capital transaction tax. Senior Finance Ministry officials also held investment fairs abroad to attract more capital, even though short-term foreign currency holdings needed to be reduced. The officials' action reflected the continuing trauma of the 1997 currency crisis.

As a senior economic advisor, I provided reports to President Lee on a variety of fiscal and financial issues. I touched upon regulation of capital transactions several times. The finance ministry and I had a different opinion on foreign exchange rates and regulation of capital transactions. In addition, the ministry did not want to create controversy as it was preparing for the 2010 G-20 Seoul Summit to be chaired by Korea.

The atmosphere began to change with an IMF report titled "Capital Inflows: The Role of Controls" on February 19, 2010. In the report, the IMF stressed the need to regulate capital inflows and impose tax on short-term debt, signaling a reversal in its attitude toward market exchange rates and capital liberalization although it was not an official stance. The report was a harbinger of a sea change to the international financial order and we were able to prepare for it in advance.

On March 23, I presented a report titled, "Review of Economic Situations and Preemptive Actions" to the President. I argued, "Despite the positive atmosphere about economic situations, there are negative signs regarding growth, exports, and unemployment from 2010. Therefore, we need to reexamine the situations and adopt a strategy to consolidate our hard-won victory through preemptive actions. Our efforts over the past two years are likely to come to naught without such actions. We have to carefully devise an exit strategy and at the same time revisit policies for foreign exchange rates, tax cuts, and the budget. In particular, all of our efforts will end in vain unless we effectively deal with the issue of speculative money finding shelter in Korea for their investments into emerging economies through preemptive policies. A variety of measures are available from regulation of non-deliverable forwards and control of currency positions to taxation of bank liabilities and capital transactions. Not only the IMF but the US, the UK, Germany, and China call for the need to impose tax on capital transactions. Brazil already charged 2% tax on currency transactions by foreign investors to stabilize its foreign exchange rates from 2009, and the US announced it would impose a 0.15% tax on bank liabilities."

Around that time, another presidential advisor on international finance, Shin Hyun Song, who teaches at Princeton University, gave a report to President Lee on taxing bank liabilities. His view was similar to mine, except for one thing. He insisted that a bank levy would be more effective than a capital transaction tax because the main agent of sharp movements of short-term money was banks. We decided to introduce bank levy first and then wait and see before imposing capital transaction tax.

First, leverage caps, which had been announced on June 13, 2010, were introduced in October, 2010 on banks' foreign exchange derivatives positions. The caps required domestic banks to limit their foreign exchange derivatives position at 50 %

of their equity and foreign bank branches, at 250%. Since then, they had been tightened twice by 10% each to 30% for domestic banks and by 50% each to 150% for foreign bank branches. In addition, foreigners were subject to withholding taxes on their bond holdings from January 2011 at 14% on interest income and 20% on gains from trade. In August of the same year, a bank levy was introduced on non-core foreign exchange liabilities of banks with the rate varying between 0.2% for liabilities shorter than one year, 0.1% for those from one to three years, and 0.05% for those longer than three years. The earnings were channeled into the foreign exchange stabilization fund. The introduction of the bank levy in 2011 became the government's final macro-prudential action.

Seeing currency speculation and cross-border movements of short-term money inundating in the foreign exchange market, I think we should have introduced a capital transaction tax from the beginning. We need to suppress the offshore currency forward market by banning residents, including local banks from making deals in the market and tighten regulation of the local forward market. Also, we need to be better prepared for a crisis by increasing the foreign exchange stabilization fund through increased bank levies. The carefully designed macro-prudential measures reflected economic indices agreed at the G-20 Seoul Summit and laid the firm foundation for regulation of cross-border movements of capital.

Sovereignty over forex rates: G-20 Seoul Summit agreement

Foreign exchange rates are one of the most critical variables for businesses operating in a small, open economy like Korea's. Putting a brake on excessive cross-border flows of funds requires international agreement on exchange rate operations. The Korean government had been under pressure from the IMF and the US to refrain from intervening in the currency market. It was my toughest challenge in managing international finance. Against this backdrop, the agreement on the principles of government intervention on foreign exchange rates reached at the G-20 Seoul Summit on November 11, 2010 brought a Copernican change to the world's attitude toward the rates.

The G-20 Seoul Summit was meaningful for us on two fronts. First, we switched our role from rule-taker to one of the rule-makers by steering an international conference which decided an important international order for the first time in our history, thereby heightening the country's stature on the international stage. Second, we faithfully acted as the intermediary on behalf of periphery nations in setting new principles on foreign exchange rates, which were major obstructions to periphery nations.

The summit participants agreed to three principles on foreign exchange rates: 1. They would move toward enhanced exchange rate flexibility to reflect underlying economic fundamentals and refrain from competitive devaluation of currency, 2. Advanced economies, including those with reserve currencies, would be vigilant against excessive volatility and disorderly movement in exchange rate, and 3. In circumstances where countries are facing undue burden of adjustment, policy responses in emerging market economies with adequate reserves and increasingly overvalued flexible exchange rates may also include carefully designed macro-prudential measures.

Before the Seoul Summit was held, an agreement was reached on the foreign exchange rate principles at the G-20 Finance Ministers' and Central Bank Governors' Meeting in Gyeongju on October 23, 2010. I was moved when Senior Secretary to the President for Economic Affairs Choi Joong Kyung telephoned me with news of the agreement. He advocated sovereignty over foreign exchange rates and priority to external balance. The agreement was meaningful personally as well because it ended a 25-year long journey. It began with the Plaza Accord I had witnessed as a financial attaché in New York in 1985. Six years later, as the Director General of the International Finance Bureau of the Finance Ministry, I collided with the US over foreign exchange rates and then the currency crisis hit Korea in 1997. In 1991, I first argued for sovereignty over foreign exchange rates and in 1997 I realized that the sovereignty laid the foundation for national governance.

Senior Secretary Choi who made tremendous efforts to forge the agreement in Gyeongju and Assistant Minister Shin Je-Yoon, who had been committed to the principles from the G-20 Washington Summit on November 15, 2008, steered historic achievements in international finance. I would like to pay my respect to Minister of Finance Yoon Jeung-hyun who showed leadership to reach the agreement as the chairman of the G-20 Finance Ministers' Meeting in Gyeongju.

The Gyeongju agreement came out of a long process. Under a rotating system to decide who should chair the G-20 finance ministers' and central bank governors' meeting slated for 2010, it was an Asian country's turn. At a meeting in Madrid in May 2008, I met with the finance ministers of China and Japan and we agreed that I should be the chair. This was because Chinese Finance Minister Xie Xuren was newly appointed to the post and Japanese Finance Minister was scheduled to chair the Asia-Pacific Economic Cooperation meeting.

The decision for me to hold the chairmanship simply came by a stroke of luck. At the extraordinary G-20 meeting of finance ministers and central bank governors in Washington on October 11, 2008, Korea and the US held prior consultations for Korea's chairmanship and at the regular G-20 finance ministers' and central bank governors' meeting in Sao Paulo held on November 8-9, Korea was decided as the next chair country following the UK. The first G-20 Summit was held in Washington on November 15, 2008, during which time US Assistant Secretary for International Affairs Clay Lowery told Assistant Minister Shin that the US intended to maintain the troika structure of the G-20 finance ministers' meeting—a three-member steering group of past, present, and future chairs—into the G-20 summit meeting.

Before world leaders agreed to have the G-20 structure for summit meetings, French President Nicolas Sarkozy insisted on Group of Fourteen (G-14) while Japan opposed a G-20 format, due to its testy relations with China. The G-14 system included the G-7 countries and BRICs, but did not guarantee membership for the remaining three. The probability of Korea having a seat was very low. With no certainty of having a G-20 or G-14, Senior Presidential Secretary for Economic Affairs Bahk Byong-Won, Senior Economic Advisor SaKong Il, and I attended a meeting chaired by President Lee. I contended that given the dynamics of international politics, G-14 was less probable since it could threaten the US leadership and G-20 was the only option for us. President Lee concluded that the finance ministry should pursue G-20 and advisor SaKong Il should press for G-14, and would visit France and the UK to make that happen.

US President George W. Bush made a surprise visit at the extraordinary meeting of finance ministers and central bankers on October 11, 2008 which was being held at the same as the annual IMF meeting. Seeing it, I realized that President Bush had chosen the G-20 system as the mechanism for international cooperation to deal with the ongoing crisis before he left office at the end of the year.

Aside from the elevation of the finance ministerial meeting to summit level, whether we could hold the chairmanship for summit meeting was uncertain due to opposition from Japan. However, it did not raise an objection to our chairmanship at the Korea-China-Japan summit meeting on finance held in Fukuoka, Japan on December 13, 2008, seeing the decision was almost reached in favor of G-20 around that time at the US leadership. In addition, President Lee did all he could do, including appealing for friendship with President Bush and President Barack Obama, which was a big help to make the Seoul Summit a success.

The initial G-20 Summit was held under the banner of Summit on Financial Markets and the World Economy in Washington on November 15, 2008 where global leaders discussed ways to enhance international cooperation to overcome the 2008 crisis. President Bush exercised leadership to make it happen before his term end at the end of the year. The Washington Summit was followed by other summit meetings in London in 2009 and Seoul in 2010. Since then, the summit has been held on an annual basis, providing the most important forum for discussion on international order.

In the run-up to the Gyeongju finance ministerial meeting and Seoul summit meeting in 2010, I submitted a report to the President, titled "G-20 Agenda on Foreign Exchange Rates and Strategies for Relations with the US, China, and Japan" on October 13. The report sought four courses of action. It recommended: 1. the G-20 establish an international mechanism to enhance exchange rate flexibility to reflect underlying economic fundamentals; 2. the US pledge not to debase the dollar and refrain from conducting another quantitative easing worth US$1 trillion with zero interest rate; 3. China manage the yuan with flexibility based on economic fundamentals; and 4. Japan, Brazil, and other developing countries join in the international cooperation in these efforts. I sent the report to the finance ministry as well in order for the contents to be reflected in the leaders' declaration. Finally, the G-20 Seoul Summit was held on November 11 chaired by Korea and the agreement on foreign exchange rates was reached in cooperation with the US and the IMF.

The G-20 system is significant in terms of international politics. Around the inception of the Bretton Woods System in 1945, the world was a unipolar system dominated by the US. The Group of Five, consisting of the US, the UK, France, Germany, and Japan, was born out of the need to find ways to overcome the oil shock in 1974. The group was expanded to the Group of Seven (G-7) with Italy and Canada joining. The emergence of the BRICs (Brazil, Russia, India, and China) with vast land, population, and resources threatened the representativeness of G-7 in the 1990s. The need for a new forum for consultation to avoid recurrence of the Asian financial crisis also rose. The G-20 meeting of finance ministers and central bankers was founded in 1999 against this backdrop.

Collectively, the G-20 countries represent 60% of the world population, 85% of the world GDP, and 80% of the world trade. The group consists of five countries in Asia (Korea, China, Japan, India, and Indonesia), five in Europe (the UK, France, Germany, Italy, and the European Union), five in America (the US, Canada, Mexico, Brazil, and Argentina), and other five countries (Russia, Turkey, Saudi Arabia, South Africa, and Australia).

Korea rose to a rule maker from a rule taker by hosting the G-20 Summit to set a new international order as the chair for the first time in Asia and among developing countries. It was a blessing in our history as well as a significant change in the international power dynamics.

| Financing for overseas projects: Fostering mega-banks

The fourth strategy to improve the business environment is to foster globally competitive large banks capable of providing active support for businesses. They can also play a leading role in developing Korea's financial industry.

The need to foster large banks was first raised by McKinsey Korea in its report to the Presidential Transition Committee in 2008. The consulting firm recommended fostering a "champion" bank that would provide massive financing for overseas projects, helping Korea become an advanced nation. The firm suggested merging of policy lenders Korea Development Bank and Small and Medium Industry Bank, known as Industrial Bank of Korea (IBK), with Woori Bank to create a "key player" with 500 trillion won in assets, ranking 10th or higher in Asia and 50th or higher in the world. The synergy would be imposing with KDB's project financing, IBK's small and medium-sized corporate business with Woori Bank's large corporate and retail banking blended together, McKinsey stressed. At that time, Woori Bank was the largest bank in the country, with Korea Deposit Insurance Corporation (KDIC) as a major shareholder. It ranked 13th in Asia and 71st in the world.

The then president-elect Lee Myung-bak received a modified version of the McKinsey report; the suggestion to merge KDB and Woori Bank and omit IBK, the small and medium enterprise-specialized bank, to avoid possible political controversy. The idea of a having a "champion bank" also was changed into "mega-bank".

Widespread discussion on a mega-bank ensued, motivated partly by Korea's need to provide a large performance bond to the United Arab Emirates (UAE) to export nuclear power plants and massive project financing to build such plants in Turkey. In 2009, the UAE demanded a performance bond issued by one of the world's top 50 banks with an AA or higher credit rating as a precondition for a contract to import nuclear power plants. Korea did not have such a bank and was able to provide a government guarantee for Korea Electric Power Corporation since it was state-owned. Facing the demand from the client, we had to pay a dear price to secure the performance bond from Standard Chartered. Taking the occasion of receiving the order from the UAE, the Korean government unveiled a plan to nurture nuclear generation into an export industry which ranked among the top three in the world. The plan targeted the export of 10 nuclear power plants by 2012 and 80 by 2030, thereby taking up 20% of the world's nuclear power plant construction market. Minister of Knowledge Economy Choi Joong Kyung presented the plan to President Lee on February 8, 2011. A decision also was made on combining KDB and Woori Bank into a mega-bank capable of financing large-scale projects such as construction of nuclear power plants overseas.

I assumed responsibility for the banks' merger and development of the new institution into a mega-bank by taking the posts of Chairman and CEO of KDB Financial Group and President of KDB Bank on March 11, 2011. Initially, I turned down the offer twice. I had opposed the privatization of KDB since the idea was first broached in 2007 election campaigning. But, my personal convictions had to take a backseat to the request from the Office of the President.

Before taking office, I reflected on the privatization idea from scratch and submitted a plan to develop a mega-bank capable of financing large offshore projects, which was approved by the President.

As Chairman and CEO of KDB Financial Group, I drafted a plan called "Pioneer Bank of Asia." In the plan, I stressed that Korea needed to have a large corporate and investment bank to play a role not only in the domestic market as the top bank but in the world, where it should be in the top 10 in Asia and top 50 globally. If merged with Woori Bank, KDB would be positioned to become a champion bank with a balanced business portfolio in retail, corporate, and investment banking sectors, and serve as a pioneering partner for Korean firms to finance their overseas projects such as construction of nuclear power plants and high-speed railways. The plan was intended to transform KDB into a globally competitive financial group with a balanced portfolio in a short time through M&As as were the cases of US JPMorgan Chase and Singaporean DBS. It was a rare opportunity which could be seized by a simple decision of the government. Meanwhile, mergers between private financial groups would demand massive restructuring to lower redundancies in personnel and branches with the synergy prospects very limited.

Also, the feasibility was low due to large shares held by foreign investors.

Against this backdrop, the plan on KDB Financial Group's purchase of Woori Financial Group was announced on May 17, 2011. It ignited fierce resistance from the group's labor union and opposition parties. Opposition came from the academia, too, which argued that the effect would be limited. The opposition parties complicated the situation for the government. I proposed an alternate approach. It envisaged slow, but independent growth of KDB by raising capital through initial public offering (IPO), strengthening retail banking operation in the domestic market, and securing M&As overseas. The drive to merge the two financial groups ended with submitting a report to the National Assembly that KDB Financial Group would not participate in the bidding to buy Woori Financial Group on June 14. Soon after, we lost the bid to Japan for nuclear power plants in Turkey due to the inability to provide large-project financing.

Following the serial collapse of banks amid the economic crisis, a new sort of banks emerged. With government as a major shareholder, banks were raising capital through IPOs in the capital market on the backing of government credit. Upon the advice of Goldman Sachs, I pushed for IPO of KDB Financial Group with a "50% plus one share" plan to secure at least 50% of the group for the government. Opposition parties and the labor union objected to the plan and time passed without decision by the government. Goldman Sachs was confident that an IPO would be a big success. It estimated the share price would reach 1.5 times of the price-to-book ratio given the high demand overseas. At that time, the private commercial bank's share price was only 0.8 time of the ratio at highest.

Tasks within my control were to expansion of domestic retail banking and pursuit of M&As overseas. In fact, expansion of retail banking was not an option but a requisite since KDB had to shore up its liquidity coverage ratio from 30% to over 100% by 2015 in order to receive fair credit ratings in the global market. The group also needed to reconfigure its financing structure by raising the portion of deposits from 10% to 30% while reducing the high dependence on industrial financial debentures and offshore borrowing to about 30% each.

KDB had only 48 branches nationwide. So, it was impossible to reinforce retail banking through conventional means against rivals operating about 1,000 branches on average. We found a way in branch-less direct banking, which was being implemented by HSBC in Seoul. Based on the advice of ING Direct, which was enjoying huge success in the US, we launched KDB Direct which unconditionally paid 4.5% on deposits on September 29, 2011. The motto was "Simple Product, Independent Operation, and Unique Hiring" and the goal was to raise 100 billion won within one year. We hired ten high school graduates to market the new product. We started it on a small scale, mindful that HSBC's direct banking was underperforming. We hired students from specialized vocational high schools to fill bank clerk positions, seeking potential, not high academic results. I told the recruits, "You are founders, pioneers, and partners." The direct banking team was allowed a high degree of autonomy in terms of organizational matter, working rules, and wages. The result was a mega-success. We recruited 30 extra clerks with the deposit exceeding 100 billion won on November 2, a month after launch and raised the workforce to 100 as the deposits broke the 1 trillion won mark in May 3, 2012, seven months after the launch. The deposit continued to grow, reaching 5 trillion won on September 21, 2012; 7.5 trillion won at year-end; and nearly 10 trillion won on April 4, 2013, the day I retired from the chairman post.

Fifteen deposit products were integrated into KDB Dream paying up to 3.5%. We decided to lower the operating cost of each branch to 1.2 billion won. To save on rent, branches shared office with KDB Daewoo Securities, the group's affiliate or operated above ground level. The staff per branch also was reduced to about five. In comparison, other commercial banks were operating their branches with 12 employees at an operating cost of 6 billion won. The deposits at the branches averaged 150 billion. KDB Dream was a channel to transfer the cost saved through belt-tightening to customers in the form of higher interest rates. We depended on "mouth-evangelist" to promote the product and the result was a huge success, too.

Robust performance by retail operation and strong lending boosted KDB's total assets by 26.3% from 113.2 trillion won in 2010 to 143.0 trillion won in 2012 while growth for other commercial banks remained at 7.2% on average during the same period. These accomplishments were important for the company's share price to be fairly valued when the bank went public.

In addition, the company acquired the Royal Bank of Scotland

Uzbekistan. Acquisition of an Indonesian bank also was pursued but failed. As the first step to expand across Europe, we reshuffled KDB Bank Hungary into KDB Bank Europe.

The inauguration of a new administration in 2013 changed everything. The new government decided to disband the KDB Financial Group and consolidate it with the Korea Finance Corporation, which had been separated from KDB previously, to found a new policy financing institution.

KDB Financial Group had a total workforce of 7,200 and six affiliates—KDB Bank, KDB Daewoo Securities, KDB Life Insurance, KDB Capital, KDB Asset Management, and KDB Infrastructure Investments—and total assets of 184 trillion won. Many foreign consulting firms thought KDB could become the best financial group in Asia. The window of opportunity would not last long and would not open easily again. I felt the country's financial industry development would regress if the attempts failed. Behind the misguided decisions were misunderstandings about policy financing and retail banking, which was very regrettable.

All my efforts to advance KDB Financial Group into a world-class financial group did not have enough time to bear any fruit. Nevertheless, I cherish the memory of that time I spent at KDB, which was an opportunity to realize my dream to manage a business after retiring from public life. The experience I had with about 100 clerks and managers who strived to design and promote KDB Direct will be long remembered. The efforts my colleagues made in preparing the group to go public left me with unforgettable memory as well.

I finally retired on April 4, 2013, ending the 43 year-long public life, and "went with the wind."

| Social capital build-up:
Trust decides 20% of growth

Social capital is vital to a business environment. It coordinates relationships among interest groups and enables norms, trust, and solidarity to work to encourage cooperation in society. We need to accumulate social capital based on the rule of law and trust to reinforce the country's economic capability. The effect of low social capital on business environments is readily seen in the consequences of militant labor strikes. Korea has industrialized its society based on traditional paternalism, rather than on the rule of law. Law of the masses and law of emotions take precedence over politics, the economy, and diverse sectors of society.

In *Trust*, Francis Fukuyama argued economics determines 80% of an economy and trust decides the remaining 20%. He divided countries into "high trust" society with strong community solidarity, naming Japan and Germany, and "low trust" society with low community solidarity, citing Korea and China. Certainly, we lack the invisible social capital that determines the remaining 20%.

Social capital of the rule of law and solidarity can be accumulated by establishing laws and regulations based on honesty and institutions in accordance with global standards.

According to a philosophy of law, someone may commit a crime by making a law an average person cannot observe. Laws which benefit the observers and institutions meeting the international standards are important factors to ensure the best business environments when the global economy becomes borderless.

If the rule of laws and regulations based on honesty is firmly established, violent labor-management disputes will disappear, crippled political functions will be restored, and the productivity of the Korean economy will jump. A KDI report contended that the economy would grow another 1% without illegal labor strikes. The number of business days lost to labor disputes in 2008 fell below 1,000 after staying above 1,000 days from 2000. The number could fall further if both labor and management observe the law. The violent labor disputes involved union workers, who represent only 10% of the national workforce. The clashes aggravated social divide and hindered the efforts to resolve disadvantages facing irregular workers, who account more than 30% of the total workforce. In a bid to deal with the problem, some called for a revision of the labor relation laws in accordance with International Labor Organization conventions. However, no progress has been made and the rule of law continues to give little respect in labor disputes, which has further aggravated the business environment.

A country needs to have systems that meet global standards when it opens up and integrates with the world into one global village. The existence of such systems is an important determinant to the quality of the country's business environment. It is especially important to have laws and regulations on roads, signs, and transportation in line with the global standards in order to facilitate the travel and tourism industry. I believe systematic realignment is the very first step toward accumulation of social capital and heightening of external competitiveness.

Establishment of laws and regulations based on honesty and systems in accordance with the global standards is essential for accumulating social capital. As a former law student and drafter, I strongly believe that Korea cannot become an advanced nation as long as law of the masses and law of emotions take precedence and systems remain below global standard, suppressing competitiveness. Accumulation of social capital is the prerequisite for entry into the ranks of advanced nations.

| Mobilizing externally: Korean diaspora and FTA

In terms of the number of countries where they relocated, ethnic Koreans constitute one of the biggest diasporas in the world. More than 7 million ethnic Koreans live in about 160 countries, a consequence of the tragedy in our history. They could be an invaluable asset considering Korea's dramatic slowdown in population growth and expectations of increasingly severe labor shortage in the decades ahead. That was the motivation behind granting dual citizenships and allowing unrestricted entry and departure for overseas Koreans as part of the population growth policy in 2010.

Another track in looking abroad is free trade agreements. FTAs provide us an opportunity to expand the scope of geographical areas under our economic influence as far as we want. Starting from the one with Chile in 2004, we have concluded FTAs with the ASEAN, India, the EU, the US, Turkey, Australia, and Canada. Also, negotiations with China and Japan were started. The geographical area covered by Korea's FTA portfolio is larger than any other country. The size of potential markets will have to be increased further by playing an active role in the planned Northeast Asian FTA and the Trans-Pacific Partnership.

Korea is the only country to transform itself from international aid recipient to a donor. On November 25, 2009, it became a member of the OECD Development Assistance Committee (DAC). Unlike other advanced countries, Korea provides not only official development assistance (ODA) but also its economic development know-how, which has been dubbed a "miracle." Saemaul Undong, the country's community-driven development program in the 1970s, receives attention especially. In October 2008, 22 ministerial level officials from 21 African states gathered to attend the Korea-Africa Economic Cooperation Conference. The Korean government established a unique ODA plan that combined financial support and programs to share its development experience, which was well received by the participants. Involvement by private organizations and religious groups in particular will increase the effect of those efforts especially in narrowing the gap between "obesity" of advanced economies and "malnutrition" of developing economies. Youth volunteer programs incorporated into ODA plans will provide work opportunities and cultural enrichment in other countries, which will be a valuable asset for Korea to use to achieve further growth.

20

We Survived Stronger: Top 7 Exporter

Korea became stronger sailing through the global economic crisis. It was unimaginable before the crisis for the country's export volume to be the seventh highest in the world, the credit rating to surpass Japan's, and the country to be the first to transform itself from a recipient to a donor. Korea has transformed itself from a shrimp torn by fighting whales at the dawn of the 20th century to a dolphin, a small but smart creature passing the global economic crisis in the 21st century. The country survived an unprecedented survival game to become stronger and took over rivals, turning the crisis into an opportunity. Fast-track action to cope with the economic crisis helped revive the economy at the fastest pace in the OECD. Consequently, positive growth returned while others were still struggling with contraction. Through preemptive, decisive, and sufficient measures, it lifted its ranking in the world in terms of export, R&D, and credit rating, and raised its stature on the global stage over capital export, setting of the international order, and foreign assistance. The historic shift of power is really taking place!

The vigor and spirit which enabled Koreans to rise from the ashes of the war and overcome authoritarian rule was the only and strong asset we had, which I would term the *get-up-and-go economics*.

In 2008, foreign media sarcastically predicted a recurrence of crisis. They described Korea's economic situation as "1997 rewind," "heading for black September," "Asia's Iceland," and "as risky as Poland" which was ranked third after South Africa and Hungary. However, they quickly switched to plaudits the next year when the economy began recovering at the fastest pace in the OECD.

CNN reported on April 24, 2009 that Korea staved off a recession through a $37 billion stimulus package in a surprise move to the market. *Bloomberg* ran a column that said, "Hats off to officials in Seoul" on July 27, 2009. *Financial Times* said that Korea was no more a loser, the economy was as big as India's with a population 20 times larger than Korea's, and the exports was bigger than that of the UK on February 24, 2010. *The Economist* reported that Korean development model set an example for developing economies; the country needed a new path on November 12, 2011.

In a report on January 18, 2010, the OECD assessed that our fiscal and financial measures, including those on foreign exchange and interest rates, boosted the economy faster than expected. In an interview on August 5, 2011, the IMF which had guided us during the 1997 crisis also praised our response, saying that the Korean government's fast and decisive measures set a textbook example on how to stimulate an economy in recession. Economists who had pounded me were speechless, and the media and politicians pressuring me to step down remained silent

We became stronger and got seven achievements in tackling the 2008 turmoil with the "get-up-and-go" spirit and by turning the crisis into an opportunity. They were; the fastest recovery in the OECD; rise as the world's seventh largest exporter; the world's highest R&D investment relative to GDP; switchover to capital exporter; highest credit rating in Asia; transformation into a rule making country; and transition from a recipient to a donor. Behind the stellar achievements was great devotion of public officials at the Budget Office, the Tax and Customs Office, the Economic Policy Bureau, and the International Finance Bureau of my ministry as well as the President's excellent leadership.

The priority given to external balance meant activity to boost domestic demand fell short. Critics said the government efforts to stabilize foreign exchange rates were done only to benefit exports and large corporations. However, the policy was unavoidable in order to manage the crisis since we believed deterioration in exports would bring much graver damage to the economy. We cannot avoid the moment of choice when deciding on economic policies, which is all the more true at times of crisis.

Fastest recovery in OECD

The emergency government measures to combat the effects of the global financial crisis i.e. normalization of foreign exchange rates and lowering of interest rates and 73 trillion won worth of fiscal stimulus put Korea a year ahead of fellow OECD member states in terms of recovery. In 2009 the Korean economy expanded 0.3% after the crisis. Meanwhile, other OECD states contracted by 3.5%. In the next year, they expanded by 3.0% and Korea's jumped 6.3%.

In a report titled "How has Korea performed better than expected? A comparison among OECD countries" released on January 18, 2010, Randall S. Jones, Head of the OECD's Korea/Japan Desk, highlighted the steps Korea took to recover from the global economic crisis faster than in other OECD country. They included: 1. a more than 30% decline in the won in effective terms, which increased Korea's competitiveness in world trade, leading to large export market share gains; 2. a rebound in exports, which helped boost output to surpass its pre-crisis level; 3. domestic demand recovery, thanks in part to large-scale fiscal stimulus amounting to 6% of GDP, the largest in the OECD area; 4. fiscal stimulus, which boosted employment by an estimated 200,000 in 2009 and thus contained unemployment and helped sustain private consumption; and 5. easing of monetary policy, which pushed real short-term interest rates into negative territory in early 2009, encouraging investment and easing the debt burden.

In an interview on August 5, 2011, Subir Lall, Chief of Korea Division in IMF's Asia and Pacific Department, praised the

Korean government's response as "quick" and "decisive," saying that it set a "textbook example" on how to use "fiscal policy to help stimulate the economy when it is slowing down." He explained that the rebound in exports had positive impact on the country's export-driven, open economy and thanks to their sound financial base, companies increased output, expanding market shares, and the movements in foreign exchanges rates were favorable for them to improve competitiveness.

The debt ratio of both the government and the corporate sector is one of the lowest in the world despite such aggressive and decisive fiscal and financial measures taken so far. According to the OECD data, its public debt ratio remained low at 35.5% in 2012 while the ratio reached 218.8% in Japan, 102.1% in the US with the overall figure for the OECD averaging 107.4%. Over the course of repelling the crisis, national debt grew 20.7% on average for the club, but it rose only 5.1% for Korea. We seem to have been too frugal. In addition, the debt-to-equity ratio of listed companies remains at the world's lowest level of below 90%.

┃ World's seventh-largest exporter

Korea became the seventh-largest exporter in the world in 2010, emerging as a new powerhouse amid the wreckage of the global crisis. In 2009, Korea's exports shrank 7.8% while that of its OECD cohorts fell 10.9% on average. The next year saw export growth of 15.5% and 12.4%, respectively. As the result, Korea's trade surplus surpassed that of Japan for the first time and its economic size neared that of India, which boasts population as much as 20 times larger than ours. Crisis was an opportunity for Korea to move forward overtaking the rivals.

The trade performance was attributable to improvements in price competitiveness resulting from adjustment of foreign exchange rates to reflect the actual conditions of the economy, and in technology competitiveness due to larger R&D investments. Both the OECD and the IMF cited foreign exchange rates as a main driver. The Trade Day ceremony was held on November 30, 2010 to mark the country's achievement to become the world's seventh largest exporter with US$360 billion in exports and US$40 billion in trade surplus. Attending the event as the Senior Economic Advisor to the President, I was deeply moved by the achievement. I also remembered the harsh criticism and pressure on me to resign in 2008 as I attempted to normalize foreign exchange rates, and the opposing arguments of the BOK and those based on the US-anchored economic theories.

Korea's exports continued to rise from the 12th largest in 2008 to the ninth in 2009 and the seventh in 2010, reaching US$363.5 billion in value and 3% in global market share. That year, sales revenue of Samsung Electronics surpassed that of HP to become the largest in the world and beat that of the top 15 Japanese electronics makers combined. Hyundai Motor Company also posted the biggest operating profit in the industry in 2010 and boosted its share in the US market from 3.7% in 2008 to 4.6%. According to the OECD data, Korea ran a US$30.1 billion surplus in trade of goods in 2011, beating Japan which ran a US$20.2 deficit. It was the first time that Korea beat Japan in the goods trade category. In 2013, Korea registered a US$70.5 billion current account surplus, exceeding Japan's US$33.9 billion surplus, which, too was the first lead of Korea over Japan.

| World's highest R&D investment

In 2012, Korea's R&D investment relative to the GDP was higher than any other in the world. External competitiveness is determined by price competitiveness in the short-term and by technology competitiveness in the long-term. After rising to seventh place in the world, the country's exports remained strong despite strengthening of the won thanks to vigorous technology development and investment. According to the OECD, Korea's R&D investment relative to the GDP was 3.21%, coming fifth in the world in 2008. Its rank rose to the third in 2010 and then to the top in 2012 with the share reaching 4.36%, followed by Israel at 4.20%. Japan was fifth (3.34%), the US 11th (2.79%), and China 19th (1.98%). The OECD average was 2.40%.

A small country that lacks natural resources and has an open economy must rely on technology to compete globally. Technology also is our only means to overcome a situation where excessive foreign capital inflows appreciate the won. With this in mind, we planned to raise the share of R&D out of GDP to 5% in 2008. For this, we decided to increase government R&D investment by at least 10% every year until it reached

1.5% of GDP and lower corporate taxes according to the stage of activity from preparation and investment to research in order to boost private R&D spending to 3.5% of GDP. As the result, we became the top R&D investor in four years. Korea's technology trade deficit widened from US$3.1 billion in 2008 to US$5.7 billion in 2012. This suggests the effects of the increased R&D spending have not been fully materialized. To make the most of the investment, we need to continue to reinforce the infrastructure for trade in intellectual property rights and financial technologies, too.

Public R&D investment which accounted for 1.09% of GDP and private spending, 3.27% in 2012 prove that we are on the right track. In terms of value, however, we still have a way to go. In that year, the US spent an overwhelming amount of US$415.2 billion into R&D, ranking first in the world. This was followed by Japan, the second with US$199.8 billion; China, the third with US$134.4 billion, and Korea came sixth with US$49.2 billion.

According to 2012 EU statistics on private sector R&D investment, Volkswagen topped the list with 9.5 billion euros. Samsung Electronics was second with 8.3 billion euros, followed by Microsoft and Toyota, which ranked third and fifth, respectively. Other companies need to utilize lowered corporate taxes to significantly boost their R&D spending in order for the country to sustain the remarkable achievement of rise as the seventh largest exporter in the world.

| Switchover to capital exporter

Korea has been establishing itself as a capital exporter. In 2008, the country ran a US$5.8 billion current account deficit and held US$30.1 billion in net borrowing. However, a surplus in the current account with capital lending exceeding capital borrowing followed for the next five consecutive years. In 2012, the current account surplus amounted to a new high at US$48 billion; and in 2013, the net lending broke the record to reach US$185.6 billion. Foreign exchange reserves rose from US$201.1 billion in 2008 to US$360.0 billion in 2014.

The country ran a current account surplus for four years in a row from 1986 thanks to the "three lows," namely low value of the dollar to the yen, low oil prices, and low interest rates. It was the first current account surplus since economic development plans began in 1962. After that, it remained in the black for ten years from 1998 thanks to on high exchange rates of the won before lapsing into the red in 2008 due to the exchange rate falling below 1,000 to the dollar in 2006. Korea has been a net creditor since 2009.

Data shows that the country's current account balance deteriorates and capital borrowing surpasses capital lending when the won's exchange rates do not effectively reflect economic fundamentals because of cross-border movements of capital. This occurs especially when the relative ratio of the yen to the won against the dollar drops to 1 to 10 or below. We have no other option but to prevent the won from strengthening and build up foreign reserves as much as possible when countries with a reserve currency begin to ramp up their currency printing presses. That is the only option allowed for a small, open economy.

We still maintain capital importer's mindset, which is probably due to the lasting emotional scars of the 1997 currency crisis. This was demonstrated by the 2009 action to grant tax exemption on bond interests for foreign investors and investment fairs to induce foreign capital. From now on, we have to strive to export our capital and enhance control of inflows of short-term money. We should not forget how foreign capital flows may cause another currency crisis. Korea may quickly change into a net debtor once it fails to shed the capital import's mindset and continues to maintain the exchange rate at an appropriate level. We have to keep the lessons of the 1997 crisis in mind and be aware that the time has come for us to aggressively export capital, while retaining exchange rate momentum.

| Asia's top credit rating

In September 2012, Fitch Ratings raised Korea's rating by two notches to AA−, a notch higher than those of Japan and China, excluding city states. Japan had to see its rating slide to A+ after tumbling two notches from 2009 and China remained at A+. The decision was based on several factors. Korea's national debt ratio fell in the world's lowest 30% level while the OECD average hovered at 100%, and the corporate debt ratio was also in the bottom tier in the world, below 100%. In addition, the country held more than US$180 billion in net credit and more than US$360 billion in foreign reserves.

Moody's put KDB along with HSBC and the Bank of Tokyo-Mitsubishi UFJ at Aa3, the highest, in August 2012. Deutsch Bank, which had been at the top, followed at A2, two notches below. Goldman Sachs was three below at A3 and Citigroup was five below at Bbb2. The capital adequacy ratio of KDB was 15.80%, higher than those of HSBC and the Bank of Tokyo-Mitsubishi UFJ. In this sense, it was fair to say that KDB was the most creditworthy bank in the world, which was unimaginable in the past.

As the Chairman and CEO of KDB Financial Group, I was surprised and deeply moved by the news. Banks I had highly regarded in 1986 when I was in New York as a financial attaché were ranked below KDB, and Citigroup, which had helped the country at times of crisis, was as much as five notches below. This attests to the saying that the strong don't always survive but survivors become the strong.

Private companies' credit ratings rose sharply, too, especially from those during the time of the 1997 crisis. Today, Samsung Electronics, Hyundai Motor Company, and POSCO boast solid financial base. Manufacturers' debt-to-equity ratio dramatically fell to about 100% from 396.2% in 1997, and the ratio of about 700 listed companies fell below 90%. The manufacturing sector's interest coverage ratio soared to about 500% from 129.1% in 1997.

All in all, we have achieved remarkable improvements in the international financial market. Not only sports champions, Pak

Se-ri in golf, Kim Yuna in figure skating, and Park Tae-hwan in swimming but many economic players became world champions although many in Korea are unaware of this.

| Rule maker: First non-Western chair of G-20

Korea was the first non-Western state to chair a conference under the new G-20 system, something I never imagined would happen. Korea has transformed itself from a shrimp torn by fighting whales at the dawn of the 20th century to a dolphin, a small but smart creature in the 21st century.

Korea joined the ranks of "rule makers" for the world by chairing the G-20 Seoul Summit in 2010. It was the first time neither a G-7 country nor a Western state had ever chaired the G-20.The agreement on exchange rate principles reached at the meeting will go down in history. It was an the opportunity for the country to heighten its stature on the global stage as well as faithfully play the intermediary role for other periphery countries in easing their difficulties regarding foreign exchange rates. The leadership President Lee Myung-bak showed will be remembered for long time.

| First shift from recipient to donor

Korea is the only country in the world to have transformed

itself from an aid recipient to an aid donor. Korea sent a letter of intent to the OECD DAC in August 2008 before submitting an official application in January 2009. The nation joined the DAC on November 25, 2009, as the second Asia member after Japan.

Korea's foreign aid started with the establishment of the Economic Development Cooperation Fund in 1987, which provided aid in the form of concessional loans. Grants were provided after the Korea International Cooperation Agency was founded in 1991. The country began making contributions to the International Development Association (IDA), a member of the World Bank Group involved in the provision of concessional loans, in 1978. I attended the IDA meeting to discuss Korea's contribution as the Director General of the International Finance Bureau in 1992. It is safe to say that the OECD DAC was the first international aid organization providing Korea to permit its official attendance.

Since the nation's founding, Korea has received US$12.6 billion in aid, most of which came from the US. Its five-year economic development plan projects were mostly funded with concessional loans from the World Bank. Without foreign aid, Korean economy would not have been able to ascend to the level we see today. The country has transformed itself from a recipient to a donor offering both loans and grants. It has been steadily raising the share of aid out of GDP to 0.3%. The share remains small yet, but the country will increase the share until it matches that of other advanced countries. Unlike other advanced countries, Korea provides its own type of ODA. It combines financial support and programs to share its development experience. Also it provides development know-how gained through *Saemaul Undong* for poor African nations. These efforts are well received by the recipient countries. We are helping them realize the dream of another miracle that will go down in the human history.

POLITICAL ECONOMICS TO ADVANCE

2 I

2015 Peak vs. 2050 Richest

In September 2009, Yukiko Fukagawa, who teaches at Waseda University, predicted the Korean economy might peak around 2015. In the book *Megachange: The World in 2050* published in March 2012, *The Economist* predicted that Korea would become richer than the US, Japan, Germany, any others in the world in 2050. One prediction is based on the intuition of a long-time researcher. The other is based on statistics.

I have reflected on the two different views. The pessimism has a few sources: a working age population that is expected to peak around 2015, the world's fastest aging population and young people losing hope for the future. Comparison with Japan in the 1990s suggests the economic apex of Korea coming around 2015. The optimism is based on the assumption that controlled globalization under which liberalism does not progress nor regress significantly will continue and growth in labor force, investment stock, and total factor productivity will continue on the same trend measured through statistics until 2009. If real per capita GDP of the US at 100, Korea will top the list with 105.0 in 2050 according to the outlook. Germany will come third with 87.7; Russia, fifth with 71.9; Japan, eighth with 58.3; and China, ninth with 52.3.

For now, we cannot say which prediction is right. The variables for assumptions and predictions are past trajectories; not dynamics for the future. One thing for sure is that our future may be bright or dark if the premises and assumptions are correct.

| New abnormal and Asian century

In this 21st century, the global village faces new megatrends, which was unseen before. Exemplary are Asia's rise and historic power shift, and low growth and polarization. Since these are new phenomenon, uncertainty for us will rise, making adaptation to the new trends more difficult.

The Economist's book predicted the Asian century would peak in 2050. It estimated Asia's share of the world's GDP would double to 48.1% in 2050 from 27.9% in 2010, but those of North America and Western states would decline from 21.5% and 18.7% to 12.3% and 8.9%, respectively. Per capita GDP would grow by 4.7% in Asia, 4.4% in sub-Saharan Africa, 3.9% in the Middle East and North Africa, 3.3% in Latin America, and 3.2% in Eastern Europe, and along with India, China would recapture the dominant position it had held for 2,000 years in the past, it argued.

Pessimistic outlooks for advanced economies make the future look darker. Professor Nouriel Roubini at New York University asserted that low growth, austerity fatigue, excessive ownership would obstruct economic activities, bringing a new economic order, namely the "new abnormal" era. In the "new abnormal" era, increasing uncertainty will make economic forecasts more difficult, he says.

In this new era, it is increasingly true that the strong don't always survive but survivors become the strong. Zero interest rates and quantitative easing were phenomenon of a new form of currency war, and we do not know where it is heading. They may be adding fuel to the bubbles that sparked the crisis, deepening the problems even further. The international financial order which could be controlled came to an end in 1971. We may have crossed the Rubicon.

For us, historic power shift, low growth, and polarization pose an opportunity and a challenge at the same time. We achieved industrialization and democratization in a generation, rising from the ashes of the war, boosted exports from the 12th largest in the world in 2008 to the seventh largest in two years, and increased R&D spending relative to GDP from the fifth highest to the top in four years. If we maintain the spirit and vigor which made such achievements possible, the optimistic outlook will turn into reality. If we miss the once-in-a-lifetime opportunity and follow in Japan's footsteps, the pessimistic prediction will be realized. We should not forget that an opportunity and a challenge lie ahead of us.

Economics of conflicts:
Much food, many problems

In *Megachange: The World in 2050*, *The Economist* suggested two aspects of economic disparity between rich and poor: leveling among nations and polarization among nationals. Under this scenario, income disparity between nations will be dramatically lower while that within national borders will widen. The magazine predicted per capita income of Asian countries will jump from 12% of the US level at present to 40% and that of sub-Saharan countries, from 5% to 14%. However, it expected within the US, the richest 1% of the American people will control 24% of the national wealth in 2007, significantly up from only 8% in the 1970s. Different levels of education and skills as well as excessive growth in the financial industry are the dividing factors. Even if the difference in developmental levels of industries is steadily resolved, economic disparity will only be widened in line with technological progress.

Economic polarization casts dark shadows of conflicts. The "Occupy Wall Street" movement that began on September 17, 2011 and the chant, "United States of the 1%, by the 1%, for the 1%" mirror the conflicts we face in this century and the public anger at Wall Street, the epicenter of the global economic crisis. Behind them is polarization.

In *The Skeptical Environmentalist: Measuring the Real State of the World*, Bjorn Lomborg, a Danish political scientist interested in using statistics in the environmental arena, stated as follows:

『My claim is that things are improving ... Fewer and fewer people are starving. In 1900 we lived for an average of 30 years; today we live for 67 ... "A good story is usually bad news," writes a textbook for journalists. Although it is not easy to explain, we all seem to be curious about and fascinated by bad news ... Coupled with the finely tuned PR units of the environmental organizations and problem-oriented research, this can provide serious bias towards a negative appraisal of the state of the world ... But how is it possible to believe that things are getting worse when objective figures show the exact opposite? This apparent paradox seems to be a consequence of prosperity often described by the expression: "No food, one problem. Much food, many problems."』

It is not hunger, but jealousy which is most difficult to put up with. When we are hungry, there is only one problem; but when we are full, there are many problems. Intensifying polarization undermines economic growth and causes a heavy fiscal burden to resolve conflicts. Although we have to raise tax revenue and cut spending to deal with this, we cannot but give up raising revenue and increase spending due to populism. The national debt ratio of the OECD countries now exceeds 100%, up from 75% before the crisis. Given this, deepening polarization will be a great burden on the fiscal position of their economies.

Raging populism on the rise

Low growth and polarization are the trends facing the humankind in this century and thus cannot be resolved easily. Polarization causes conflicts, which may transform into struggles, which in turn evolve into the economics of jealousy under the disguise of justice. Combined with populism, the economics of jealousy may lead public opinion, driving us into co-destruction in the end. Regardless of where we belong to between the both ends of a polarized world, we feel depressed by polarization.

In *Economics of Justice and Jealousy*, Takeuchi Yaso, a Japanese economist, states that jealousy sometimes is disguised as justice. Distorted justice taking putting 900 million yen in tax on 1 billion yen income for granted is a product of jealousy, which causes drain of brain and economic vigor and absurdly results in increased taxes on the remaining poor.

In our society, conflicts are fast developing into hatred, driving us into co-destruction. The Korean Teachers and Education Workers Union members opted to leave schools early in the morning to push through their demands. This is a deviation from what I consider a right path for teachers. Democracy based on due process and the rule of law is now confronted by challenges. Under the name of democracy, people often commit acts of misdemeanor in an easy belief that they are out of the reach of laws. Democracy has become a convenient excuse for those who commit illegal acts to avoid legal judgments and this is rampant in politics, economy, media, and the rest of our society. Social network services provide channels for those who say only what they wish to say and listen only what they wish to listen to hurl abuses lawlessly.

Tax rate cuts implemented to cope with the 2008 economic crisis were condemned as what benefits the rich; normalization of the won's value was blamed an act that would help lose market confidence; Minerva, a blogger who recklessly spread false information on the internet, was hailed as a "national mentor." Jealousy under the disguise of justice was entirely behind the criticism of crisis management policies. Opponents only listened to what they would like to hear and only want to talk about what they want. They might have thought of me in the same manner. There were no wise men to play a mediating role.

Things haven't changed so much. Calls for a democratized economy touted as justice are driving corporations out of the country, thereby diminishing jobs while benefiting foreign capital only. Conflicts are not bringing justice; but the disguised justice is causing conflicts. Populism is undermining majoritarian democracy; and calls for economic democratization is pressuring down on economic facilitation. The justice and prioritization of people's well-being that demonstrators called for during the 2008 protest against the import of US beef were justice for themselves and their supporters. I sometimes wonder if they still do not eat US beef.

Democracy is a simple compound of demo (people) and cracy (rule), and does not include the meaning of ism or ideology. Democracy is neither political goal nor philosophy nor ism, but political system for people's rule. Currently, however, most of the Korean people accept democracy as philosophy or ideology for people's rule. The official name of North Korea is the Democratic People's Republic of Korea. According to a recent survey, the US was ranked 21st in the world in terms of the level of democracy while South Korea was put higher at 20th and the first in Asia. How democratized the Korean society is!

| Legacy of tragic history

Seeing conflicts and hatred on the rise in Korean society, I wonder why. Sometimes, I am scared that we have certain characteristics running in our blood for fomenting conflicts and hatred.

After one demonstration, a police officer bled from being beaten with a high-heel shoe. Would this possibly happen in other societies? In another clash, demonstrators wielding bamboo spears challenged soldiers in a grave act breakdown of law and order. The overly aggressive behavior is not confined to the streets. Inside the National Assembly building, lawmakers have fired tear gas and smashed down doors in order to obstruct the proceedings of political rivals. How can they be entrusted to draft legislation in an appropriate manner? In contrast, there was a case of police in the US fatally shooting an ethnic Korean taxi driver who had ignored orders to stop his vehicle. And members of Congress were arrested for participating in an unlawful protest at the US Capitol. What would the Korean demonstrators think of these two episodes? Does the contrast testify to the "level of democracy" survey that puts Korea higher than the US?

Seeing so much civil disobedience, I think about our tragic history and its legacy. Under the corrupt dynasty, colonial rule, and authoritarian rule in the past, murder, arson, and tax evasion were once treated as acts of patriotism. Our history of upended values seems to have left us a legacy of ignorance to the rule of law. People were subjected to wrongdoings of corrupt officials, members of the ruling class betrayed their country; and presidents violated the Constitution in the past. The past has gone and the time has changed. President Park Geun-hye was elected by a majority of voters in 2012. Those who voted against her have to wait until the next presidential election. This is the essence of the representative democracy based on the majority decision rule. President Park is not a queen of a corrupt dynasty or Japanese Governor General of Korea and did not hold her presidency on the basis of force and authority.

We are under the rule of a free democratic Republic of Korea, not of a corrupt dynasty, Japanese Governor General of Korea, or an authoritarian regime. When attempting to fix the rules on walking on the left side of the sidewalk and giving the green light to cars turning left first, I saw the legacy of the Japanese Governor General of Korea in our lives. We are still haunted by the tragic history and its legacy. Tendency to self-abuse and self-degradation is the only explanation for the on-going conflicts and hatred. The April 2014 Sewol ferry sinking that claimed more than 300 lives, most of them students, had to be concluded by punishing those responsible for the disaster. However, it has come such a long way to an issue of the so-called "bureaucratic mafia" or "savage officials," which points the finger at public officials who have no connections with the ferry accident.

The rule is simple: Punish those who did wrong. There is no point of discouraging the morale of other officials working diligently. There is an old Korean saying, "If you want good farmhands, feed them well first." Many attribute much of the miraculous achievements Korea has accomplished in industrialization and democratization in only one generation to elite bureaucrats. How closely are the Senior Civil Service Examination and the Sewol ferry sinking correlated? Can we prevent such a disaster from happening again if we continue to only chastise public officials? Why does nobody tell about the operation of a rational market pricing mechanism? By when could we possibly be freed from this legacy of conflicts and hatred escalated by ourselves? The deeper I delve into this matter, the more depressed I feel.

22 Political Economics for Advanced Nation

How can we develop the country into a first-class advanced nation? What political economics is needed to do so? Can we succeed without fixing political systems and social practices that are exacerbating conflicts and hatred?

Continued abundance and peace give rise to indolence and decadence, which results in populism disguised as justice and goodwill. The global economic crisis was a result of such populism. The Roman Empire, which boasted enormous wealth, and the Soviet Union, which had touted equality, collapsed in the end.

Low growth and polarization are dominant trends grabbing the whole world in an historic power shift. Korea cannot become an advanced economy unless it effectively deals with low growth and polarization, and it cannot march toward the future without overcoming the tragic legacy of conflicts and hatred from the past. We should first have confidence in our ability and realize our potential. No one will do it for us. The time has come to have new political economics charged with a get-up-and-go spirit in politics, economy, and society in order to address emerging uncertainties and further advance the country.

| Beyond polarization and conflicts: Risks and opportunities

History shows that an economy cannot operate properly without proper political systems. I have been in such situations many times with the economy immobilized by political obstacles or social problems. To ride the new megatrends in the 21st century, we must devise new strategies not only for politics but for the economy and society.

An old Korean adage says there are no millionaires or dignitaries through three generations. There have been few dynasties which lasted over a century. In the era of the historic power shift, we must overcome risks from low growth and social conflicts and seize opportunities that arise from them to win the current survival game.

Risks originated from economic polarization and political conflicts. Economic polarization gives rise to "a low-growth economy" marked by flagging investments, excessive household debt, and militant labor unions; and political conflicts produce "an incapable politics" through confrontations which refuse compromise and destructive workings of the majoritarian rule. Escalating conflicts destroys the rule of law in society, and then those lead to "a lawless society." The internet, a jungle in which people hear only to what they wish to hear and only talk about what they wish to discuss, is "a pariah culture."

Opportunities include the arrival of the Asian century, Korea's geopolitical benefits from its location, high entrepreneurship, and the world's highest level of education. When Korea is reunified, its 80 million people will turn into an enormous opportunity if we make full preparations. Koreans can write a new chapter in our history as they have done so far, rebuilding the nation from scratch, industrializing the economy, and advancing democratic systems.

Today, risks and opportunities lie ahead and risks outweigh opportunities. To repel the risks and seize the opportunities, the nation needs new visions, strategies, and tactics of political economics that can effectively resolve economic polarization and minimize the cost of political conflicts.

| Path toward a first class nation: Growth, balance, and open-up

The 21st century calls on Koreans to build an advanced leading nation. This represents a desperate hope and a vision for us after suffering hardship and disgrace for periods in the past. What strategies we pursue during the next 10 years will decide whether they will descend after 2015 or make the country one of the richest in the world by 2050.

The path toward the advanced leading nation vision is to work more, save more, and invest more with diligence. This is the basic foundation for any chosen strategy to succeed. The global financial crisis demonstrated that savings and investments are virtues, but borrowings and consumption are not in any case. This is the same lesson I learned from successes and failures as a public official.

I would like to suggest three strategies to develop the country to one of the richest in the world by 2050: more sustainable economic growth, increased social balance and vitality, and more globalized state open to the world.

For politics, wise men need to show their leadership; for the economy, capable entrepreneurs should exercise their frontier's spirit; for society, Koreans must build solidarity based on honesty and trust; for culture, we have to revive pioneer's mindset of the past to overcome the current cultural degradation and public officials especially have to stay aware of changes in society and commit themselves to their tasks with a strong sense of responsibility. Increased capabilities, high moral standards, spirited minds at home, and taking challenges, pioneering spirit, and exploration abroad are all necessary for us to overcome political conflicts, low economic growth, social militancy, cultural degradation, and bureaucratic complacency.

Given the country's small open economy's lack of advanced technologies and natural resources, our top priority must be external balance based on savings and investments with diligence. Instead of consumption and liquidity argued by Keynes and Friedman, supply, investment, and productivity championed by Hayek and Schumpeter will help Korea achieve sustainable development in economy and society, turning the country into an advanced nation.

| Political economics of spirited minds:
  Never up, never in

The three strategies I suggested can only succeed by adopting political economics of spirited minds that can resolve conflicts and promoting the belief that only offense brings victory. Without offense, Korea will have a tie at best, but not a victory. Never up, never in!

There are 10 necessities to realize the advanced nation vision. The most critical is rule of law. The economic requirements relate to foreign exchange rate, R&D investments, business environment. The social imperatives are social capital, housing necessity, need-based social security. The external necessities include Korean expatriates, outbound exploration, and national unification. My criteria in choosing the tasks are based on the successes and failures I had in public service. Among other important tasks, we should pour our energy and resources on these with selectivity and concentration to promise the best results.

First, establish the rule of law. This is an overarching principle of political economics necessary for any advanced nation. The principle must be the basis of all political, economic, social, and cultural activities. Nothing works properly unless the principle is strictly observed and it is the only means to resolve growing conflicts in our country. Under the law of the jungle, in which the law of the masses, emotions, lawlessness, and illegality prevail, we will otherwise pay a hefty price for the law of the masses, law of emotions, and illegality. I assume the price will be unimaginably high, although there are no estimates available.

To establish the rule of law, we should revise laws and regulations, and reorganize systems on the basis of honesty and global standards. The rule of law becomes firmly rooted only when people believe respecting laws will benefit them and make their life easier. Then, the government must enforce the laws with zero-tolerance for illegal acts. Corrupt leaders cannot enforce integrity on society. In a sense, it does not make sense to expect integrity among average individuals when we have had corrupt leaders not only in the past but even today.

A KDI study estimates illegal strikes reduce GDP by 1%. We have to upgrade labor standards to those defined by the International Labor Organization and revise relevant laws and regulations accordingly. Both labor and management must observe them. Labor unions, which represent 12% of the country's total workforce, can protect the interests of their own but those of non-unionized workers can be attained by respecting the laws. Grand compromise for the remaining 88% is needed. Otherwise, a rare opportunity will be missed.

Second, Korea must protect its sovereignty over foreign exchange rate. Any policy will become null and void if we fail to do so. The two crises in the past proved that a small open economy must treat external balance as the top priority. Maintaining exchange rates at an appropriate level is the beginning of higher external competitiveness, and current account surplus backed by appropriate exchange rates is the basis of national governance.

The agreement on exchange rate principles at the G-20 Seoul Summit in 2010 was pivotal for the international financial order. Excessive flows of capital across borders place a bigger burden on the Korean economy than others now that Korea has became a capital exporter. At present, countries with a reserve currency are waging an unprecedented currency war. A short-term means for to survive is exchange rate intervention and the long-term means is technological development.

Third, R&D spending must be ratcheted up. Technology is a fundamental source of external competitiveness. R&D investments will prepare us to break from the low-growth trend and continue to develop new growth engines. Exchange rate sovereignty as well as technology development is two main tools for us to survive the global competition. Therefore, the government must invest at least 5% of the GDP into R&D until it runs a technology trade account surplus. The government should steer development of basic science and technologies, and the private sector should focus on applied technologies.

Although Korea's share of R&D investment out of the GDP set a global high at 4.36% in 2012, the country had a more than US$5 billion deficit in the technology trade account that year. In addition, the country has never achieved a surplus in the account. In terms of amount, Korea's R&D spending represents only 45% and 15% those of Japan and the US, which come fifth and eleventh, respectively in the relation of their R&D spending to GDP. Therefore, the current tax incentives designed to expand

R&D spending must be maintained or further strengthened.

Fourth, Korea should strive to create the world's best business environment. One way for the country to accelerate its growth is to create a favorable business environment so entrepreneurs can exercise their ability freely. Maintaining business and investment environments at the same or higher level than those of competitors is a necessary condition for continued enhancement of a country's economic capabilities. A sound business environment attracts investments, which accelerate growth, which then creates jobs.

Critical to having a better business environment are proactive fiscal and financial policies, deregulation, promotion of market competition, increased investment into infrastructure. Economic vitality will grow when co-growth of large and small and midsize companies leads to unlock new champions. Without growth, Korea will have neither future nor welfare. Innovations to corporate investment and the business environment lay the groundwork for increased welfare and set the stage for addressing low growth and polarization.

Fifth, Korea must build up social capital, which are norms, trust, solidarity, and the get-up-and-go spirit to resolve conflicts and promote cooperation. Social capital is believed to increase production just as physical and human resources do. An advanced nation will be a far-fetched dream unless we address the current political and social practices that aggravate conflicts. Norms are better observed when they are devised based on the honesty of the average member of a society. Trust among the members of the society will evolve when the observance of norms rises, which will in turn strengthen solidarity in society. With the get-up-and-go spirit added, this will turn into strong social capital.

For this to happen, I suggest three: healthy debate and compromise between leftists and rightists; thoughtful use of the Internet for greater solidarity; and nurturing spirited young people.

Healthy debate and compromise is imperative for resolving social conflicts. This is especially true with the problems caused by populism under the majoritarian democracy. Interest groups and political parties should consist of rational-minded people, not extreme conservatives or violent leftists. Otherwise, Korea cannot break free from the tragic legacy of the past filled with destructive confrontation and fighting. Obsession with vested interests and fighting disguised as justice will lead us to co-destruction. As for critical issues facing the Korean society like reforms of tax, pension, and health insurance, an option is "techno-democracy" which places unelected and rational-minded experts at the forefront of discussions and decision-making.

Internet sites filled with abusive words and pornography may degrade the overall quality of the whole society. Certain groups of people only want to say whatever they want and listen to only what they want to hear, aggravating social conflicts and hatred. Use of real name on the Internet is one of the solutions to this problem.

Young people will lose their ambition and hope when there is no need to compete. In Japan, many point to young people who have lost ambition as a major cause of the Lost Decade. The blame is being placed on *Yutori kyōiku*, meaning "education that gives children room to grow," Japanese version of high school standardization.

Japan has shelved its standardized education system after 40 years. Today, Korea is the only country that still has the approach. Under the system, the future of high school students is determined by the result of their one-time university admission test. This is too harsh as well as unfair especially to students from low-income families, who cannot afford private test preparation classes. Indeed, the fundamental cause of excessive dependence on private tutoring in Korea, a cause for the country's falling fertility rate and growing wage pressure, is the high school standardization policy. One plausible option for secondary education is to let local governments and parents take the initiative. Complete standardization is not feasible for high school education unless we use random assignment for university enrollment or for jobs just like we do now for high school enrollment. Unlike Korea, there are many countries which use admission test even for middle school enrollment.

Sixth, we have to provide affordable homes for newlyweds. In addition to employment and education, housing should be protected as one of the three basic rights to ensure stable livelihoods. No one can receive education or stable jobs without a place to live. Providing homes for newlyweds is also necessary to reverse the nation's low fertility rate, strengthen welfare, improve labor-management relations, and boost the domestic economy as well as the first step toward easing of polarization.

The right to housing must be protected by the Constitution. Restrictions on the green belt surrounding large cities should be relaxed to secure the lands to build homes. These homes will be assigned to newlyweds—permanent rental houses for those with lower income level and "national" sized houses for those who earn more. Excessive home pricing is the backdrop to violent labor strikes over higher wages, despite already decent pay levels. If the cost to buy a house is included, pay levels in Korea are not high at all when compared to those of other advanced countries. There are few countries in the world where house prices are higher than in Korea, and the government efforts to lower the prices are more insufficient than in Korea. One of the main duties of local governments of other advanced countries is to provide public transportation and affordable housing to low-wage working people.

Seventh, let's help those in need—feed the starving, accommodate the homeless, and treat the sick have-nots. Institutional foundation is necessary to support a fresh restart by those who had failed. Excessive welfare causes a decline in work morale and economic vitality, and ultimately in welfare itself. Without growth, welfare is not sustainable. If our companies lose the global competition, Korea cannot expect growth or distribution of income.

Sweden, one of the world's most generous welfare states, reduced welfare programs and adopted more liberalist policies. In the UK, the Conservative Party introduced the workfare scheme which provided unemployment benefits for the jobless willing to work in 1997, when it was fighting against an economic crisis with the help of the IMF. The Labor Party which took power in 1997 further developed the scheme by providing vocational training to job seekers.

Eighth, ethnic Koreans overseas are a great asset. Our tragic history left behind 7 million — presumably 10 million — Korean people scattered in 160 countries around the world. Giving them the right to free entry and exit of the country as well as the Korean citizenship are effective ways to address low fertility rate and shortage of labor. We can find a new way for further growth by establishing a network to link them, thereby building a global Korean community. In particular, a global network of Korean experts and scholars will be of great help in ushering in a brighter future.

Ninth, let's look outside the country. Having influence on wider regions through free trade is a sound way to grow a small open economy. As a capital exporter, Korea needs to pay attention to cross-border mergers and acquisitions. It also needs to increase sovereign wealth funds and makes active investment into overseas markets. ODA programs that provide not only capital but Korea's development experience are a good opportunity for our young people to experience international activities and nurture global mindset.

Tenth, we have to prepare for national unification. National unification will be a blessing only when we are prepared for it. Restoration of homogeneity among the Korean people and improving the quality of life of the North Korean people and their economy through expansion of exchanges between the two Koreas must precede political unification. By doing so, we can achieve national unification earlier than later at a reduced cost.

Given the current political dynamics surrounding the country, unification will never come easy. Korea is the only divided nation in the world and directly linked with the US, China, Russia, and Japan—the most influential in the world now—by land or sea. We should not forget that Korea suffered the colonial rule by Japan and a war when the US decided to withdraw its military presence on the peninsula just after our independence. One Chinese political scientist once said Korea has diplomatic significance since it is a US alliance. When the country was isolated from the world due to the closed-door policy, it was colonized by Japan, and when the US reduced its forces from the country, the land was devastated by a war. The national division in 1945 is a clear indication of what consequence we will face if we fail to unify the country by ourselves. Rights and freedom are not something for granted, but something that we must achieve. People who forget its history will disappear.

23

Way Forward:
Let the Outcomes Speak

『Commit your way to the Lord; trust in him and he will do this: He will make your righteous reward shine like the dawn, your vindication like the noonday sun』(Psalm 37:5-6)

The role of building a first-class state rests primarily with the bureaucrats. When these public servants are fully awake, the state can overcome the usual populism that pervades in any democracy and execute a needed political economy with enterprising drive. With the bureaucrats working on full alert for the future in spite of criticism, such a state may look for a brighter future leading to a first-rate country.

The 43 years of my public-service career is filled with a lot of criticism and blame entailing a vortex of many controversial policies and programs. I had to take responsibility for administrative action and write letters of resignation on three occasions, and I was demoted once. My first resignation letter was written in my capacity as division director in charge of the introduction of the value–added tax provision. The second time was in 1997 when my role as Vice Minister was questioned over government's countermeasures against the Asian Financial Crisis. In 2008, I wrote the third letter in the wake of the Global Economic Crisis, this time as the Finance Minister, for pushing exchange rates up while cutting tax rates. And, earlier in 1992, I was demoted amid controversial negotiations with the United States over opening of Korea's financial market.

Assessments of the outcomes of my misfortunes varied at the times, but yet I was in the roles and posts that could not dodge accepting responsibility under the given political realities. The 2008 letter was written under criticism that amounted to a demand for my resignation. However, eventual success in surmounting the 2008 global crisis prompted plaudits from abroad such as "hats off to officials in Seoul" and "a textbook example." In spite of the eventual vindication, the initial wound that was inflicted worked its effect on me. I presume that it's an inevitable fate in the career paths of public officials.

With much dream and ambition, I began the life of a government employee in a rural tax office, only to run into the harsh agony and difficulties. I still retain the brown envelope of my first salary payment, dated November 1970. It contained 23,544 won, equivalent to US$75 at that time. This meager pay, the critical point of my agony, was an amount that barely covered my monthly boarding–house charge alone. With this pay, I couldn't even think of doing the son's filial duty to my parents; I agonized over whether I could or should continue this government job any longer. Somehow, my future assignments eventually spanned 43 years. In 2007, I even participated in the move to advance a new regime in Korea; upon success in this move, I had the opportunity to spearhead economic policies of my belief and design.

During the days of my working-level assignment, my primary duty was to deal with the fiscal needs of the national treasury and the shaky financial structures of industries. My tenure fighting the 1997 Asian currency crisis would have been enough for any Finance Ministry official but I had to grapple with the 2008 meltdown a decade later. It was a thorny career path to say the least. Now, having ended my career, I am tempted to lay out this writing for future colleagues, showing them my painful career experiences as lessons to think about or something to emulate if they desire. My point in brief is: Act with convictions and let the outcomes speak!

| The unforgettable 2008!

When I confronted the global economic catastrophe, I gave every morsel of my energy to directing countermeasures, deciding it would be my last service to the country before stepping down as Finance Minister. "Stepping down" may not be an accurate description; I was expelled, to be correct. Tons of harsh criticism, accusations, and blame paved the road to my firing. Of course, much of it was unfair and I regretted the treatment. But, in fact, I felt good when I left the post because I had implemented nearly all of the major policies that I had designed.

One day after leaving the post, I stopped in a back-alley restaurant in Seoul that I had frequented during my earlier government-work days. There on the walls, I saw an array of nasty comments about me. They amounted to: "Man-Soo, you conservative sympathizer, stop catering to the rich." On the online media outlets, someone named Minerva, who commanded national attention, thrashed out plausible commentaries about my performance for days and days. His commentaries turned out to be nothing but compositions of bits and pieces that he had dexterously collected from a number of other internet media sources. Still, one university professor would extended credibility to this self-professed authority's online writings by calling him "the nation's master teacher." Name-callings too were wild and colorful: "Old Boy," "King Man-Soo," "Kang the Stubborn," and "Economic President," just to name a few. One daily newspaper published opinion pieces numerous times a month criticizing my performance with the single identical demand for my exit.

Battling the national economic crises was strenuous enough in itself, but in fact I had to spend an enormous amount of time and energy in confronting criticism from politicians and the media. Believe it or not, I also had to fight against the Bank of Korea and even US-anchored economic theories, perhaps a fight more strenuous. The Bank of Korea took on policies opposite to mine on such major issues as interest rates, exchange rates and prices. A group of 118 professors of economics said I was the prime culprit behind the nation's economic woes and called for my immediate removal. The opposition members of the

National Assembly even resorted to staging a rally in front of their National Assembly building demanding my exit. Not many officials might have ever faced such criticism, accusations, and calls to resign or be fired as much as me.

During the 2008 crash, despite pressing time I went to church every day to attend early-morning prayer service and made the same plea each time: "O Lord, take away the road if not the right way; if it's the right road, let me take it and move along straight forward without minding the obstacles, if any." That's the way I proceeded during the turmoil. While even the ruling party and the presidential staff posed threats to me, President Lee Myung-bak didn't waver as my sole supporter. Yet the stark realities of politics were odd, indeed. They wanted to punish the person who planted the seeds of recovery. Later, those who merely picked the fruits later collected applauses from the oblivious public, neglecting the time lag of economic policies. My predicament around that time was evident in the entry scribbled in my diary for November 24, 2008: "early morning prayer, nothing to rely on, tears and tears, triumph in the name of Jesus, crisis as opportunity, obstacles as stepping stones." Thus, I chose the thorny road of struggles by committing my way to the Lord with the belief that the Lord will eventually make my righteousness shine like the noonday sun.

I don't see myself as being stubborn or obstinate. What is right is right always everywhere, and what ought to be accomplished should be done regardless of the difficulty or who says what. One of my traits merely happens to be nonstrategic foolhardiness. In my work, I utter yes or no without any ambiguity; the direction that I hand down is legible and clear; and execution of any task is preemptive and decisive. This modus operandi didn't always jibe well with some people though, hence the familiar criticism for my being self-righteous. In contrast several of my staff members often confided that it was easier to work with me. I did not like the nickname "Kang the Stubborn," but it stayed with me wherever I moved.

On the day when I assumed the post of Minister of Finance, I made a set of personal goals for three key tasks —establish a sustainable foreign exchange rate, accomplish the current account surplus, and abolish the infamous political violence, namely the comprehensive real estate property tax. I resolved these three at the minimum accomplished when I leave the post, and that's exactly what happened, though half was done on the property tax. In my life, it was the most fearsome, gutsy, and time-consuming period from start to finish. With that assignment, I knew I wouldn't last long, hence my decision to be bold and blunt from the beginning point. On February 10, 2009, I left the ministry building on the outskirts of Seoul, feeling good about fulfilling 50 or so tasks that I had assigned to myself. Showing no reservation or regret whatsoever, my farewell message ran like this:

「Now I am leaving you, my colleagues. I came here with a feel of restlessness, but throughout we worked together tirelessly with fighting spirit.

The crisis was the kind that we had never heard of before.

But we deployed countermeasures preemptively, decisively, and sufficiently. It was a game of survival in which the strong do not always survive, but the survivors become the strong. In the broader world out there, historic power shifts are emerging.

In a sense, policies are creative destruction. Those who have enjoyed their vested rights voice their arguments, but the parties benefiting from their newly acquired gains tend to remain silent. If you work substantively, the affected people inevitably voice their opinions.

History is made by the people who take actions with a positive mind. Tomorrow's Korea will be different from today's only when you take crises as fresh new opportunities. Stick to your solemn obligations and be resolute with your convictions. Further, you can't be complacent in preparing for the future.

Please remember: Managing the current account is fundamental to running the country, and expanding the domestic demand infrastructure is the most urgent task.

What's gone remains a fond memory to me. Now I am going to a fluttering new tomorrow.」

The Korean economy, in the wake of the Global Economic Crisis, turned out to have accomplished a series of seven major feats: fastest recovery for growth, No. 7 export economy, first in R&D investment, shift to a capital export country, highest national credit ratings in Asia, a rule-maker country, and the shift from a beneficiary to a donor country. The unforgettable 2008, so much criticism and suffering! "Excuses" from Kang the

Stubborn now look like tags on the items in the list above. The outcomes speak for themselves.

Fate of public officials: Do duty, expect criticism

After I left the Ministry of Finance, many media outlets in Korea asked for interviews but I declined all of the requests. I wanted to wait until outcomes of my policies were publicly visible. I was then serving as Senior Economic Advisor to the President, also concurrently as chair of the Presidential Council on National Competitiveness. Around that time, on July 22, 2009, the New York-based *Bloomberg News* dispatched an analysis piece under this headline: "Hats Off to Officials in Seoul." The time seemed ripe for me to tell my stories. The *Monthly Chosun* carried an article headlined "Minister Man-Soo Kang, A Leader of Fortunate Destiny," based on an interview with me on August 18. On August 21, the *Maeil Business News* printed an item entitled "His convictions: One-year record parallels others' 10-year work." Then on September 2, the *Yonhap News Agency* circulated a dispatch article, "The world recognizes Korea's successful recovery from the economic crisis."

If you do your work, you inevitably draw criticism. Getting criticized for doing work is a fate of career public officials. The road to take by public officials is to do their work without surrendering to public criticism and accusations and proceed with care for the nation's future as the primary guiding light.

Good medicine often tastes bitter. Public officials with conscience and a sense of dedication should do their work without fear of fail, with passions and of course based on careful prior analysis. Criticism comes with performing your job and it becomes harsher if you work with a long-term perspective. That's the fateful destiny of public officials. As a matter of fact, the public doesn't want to see public servants going easy or doing nothing.

By nature, I didn't value colleagues who maintained extensive social networks, took moderate approaches and reached compromises very well. Do-nothing officials, by definition, haven't done anything substantive, hence there is no grounds for criticism. Incompetent officials often commit mistakes, but they can perform better if properly counseled and trained. However, officials who tend to take moderate approaches all the time are more troublesome than those who are merely incompetent. The minister who merely reacts to his or her subordinates' submissions, is thus managed by the working-level officials. The person is not an effective minister at all. The subordinates are the de facto minister in such a case. The minister, being the leader, ought to act decisively and have the results speak for themselves. This is a hard-earned lesson that I realized during my public service career.

The media, both domestic and foreign, gave me some headaches for their rash and simplistic coverage not only during the 1997 financial crisis but also with the 2008 global crisis. The domestic media fanned the crisis scenarios with a heavy dose of criticism with the foreign media following the same tracks, often deriding Korean countermeasures as being inefficient. In 2009, the foreign media began to note Korea's rapid recovery from the latest crash and turn to surplus in the current account. Their coverage made a turn, too. "Hats off to officials in Seoul" came from the U.S. media circles, and "no longer an underdog" came from the *Financial Times* of London. The OECD rated Korea's fiscal and financial policy as one of the best among OECD countries while the IMF, the institution that taught us during the 1997 crisis, praised Korea's policy as being a "textbook example."

History is written by those people who take action with courage. The complacent officials who do not do much won't attract any serious criticism, but they won't have any base to draw recognition either. They merely seek a cozy, comfortable existence. It's my belief that people prefer officials take action with enthusiasm to strive for outcomes rather than those complacent who are satisfied with keeping the status-quo. People are shrewd—they join in criticism, but they also extend applause when they see outcomes of values down the road.

▮ Last bastion of the nation: Populism, no future

Plutarch's observation of 2,000 years ago still rings pertinent and true: going against people's inclinations makes governing difficult, whereas blind embracing of misguided people's whims endangers the nation's future. The nation is forever while the governing regime is just temporary.

Competent and capable public officials constitute the nation's last bastion. If these officials compromise with populism, the nation doesn't have a very bright future. Granted compromising politics is often a necessary cost for the majority rule of democracy, it's the officials' job to help control such cost to the necessary minimum with courage and a sense of mission. Through two major crises, I found that most politicians readily offer cooperation if rational arguments are presented to convince them. These politicians seemed to value, and often respect, such officials who work with guts and a sense of mission. Although they had to be sensitive about casting votes that served their constituencies' interests, they also had to be aware of national interests, the ultimate reason for their existence.

Career officials shouldn't retain a soul of their own. Modern constitutions guarantee job security to career officials with a proviso that they remain politically neutral. The conventional wisdom says that their political neutrality means their faithful execution of the incumbent president's policies insomuch as the president is the one chosen by the people at the time. When I assumed the minister's post, I retained high-ranking officials who had opposed or criticized election pledges advanced by my candidate, Lee Myung-bak, during the campaign. It's not that I didn't have my view on their role but that I wanted to honor political neutrality with public officials. Pushing my own view isn't political neutrality. Around that time, one government official was known to have lamented that now he had to uphold new policies of the incoming administration as if he didn't have a soul. He should have learned constitutional principles for this point.

Keeping confidentiality is another major obligation, rather duty, with career officials. Recently, we saw an increasing number of breach-of-confidentiality cases initiated by career officials; their leaks of confidential government information would disrupt the routine jobs of the affected units, often incurring costly ancillary expenses. Retired career officials are required to keep government information confidential. Whistle-blowing is unbecoming to career officials, but it might be an entirely different matter if major violations have been committed.

To repeat, career officials ought to stay away from populism, stay with political neutrality, and honor confidentiality. The job security they enjoy is the reward they earned for such obligations. If public officials, the nation's last bastion, deviate from that due course, the nation may be ungovernable in its majority-rule, democratic system.

About three years after leaving government service, I had the pleasure of receiving a plaque of appreciation from the beat reporters at the ministry where they used to wield the sticks of criticism on my policies and job performance. The writing on the plaque was nothing but sweet and memorable:

『The Korean economy is a history of challenge that has blossomed amid hardship and crises. You have always stood at the forefront in facing challenges. During the 2008 global financial crisis, you led the Korean economy as Minister of Finance to rise from the crisis. You were unskilled at persuasion, but didn't give up or circumvent. Time passes by, but policies with soul last. Your devotion will be long remembered. We, the press corps who criticized sometimes and defended other times, present you today with this small plaque of appreciation.」

November 15, 2012
Members of Press Corps at the Ministry of Finance
during the time of global financial crisis

EPILOGUE

『Should this life sometime deceive you,

Don't be sad or mad at it!

On a gloomy day, submit:

Trust—fair day will come, why grieve you?

Heart lives in the future, so

What if gloom pervades the present?

All is fleeting, all will go:

What is gone will then be pleasant.』

Alexander Pushkin

Those days that hold me dearly with nostalgic ties! For a boy born in a remote mountainous village, I used to have the playful fun of picking and nibbling at the azalea blossoms on the mountain facing our village. Such memories mark my childhood days. In those early days, after the Korean War had devastated everything, we didn't have any classroom at our elementary school, so we studied under a willow tree by using cement blocks as our desks and chairs. The middle-school days weren't very different. While sitting on the rocks on the edge of a river, I used to watch the rural buses passing by stirring up misty dusts off the gravel road. The cities out there, where the busses were heading—I used to wonder with wishful curiosity what the big cities might look like.

That dream got realized when I advanced for my high-school education to the big city in our region, Busan. For a country boy, it was extremely difficult to support my education. I did so by tutoring kids. In class, I had a nosebleed after being beaten by teachers who were angry at me since I dozed off due to the tutoring work. After having a nosebleed at school, I returned to my rural home, and nursed a dream of becoming a novelist. Yet I have some sweet memories of college days in Seoul. I met a girl on one overnight inter-city train, and we used to stroll together on the Haeundae Beach in Busan—the hidden story behind my most favorite song, *Haeundae Elergy*.

My first salary after graduating from college, the meager 23,544 won (about US$75) that came in a brown pay envelope, was a metaphor of Korea's agony as a less-developed country at that time. I managed to stay in public service for more than 40 years even though I considered resigning several times. While working in New York City, I used to enjoy the ambience of Wall Street downtown clubs at invitation. On one late evening, after finishing the final exams at New York University, I had to cross the snow-draped George Washington Bridge barely passable under heavy snowfalls, reaching home at an early morning hour —one of the sweet memories from my government-work days. Yes, there was a challenging experience, too, when I worked on a successful presidential campaign to oust the decade-long left-leaning administrations. The 10 years of life as an outsider by then wasn't wasted after all.

I chose to do this writing about my experiences in the Finance Ministry upon reading acclaims from the international press in addition to the positive evaluation from the IMF which termed the Korean experience a textbook case. I believed perhaps the story written by Koreans that tells that survivors become the strong might reveal some inspiration to other peoples on this globe.

Yet one particular suffering from that era, a suffering that will remain throughout my life, rests in my heart with sadness. My daughter used to make tearful appeals to me begging for my quitting the ministerial duty while she was sitting up all nights battling abusive internet writings against her father on his handling of the financial crisis. Around the time when I finally left the governmental service, her illness progressed to the worse. She left this world after three years of battling the illness. What's left is her dad's broken heart in the verse below.

Leaving the Helpless Dad Behind

Autumn leaves fall with the evening rainfall,
On the lane we used to promenade but today me alone.
The crescent moon hangs over the mountain ridge yonder,
Gently stirring up the crisp autumn breeze.

When you battled the illness before a flickering death,
This dad was helpless, merely standing by.
Even though three years were full of pain,
I was happier then for just being with you around.

Save my daughter by taking this dad instead,
Despite my daily prayer at the early morning church,
The Lord called you first to his own will.
And leave this helpless dad behind.

Springtime comes with sprouts and autumn drops leaves,
And any union foretells ending with separation.
What mortals would dare defy such a Nature's rule,
Yet your entry to the Heaven first is my sorrow still.

Thinking of the daughter who left this world earlier,
In the autumn of 2012

INDEX